WORLD WAR II
AIRCRAFT

Christopher Chant

Above: A B-17F Flying Fortress. The B-17 was the mainstay of the USAAF bomber forces in Europe and also served extensively elsewhere (Blitz Publications)

Endpapers: US Army Air Force B-26 Marauder medium bombers. The aircraft at the top has just started to drop its bombs (Blitz Publications)

WORLD WAR II
AIRCRAFT

Christopher Chant

With a foreword by
Wing Commander Robert Stanford-Tuck, DSO, DFC

Special illustrations by
County Studio, Coleorton, Leicester

This edition published for British Home Stores plc
by Orbis Publishing Ltd 1983
© Orbis Publishing Limited, London 1975
Printed in Italy
ISBN 0-85613-210-1

Contents

Picture Acknowledgements

Colour photographs
Associated Press: Pages 112–113; Bapty: Pages 10 bottom, 16; Bibliothèque Nationale – Signal/Foliot: Page 14; Fox Photos: Page 80; Signal: Pages 22–23/Nicole Marchand, 24; US Air Force: Pages 110–111, 118; US Army: Pages 124–124; US Navy: Page 128 top

Black and white photographs
Blitz Publications: Pages 2–3, 4, 6, 8, 10 top, 12, 18, 20, 26, 28, 30–31, 32, 33, 34, 36–37, 38, 40, 42, 44, 46, 48, 52, 54, 56–57, 60–61, 62, 64, 66, 68, 70, 72, 74, 76 top/Charles E. Brown, 76 bottom, 78, 82–83, 84, 88–89, 90, 94, 96, 98–99, 100, 104–105, 106, 108–109, 114–115, 116–117, 120–121, 122, 126, 128 bottom, 130, 132, 134, 136, 138, 140, 142; Fujiphotos: Page 50; Fox Photos: Pages 58–59; Novosti: Pages 92–93, 102–103

Opposite page: Douglas SBD Dauntless dive-bombers, the US Navy's most powerful attack weapon of World War II, in flight over a Pacific atoll (Imperial War Museum)

Foreword

by Wing Commander Robert Stanford-Tuck, DSO, DFC

While reading the manuscript of this book, I was so absorbed with the various types of aircraft, their evolution, development and application, that I was sorely tempted to write about some that I had flown and knew well. However, this would have been impossible in a short foreword so I must confine myself to more general observations on this excellent book on the aircraft of World War II.

When I consider the tremendous advances made in aircraft powerplant, design and armament over the short period of the war years, I am filled with admiration for the hard-working teams in the design shops, on the factory floors and in the offices of industry and most of all for the far-sighted planners who had to forecast the operational and tactical requirements. If these were to be met, they would absorb a substantial proportion of the manpower and productive capacity of the country concerned. When the very life of a nation at war was at stake, it is not difficult to appreciate the grave responsibility that rested on the shoulders of these dedicated people.

This book is about machines—inanimate objects of great beauty and, indeed, great lethal capacity. Christopher Chant and the publishers have given us a really magnificent written and pictorial record of no less than 73 of the major aircraft of World War II. From the descriptions of the capabilities and the production of these aircraft, a clear picture of the tremendous development in their design and armament carrying capacity emerges. All who were connected with these aircraft should be justifiably proud.

It is, perhaps, a sad reflection on society that during war years man's inventive genius often reaches a peak of achievement which seems to tail off, or slow down, as he advances into a peaceful era. Indeed, had the aircraft industry been able to maintain its wartime rate of advance in design and development after 1945, aeronautics would probably be more advanced than they are today – in spite of the unquestionably brilliant achievements of the space and moon flights.

Christopher Chant's book, I think, gives us not only an informed historical account of the roles of the major air forces of the world, but also a most interesting and, indeed for me, enlightening technical record of a large number of the aircraft involved in World War II. For any aviation student, historian or plain enthusiast, this, coupled with the superb colour drawings and contemporary photographs, will make *World War II Aircraft* a book that he must have.

I for one shall look forward with great pleasure to its publication and would like to thank the author and publishers for affording me the honour of writing these few words.

Sandwich Bay
Kent
October 1975

This page: Avro Lancasters were the mainstay of Britain's night bomber offensive against Germany. Illustrated are aircraft of no. 44 Squadron, RAF Bomber Command (Imperial War Museum)

GERMANY

Below: Fighter line-up. Luftwaffe groundcrew and other personnel check a group of Messer-schmitt Bf 109E-3s before an inspection. The E-3 sub-mark was one of the Luftwaffe's mainstays during the Battle of Britain, and proved itself a worthy opponent for Fighter Command's Spitfires and Hurricanes. The type's chief operational failing was a lack of range, which prevented it from escorting bombers deep into the southern half of England

The German air force, or *Luftwaffe*, came into being officially only in March 1935, when Hitler renounced the terms of the Treaty of Versailles. The history of Germany's air arm, however, stretched back to the years immediately following World War I. By the Treaty of Versailles Germany had been forbidden to build aircraft of military purpose, or to subsidize the production of civilian types. Consequently many German designers left the country to work abroad, although the German military establishment, which envisaged the eventual rearmament of the country, kept in close touch with them and provided clandestine backing.

In 1926 the non-military restrictions on aircraft were lifted by the Allies, and immediately, Germany started to build up a secret military air arm. The heavily-subsidized state airline, *Deutsche Lufthansa*, trained large numbers of pilots and navigators in the guise of civilian personnel, and national flying and gliding clubs helped to build up the necessary background of semi-skilled flying and ground personnel, whilst also maintaining keen enthusiasm for flight. At the same time designers returned from abroad, and embryonic military aircraft soon appeared over the skies of Germany as 'fast airliners', 'long-distance mailplanes' and 'single-seat sporting types'.

These preparations were greatly advanced by the advent to power of Adolf Hitler in 1933. Hitler's close friend Hermann Göring, an air ace in World War I, was placed in charge of the programme to develop the new air weapon, a task he fulfilled with considerable energy and skill. An ambitious scheme of growth was envisaged, but only after the necessary airfield and construction facilities had been provided, and a large cadre of personnel recruited and trained. When the *Luftwaffe* was revealed to the world in 1935, therefore, it was a large-scale, well-based and powerful weapon.

The new air force entered combat for the first time in 1936, in support of General Franco's Nationalist forces in the Spanish Civil War. Here the *Luftwaffe*'s first generation of aircraft was blooded, but showed itself little better than other air forces in the war. By 1937, however, aircraft of the second generation were arriving, and these quickly gained the Nationalists a general air superiority. Valuable combat testing and tactical experience was gained with types such as the Bf 109, Ju 87, Do 17 and He 111. It was this experience that paved the way for the blitzkrieg campaigns of 1939 to 1941.

The lessons of Spain, however, also harmed the *Luftwaffe* in the long run. Such was their confidence in the second generation of aircraft that the Germans failed to press on with the third generation, with disastrous consequences in World War II: by the time the Allied air forces were getting their second wind in 1943, the Germans were exhausted. Only one of the third generation types, the Fw 190, entered service in large numbers during the war. Other types arrived in minimal quantities, and too late, to affect the course of events significantly. Such were the He 177, Me 262 and He 219.

Another lesson which the Germans misinterpreted was the supremacy of a tactical air force. Although by 1939 the *Luftwaffe* was an excellent tactical weapon, and enjoyed almost uninterrupted success in this capacity up to the end of 1941, as the war progressed the Germans discovered the need for a strategic air arm. They sorely missed this in the Battle of Britain, and in Russia it might have saved the day for them in 1942. As it was, the main protagonist of such an air force, General Wever, had been killed in 1936, and, thereafter, work on advanced heavy bombers had slowed down very considerably.

The *Luftwaffe* was also bedevilled operationally by the peculiar political/military establishment of Nazi Germany. High-ranking political figures often exerted influence over fields in which they should not have meddled, so that operational requirements were often subordinated to political expedience or whim, and decisions were constantly affected by personal relations within the high command and not made on the sounder basis of military needs alone. Admittedly this did at times have advantages, enabling men such as Willi Messerschmitt to go over the heads of the *Luftwaffe* generals to Speer or Hitler but the practice was poor in principle and slowed the production of many desperately needed types.

Luftwaffe organization, too, was badly – and to ensure political control quite deliberately badly – set up, with a strong centralized structure but totally inadequate liaison across the various branches. Thus the chain of command functioned smoothly and well in a vertical direction, but one branch rarely knew what another was doing. This made co-ordination of activities very difficult, with the result that at times research was duplicated, or a stumbling-block in one project, which might have been removed by the research of another department, led to the abandonment of the project.

All these problems came home to roost in the second half of the war. Despite the many technological superiorities of German aircraft and the brilliance of individual pilots, Germany found that she had started her war on an aeronautical base that was too narrow to support the vast conflict that followed. Consequently her *Luftwaffe* was slowly but very surely crushed, and finally strangled early in 1945 by lack of fuel.

(Unless otherwise indicated, the production figures quoted are those during the period 1 September 1932 to 8 May 1945.)

Arado 234 Blitz

The Arado Ar 234 was among the most advanced and revolutionary aircraft in service with the *Luftwaffe* when World War II ended, and was the first turbojet-powered reconnaissance-bomber to enter service with any of the world's air forces when the type's first operational sorties were flown in the autumn of 1944.

Late in 1940 the firms of Junkers and BMW were bench-running early examples of their experimental turbojet engines, and Professor Walter Blume of Arado instructed Emil Eckstein to initiate design work on an aircraft to be powered by engines of the new type. Although Eckstein left the company early in 1941, he left behind him the design for a private-venture aircraft designated E 370. This was a conventional aircraft, with a monocoque fuselage, shoulder-mounted wing, ordinary tail surfaces, a tricycle undercarriage and a jet engine mounted under each wing.

Design work continued after the departure of Eckstein, the only major change to his concept being the abandonment of the bulky, weighty undercarriage in favour of a retractable landing skid under the fuselage, with stabilizing outriggers under the engine nacelles. For take-off the Ar 234, as the type was now designated, was to be mounted on a detachable tricycle trolley. The *Reichsluftfahrtministerium* (*RLM* or Reich Air Ministry) was by now interested in the aircraft as a replacement for the *Luftwaffe's* elderly high-altitude reconnaissance types, such as the Junkers Ju 86P.

Prototype construction began in the spring of 1941, and by the end of the year the *V*1 and *V*2 were ready except for their engines. (*V* was the standard abbreviation for *Versuchs* or experimental.) The two Junkers Jumo 004A engines were not in fact delivered until February 1943. As soon as these had been installed, intensive taxiing trials were conducted, the take-off trolley proving quite troublesome. After these trials, flight-cleared engines were fitted and the Ar 234 *V*1 was flown for the first time on 15 June 1943; it was soon joined by the *V*2, 3, 4 and 5. The *V*3 was intended as a pre-production proto-

type for the 234A series, and featured an ejector seat, cabin pressurization and jettisonable *Rauchgeräte* (rockets for assisting take-off) under the wings. Soon afterwards, however, the A series was abandoned, its lack of undercarriage making ground handling too difficult.

The A series was replaced by the B series, which featured a tricycle undercarriage. The *V*9 was the first prototype for this series, flying in March 1944. The pre-production 234B-0, with provision for underslung bombs, flew on 8 June 1944, and was soon developed into the definitive 234B-2. This proved successful in operations, its

major drawback being its low rate of acceleration at low speeds, which made it vulnerable when coming in to land.

It was apparent that the 234 could absorb more power output, and the *V*6 and *V*8 tested combinations of four smaller turbojets for the projected C series. The *V*8 had a pair of Jumo 003 engines in a single nacelle under each wing, and the *V*6 had four similar engines in four distinct nacelles. Several other models were under development when the war ended, and the full potential of this aircraft had only just begun to be realized. A total of 214 Ar 234 was built.

Top: An Arado Ar 234B-2 taxis out for take-off. Note the bombs under each engine nacelle and under the fuselage, and the Rauchgeräte rocket units mounted under each wing to assist take-off at maximum loaded weight.

Above: A still from the Arado training film about the handling of B-series aircraft. The photograph shows groundcrew assisting one of the B-series prototypes (probably the V9 or 10) out of its hangar

Left: An A-series prototype (probably the V3) climbs away from take-off with the aid of its R-geräte. Just discernible under the fuselage and nacelles are the retractable main and outrigger landing skids

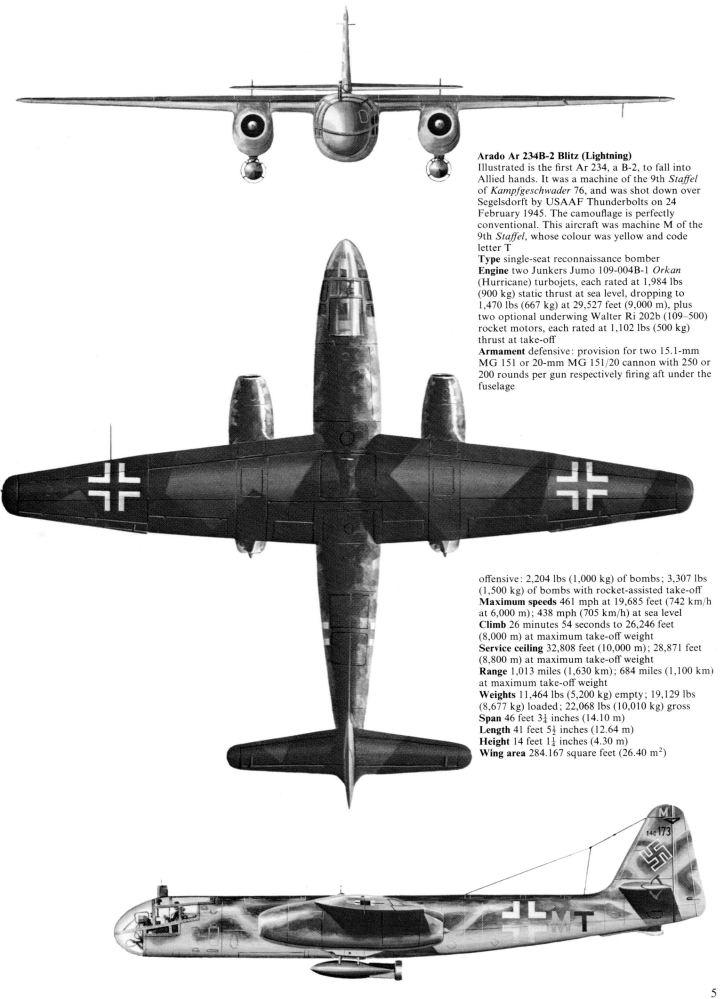

Arado Ar 234B-2 Blitz (Lightning)
Illustrated is the first Ar 234, a B-2, to fall into
Allied hands. It was a machine of the 9th *Staffel*
of *Kampfgeschwader* 76, and was shot down over
Segelsdorft by USAAF Thunderbolts on 24
February 1945. The camouflage is perfectly
conventional. This aircraft was machine M of the
9th *Staffel*, whose colour was yellow and code
letter T
Type single-seat reconnaissance bomber
Engine two Junkers Jumo 109-004B-1 *Orkan*
(Hurricane) turbojets, each rated at 1,984 lbs
(900 kg) static thrust at sea level, dropping to
1,470 lbs (667 kg) at 29,527 feet (9,000 m), plus
two optional underwing Walter Ri 202b (109–500)
rocket motors, each rated at 1,102 lbs (500 kg)
thrust at take-off
Armament defensive: provision for two 15.1-mm
MG 151 or 20-mm MG 151/20 cannon with 250 or
200 rounds per gun respectively firing aft under the
fuselage

offensive: 2,204 lbs (1,000 kg) of bombs; 3,307 lbs
(1,500 kg) of bombs with rocket-assisted take-off
Maximum speeds 461 mph at 19,685 feet (742 km/h
at 6,000 m); 438 mph (705 km/h) at sea level
Climb 26 minutes 54 seconds to 26,246 feet
(8,000 m) at maximum take-off weight
Service ceiling 32,808 feet (10,000 m); 28,871 feet
(8,800 m) at maximum take-off weight
Range 1,013 miles (1,630 km); 684 miles (1,100 km)
at maximum take-off weight
Weights 11,464 lbs (5,200 kg) empty; 19,129 lbs
(8,677 kg) loaded; 22,068 lbs (10,010 kg) gross
Span 46 feet 3¼ inches (14.10 m)
Length 41 feet 5½ inches (12.64 m)
Height 14 feet 1¼ inches (4.30 m)
Wing area 284.167 square feet (26.40 m²)

Dornier 17

The Dornier Do 17, nicknamed the 'Flying Pencil' in the English-speaking world, was one of the three bombers that formed the mainstay of the *Luftwaffe*'s tactical bombing force throughout the war. Despite this, however, the Do 17 began life as a commercial type – Dornier's response to a *Deutsche Lufthansa* requirement of 1934 for a fast mail/passenger aircraft for its European routes. By the end of 1934 the Do 17 *V*1, 2 and 3 were all being flight tested. These were sleek, slim monoplanes, powered by two BMW VI inlines, with a long, conical nose and a single fin and rudder. Although performance was excellent, *Lufthansa* decided that the accommodation for the six passengers was totally inadequate and dropped the project. The *RLM*, however, were very impressed by the prototypes' performance, and issued a requirement for a bomber version. This was forthcoming in the Do 17 *V*4, which incorporated a radio position in lieu of the old passenger compartment, a bomb-bay and twin vertical tail surfaces at the ends of the tailplane in place of the earlier prototypes' single vertical surface.

Other *V* series aircraft followed, with altered powerplants, a glazed nose and provision for defensive armament. The *V*9 had an extensively glazed nose, and was in fact the prototype for the first production series, the Do 17E-1. These machines started to come off the production lines late in 1936, and to enter service early in the following year. Produced in parallel was the F-1, a long-range reconnaissance variant without provision for carrying the E-1's 1,102-lb (500-kg) bomb-load. The E-1 and F-1 were both tested operationally in the Spanish Civil War with great success as no Republican fighters of 1937 were able to catch them. The Polikarpov I-16, which appeared over Spain in 1938, however, spelled the end of the Do 17's days of impunity.

The next production versions were the Do 17M and 17P, bomber and long-range reconnaissance models respectively. As priority for the Daimler-Benz DB 600 inline engines, with which they were to have been powered, had been allocated to fighter aircraft, Dornier re-engined their machine with the Bramo 323 Fafnir (17M-1) and BMW 132 (17P-1) radials. The lower-powered BMW engine was chosen for the 17P as it was lighter and gave greater range for the same quantity of fuel. The Bramo engine allowed the 17M version to carry a 2,205-lb (1,000-kg) bomb-load. These two models started to join the E and F models in service in 1938.

The Do 17L was similar to the 17M, but carried a fourth crew member and was intended as a pathfinder. No production orders were received, however. The 17R was a test aircraft.

The next mark of the Do 17 was the definitive Do 17Z, which offered very enhanced performance benefits over its predecessors. The origin of the new model lay in the combat experience of Spain in 1938, when it was discovered that the Do 17 was deficient in protection against attack from below, the single ventral machine-gun possessing far too restricted a field of fire to be effective. Thus a totally new forward fuselage was designed, with flat panels replacing the curved ones in the tip of the glazed nose, the cockpit being heightened and completely glazed, and the lower part of the nose deepened and extended aft to a position under the wing leading edge. This last contained a machine-gun with a field of fire superior to that possible previously.

The new fuselage was first seen on three 17S-0 high-speed reconnaissance and 15 17U-0 and U-1 pathfinder aircraft of 1938. Then the 17Z series entered production in the autumn of 1938. This was similar to the 17S and 17U, but had Bramo Fafnir radials in place of the previous models' Daimler-Benz DB 600 inlines. Various sub-models of the 17Z were produced, for bombing, reconnaissance, and training. The basic Do 17 was reaching the end of its potential as a bomber, however, and production was phased out in the first half of 1940. It is worth noting that Yugoslavia was interested in an export version of the 17Z, and this was redesignated the Do 215, a few being delivered to the *Luftwaffe* before the basic design was transformed into the greatly superior Do 217. The last variants of the Do 17 design were the 17Z-6 and Z-10 night fighters, in which the glazed nose was replaced by a solid nose mounting a cannon and machine-gun armament. No radar was carried so early in the war, and the Do 17Z *Kauz* (Screech-owl) night fighters were phased out of service in the spring of 1942.

The Do 17 served extensively with the *Luftwaffe*, but was gradually phased out of front-line bombing service in late 1942, subsequently serving as a training aircraft and glider tug. The Do 17 was also used by the air forces of Yugoslavia, Croatia and Finland. In all its versions the Do 17 was a tractable and fairly manoeuvrable aircraft for its size, and in its last versions very reliable and easy to maintain. Performance was adequate for the early years of the war, but bomb-load was always inferior to that of the Heinkel He 111 and speed lower than that of the Junkers Ju 88, the Do 17's companion front-line bombers, and only 506 were built.

Top: A Do 215B-1 in flight. The Do 215 series was basically the same as the Do 17Z, and was at first intended for export. An embargo was placed on export models, however, and the Luftwaffe took over the DB 601-engined aircraft as reconnaissance bombers in the spring of 1940.

Above: A Do 17P-1 strategic reconnaissance aircraft, powered by a pair of BMW 132N radial engines. The top photograph was in all probability taken from such an aircraft, judging by the two exhausts in the lower right-hand corner of the picture

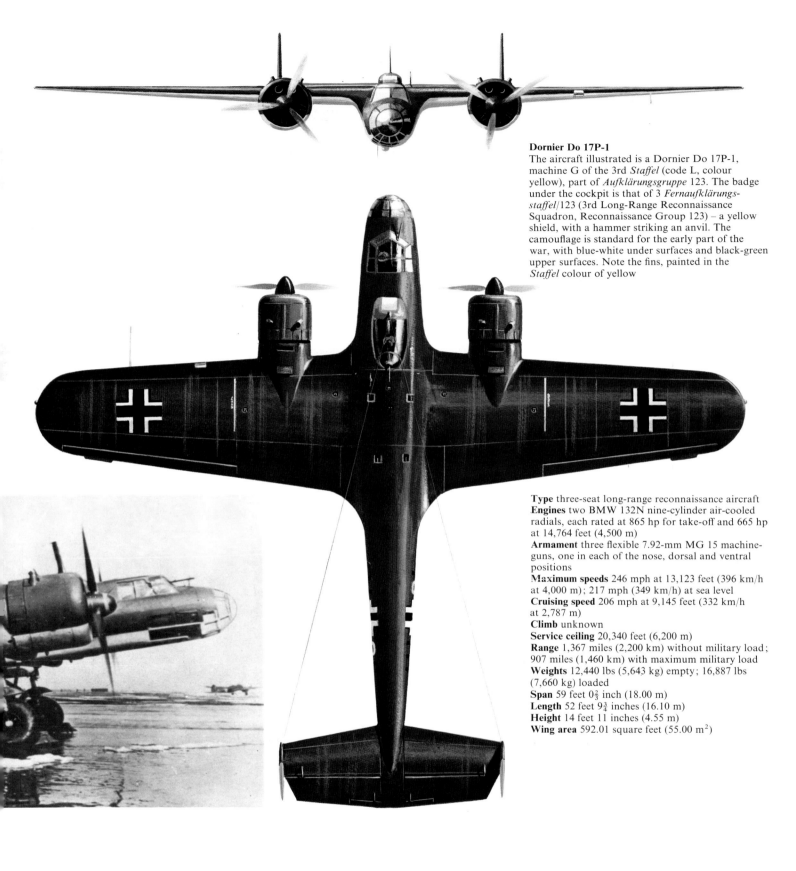

Dornier Do 17P-1

The aircraft illustrated is a Dornier Do 17P-1, machine G of the 3rd *Staffel* (code L, colour yellow), part of *Aufklärungsgruppe* 123. The badge under the cockpit is that of 3 *Fernaufklärungs-staffel*/123 (3rd Long-Range Reconnaissance Squadron, Reconnaissance Group 123) – a yellow shield, with a hammer striking an anvil. The camouflage is standard for the early part of the war, with blue-white under surfaces and black-green upper surfaces. Note the fins, painted in the *Staffel* colour of yellow

Type three-seat long-range reconnaissance aircraft
Engines two BMW 132N nine-cylinder air-cooled radials, each rated at 865 hp for take-off and 665 hp at 14,764 feet (4,500 m)
Armament three flexible 7.92-mm MG 15 machine-guns, one in each of the nose, dorsal and ventral positions
Maximum speeds 246 mph at 13,123 feet (396 km/h at 4,000 m); 217 mph (349 km/h) at sea level
Cruising speed 206 mph at 9,145 feet (332 km/h at 2,787 m)
Climb unknown
Service ceiling 20,340 feet (6,200 m)
Range 1,367 miles (2,200 km) without military load; 907 miles (1,460 km) with maximum military load
Weights 12,440 lbs (5,643 kg) empty; 16,887 lbs (7,660 kg) loaded
Span 59 feet 0⅔ inch (18.00 m)
Length 52 feet 9¾ inches (16.10 m)
Height 14 feet 11 inches (4.55 m)
Wing area 592.01 square feet (55.00 m²)

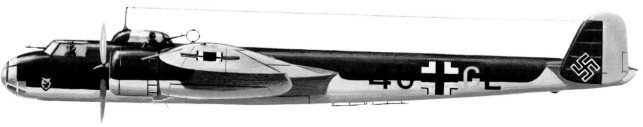

Focke-Wulf 190

The Focke-Wulf Fw 190 was Germany's second great fighter of World War II, and was in most respects superior to its front-line companion and rival for the title of the Third Reich's best fighter, the Bf 109.

Although opinion in the *RLM* was divided about the need for a successor to the Messerschmitt Bf 109, in 1938 the firm of Focke-Wulf received permission to proceed with the detailed design of a new fighter. Although inline engines, with their low frontal area, were in vogue with European fighter designers, Kurt Tank, in charge of the new project, had persuaded the *RLM* to allow him to use the BMW 139 radial, as this was already offering more power than any inline engine then in production and its use would not further strain inline engine production.

As work on the Fw 190 *V1* proceeded the BMW 139 engine was found to overheat and Focke-Wulf substituted the newer, and more promising, BMW 801 for the older engine in their plans for production aircraft. The first prototypes were too advanced to be changed, however. The 190 *V1* was flown for the first time on 1 June 1939, and immediately proved itself to be an admirable aircraft, with excellent speed and sensitive, but well-balanced, controls. The earlier fears about the BMW 139 were quickly realized, however, although the trouble was partially attributable to the fact that the engine-cooling fan had not yet been installed. The cooling fan was fitted on the 190 *V2*, but the engine still overheated. On production models a 12-blade fan replaced the 10-blade one.

The 190 *V5*, which flew in April 1940, was the first version of the *Würger* (Shrike), as Focke-Wulf had dubbed their fighter, to be powered by the BMW 801. This engine was considerably heavier than its predecessor, and Focke-Wulf had designed a larger wing for production aircraft to keep weight loadings down. After an accident, this larger wing was fitted to the *V5*. This resulted in a slight reduction in speed, although rate of climb was greatly improved and handling characteristics restored to the precision of the first prototypes. The *V5* was in most

respects similar to the first production models, and differed principally from the *V1* and *V2* in having a slightly larger wing and tailplane, with a fuselage four inches longer. To compensate for the greater weight of the new engine, the cockpit was moved further back. Nevertheless, the Fw 190 remained a very pleasing aircraft visually, beautifully streamlined, with as narrow a fuselage as it was possible to design around the bulky radial. One of the new fighter's most distinct advantages over the Bf 109 was its inward-retracting undercarriage, giving it greater stability on the ground compared with the 109's outward-retracting landing gear.

JG 26, the *Luftwaffe* unit detailed to develop the type operationally, had a very difficult time early in 1941: there was constant trouble with the engine, its cooling and the propeller. These problems were eventually resolved and the *Geschwader* went into action in September 1941. The new fighter proved very successful, outclassing the RAF's Spitfire Vs in almost every respect. The Fw 190A series went through many models, with increased power, better armament and provision for underslung bombs. With this last modification, Fw 190s made a large number of hit-and-run raids on British targets. These caused little real damage, but meant that the RAF had to resort to standing patrols, with their attendant strain on fuel stocks and aircraft serviceability.

The two definitive A-series models were the 190A-3 and 190A-8. The first was a pure fighter with four 20-mm cannon and a speed of 418 mph (673 km/h); the second was a fighter-bomber which could carry a 551-lb (250-kg) bomb and had a speed of 408 mph (657 km/h). The 190F series was derived from the A, and was intended as a close-support series, with up to 1,102 lbs (500 kg) of bombs or underwing armament of two 30-mm MK 108 cannon in addition to the standard fuselage- and wing-mounted machine-gun and cannon armament. The 190G series was also derived from the A, and was designed as a long-range fighter-bomber series.

The 190B and 190C series never materialized

except as prototypes, although these were very important in the overall development of the 190: the major combat disadvantage of the early production series had been inadequate performance at altitude as a result of the BMW radial engine, and the B and C were designed around the Daimler-Benz DB 603 inline. Tests with this engine, specially boosted with methanol-water (MW-50) or nitrous oxide (GM-1) injection, proved generally satisfactory, and the lessons were incorporated in the 190D series, the only inline-engined 190 series to enter widespread service. The major distinguishing feature of the *Dora*, as it was dubbed by the *Luftwaffe*, was its stretched fuselage compared with earlier models. The inline engine was very neatly cowled in a nose that kept the radial-engined shape of its predecessors by having an annular radiator instead of the more usual bath type. To compensate for the longer nose (the D series is generally known as the 'long-nosed' series), the rear fuselage also had to be lengthened. The definitive model of the D series was the 190D-9, a fighter-bomber with a medium cannon and machine-gun armament but a maximum speed of 426 mph (686 km/h) and range of 520 miles (837 km) on internal fuel. All the D series had Junkers Jumo engines.

Throughout its career the Fw 190 proved a remarkably successful machine, capable of adaptation to the most difficult missions (such as torpedo-bombing). It was fast, possessed a good range, was very manoeuvrable and very sturdy. Production amounted to 20,001 aircraft.

The final versions of the basic Fw 190 philosophy were the D series-derived Ta 152C and 152H (the Ta for Kurt Tank), respectively medium- and high-altitude fighters. The 152H-1 was capable of 472 mph (760 km/h) and an altitude of 48,550 feet (14,800 m).

Below: The first Ta 152 captured by the Allies, a Ta 152H-0. This was derived from the 'long-nose' inline-engined Fw 190D series, and was intended as a high-altitude, very high performance interceptor fighter

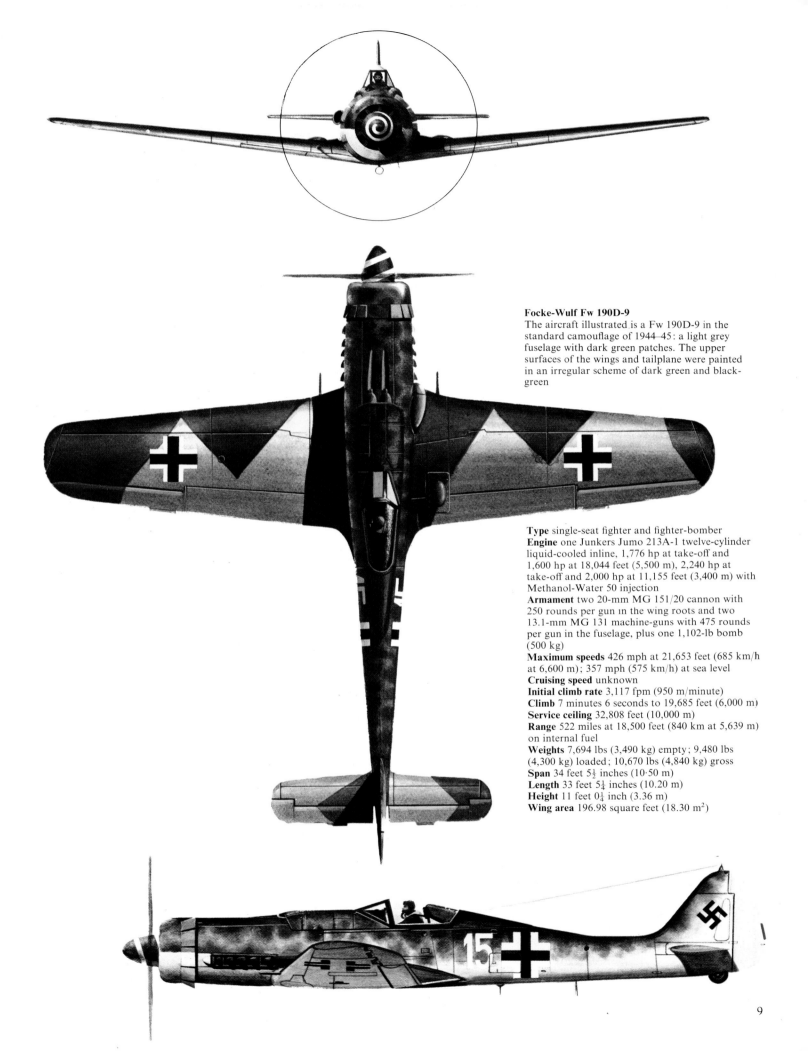

Focke-Wulf Fw 190D-9
The aircraft illustrated is a Fw 190D-9 in the standard camouflage of 1944–45: a light grey fuselage with dark green patches. The upper surfaces of the wings and tailplane were painted in an irregular scheme of dark green and black-green

Type single-seat fighter and fighter-bomber
Engine one Junkers Jumo 213A-1 twelve-cylinder liquid-cooled inline, 1,776 hp at take-off and 1,600 hp at 18,044 feet (5,500 m), 2,240 hp at take-off and 2,000 hp at 11,155 feet (3,400 m) with Methanol-Water 50 injection
Armament two 20-mm MG 151/20 cannon with 250 rounds per gun in the wing roots and two 13.1-mm MG 131 machine-guns with 475 rounds per gun in the fuselage, plus one 1,102-lb bomb (500 kg)
Maximum speeds 426 mph at 21,653 feet (685 km/h at 6,600 m); 357 mph (575 km/h) at sea level
Cruising speed unknown
Initial climb rate 3,117 fpm (950 m/minute)
Climb 7 minutes 6 seconds to 19,685 feet (6,000 m)
Service ceiling 32,808 feet (10,000 m)
Range 522 miles at 18,500 feet (840 km at 5,639 m) on internal fuel
Weights 7,694 lbs (3,490 kg) empty; 9,480 lbs (4,300 kg) loaded; 10,670 lbs (4,840 kg) gross
Span 34 feet 5½ inches (10·50 m)
Length 33 feet 5¼ inches (10.20 m)
Height 11 feet 0¼ inch (3.36 m)
Wing area 196.98 square feet (18.30 m²)

Focke-Wulf 200

That the Focke-Wulf Fw 200 proved so potent a weapon in Germany's campaign against Allied shipping was entirely providential, as the aircraft had been designed solely as a commercial transport. The *Condor* was the result of discussions between *Deutsche Lufthansa* and Dr Kurt Tank of Focke-Wulf; the Fw 200 *V*1 flew for the first time in July 1937 and was soon followed by two more prototypes. The third prototype became Hitler's personal aircraft. The subsequent Fw 200A series was used mostly for experimental purposes, and several notable long-distance flights were achieved during 1938 with machines of the series. Introduced in the autumn of 1938, the Fw 200B series featured increased weights and BMW 132 engines in place of the earlier series' Pratt & Whitney Hornets. During the war, the B series was taken over by the *Luftwaffe*.

During 1938 the Imperial Japanese Navy had evinced interest in a version of the Fw 200 for long-range maritime-reconnaissance, and the Fw 200 *V*10 was converted to the Japanese specification although never put into production. When war broke out in 1939, the *Luftwaffe* found itself without an equivalent aircraft as the Heinkel He 177 had not started its trials. Focke-Wulf therefore proposed a derivative of the Fw 200 *V*10 to fit this role. The *Luftwaffe* was very interested in the idea, which received the designation Fw 200C. Like the Japanese aircraft, the C series featured a long gondola under the fuselage for the necessary reconnaissance equipment, but also had improved engine nacelles and twin-wheeled main undercarriage units. The first few C series machines were converted from B series aircraft already under construction, and were finished without armament as transports. Later aircraft of the series were delivered with a light defensive armament and bomb racks for a moderate offensive load. These machines were delivered to I *Gruppe* of *Kampfgeschwader* 40, which was to be the chief exponent of the *Condor,* in the spring of 1940. In August and September 1940 the unit sank more than 90,000 tons of shipping.

The pre-production Fw 200C-0 series was replaced on the production lines by the Fw 200C-1, which had a ventral gondola unlike the earlier machines. This had provision for a cannon and a machine-gun, plus an internally-carried cement bomb to test the accuracy of the bomb sight before the four externally-carried HE bombs were used. The forward dorsal turret was also replaced by a raised cupola, still fitted with the same light machine-gun.

The next *Condor* model was the Fw 200C-2, which had improved engine nacelles to reduce drag when the underwing bomb-load was carried, together with faired bomb racks. The Fw 200C-2 was only a stop-gap, however, pending the delivery of the first Fw 200C-3 aircraft, which was intended as the definitive model.

The Fw 200C-3 featured a considerably strengthened fuselage and wing, which had proved very weak for combat operations. The bomb-load was also increased, as was the defensive armament: a cannon-armed, forward dorsal turret (in the Fw 200C-3/U1) later replaced by a low-drag mounting with a 13.1-mm machine-gun (in the Fw 200C-3/U3), two beam machine-guns and improved armament in the gondola.

The Fw 200C-4 was built in larger numbers than any other model, and differed from the C-3, being fitted with a variety of air-sea search radar installations. The last model of the *Condor* was the Fw 200C-8, which was designed to carry the Henschel Hs 293A guided missile. Other *Condor* adapted to carry this weapon were redesignated Fw 200C-6.

All in all, the *Condor* proved quite successful. This is all the more remarkable as the machine was originally designed for light civilian tasks. The fuselage and wing structure weaknesses were never fully eradicated, and, as the type was not intended for intensive combat operations, serviceability always remained low, usually well below 50 per cent of the aircraft of any unit.

Focke-Wulf Fw 200C-2 Condor

The aircraft illustrated is an Fw 200C-2, the aircraft of the *Staffelkapitän* of the 1st *Staffel*, I *Gruppe*, *Kampfgeschwader* 40, whose unit emblem was the world globe surrounded by a yellow ring, painted under the cockpit. Camouflage is the standard *Schwarzgrün* (black-green) and *Dunkelgrün* (dark green) upper surfaces and *Hellblau* (light blue) under surfaces

Type five- to seven-seat long-range maritime-reconnaissance bomber

Engines four BMW 132H nine-cylinder air-cooled radials, each rated at 1,000 hp for take-off

Armament defensive: one flexible 20-mm MG FF cannon in the front of the ventral gondola, and three flexible 7.92-mm MG 15 machine-guns, one in each of the rear gondola, front upper and rear dorsal positions

offensive: up to 2,756 lbs (1,250 kg) of bombs

Maximum speed 264 mph at 8,645 feet (425 km/h at 2,635 m)

Cruising speed 236 mph (380 km/h)

Initial climb rate 1,870 fpm (570 m/minute)

Climb 2 minutes 18 seconds to 3,281 feet (1,000 m)

Service ceiling 24,401 feet (7,440 m)

Range 2,759 miles (4,440 km)

Weights 28,560 lbs (12,950 kg) empty; unknown loaded; 50,045 lbs (22,700 kg) gross

Span 107 feet 9½ inches (32.85 m)

Length 76 feet 11½ inches (23.46 m)

Height 20 feet 8 inches (6.30 m)

Wing area 1,290 square feet (119.85 m²)

Left above: An Fw 200C-3/U2 Condor, aircraft K of the 8th Staffel, III Gruppe, of an unidentified Geschwader. The C-3 sub-mark introduced a strengthened fuselage and wing structure, more powerful engines, and a front dorsal turret. The U2 modification added a Lotfernrohr 7D bomb sight in the nose of the ventral gondola, with a consequent improvement in bombing accuracy from altitudes in the order of 9,842 feet (3,000 metres). The installation of the new sight entailed the replacement of the nose-mounted ventral 20-mm cannon with a 13.1-mm machine-gun

Left: Groundcrew refuel Condor P of the 1st Staffel, I Gruppe, of Kampfgeschwader 40, the most successful unit equipped with the Fw 200

11

Heinkel 111

Although several other German bombers of the World War II period first made their appearance in a civilian guise, the Heinkel 111 was notable for being designed from the outset both as a bomber and as a passenger aircraft. Designed by the brothers Siegfried and Walter Günter in 1934 to a *Deutsche Lufthansa* specification for a passenger transport to supplement the He 70, which was too small for certain routes, the He 111 had allowances for military uses built into it from the outset. In fact the first three prototypes, delivered in 1935, were basically military models, with provision for both offensive and defensive armament. These three prototypes differed from each other principally in the shape of their basically elliptical wing planforms. The first civilian prototype, the He 111 *V4*, first flew late in 1935, and was intended as the forerunner of the He 111C airliner series. In common with the early military models, the *V4* had a long, finely-streamlined nose, quite unlike the fully-glazed nose of later military series. The chief external differences between the military and civilian models were the glazed bombardier's position in the extreme nose and the open dorsal position in the former models.

The first military series was the He 111A, of which only 10 were built in 1935. Performance with full military equipment was disappointing, especially with the retractable ventral 'dustbin' gun position, and the low-powered BMW VI 6, OZ inline engines. The shortage of power was rectified in the next model, the He 111B, which had two Daimler-Benz DB 600 engines. Service deliveries of this much-improved aircraft began in the winter of 1936. The He 111B was one of the first German types to see action in Spain, where its high speed (230 mph or 370 km/h) made it almost invulnerable to Republican fighters. Its bomb-load of over 3,000 lbs (1,361 kg) was also quite heavy for the time. At the same time, Heinkel was delivering civilian machines of the He 111C and G series to *Deutsche Lufthansa*, which decided that the type was uneconomical to run.

Early in 1937, Heinkel decided that with the latest DB 600 engine mark, the He 111's performance could be enhanced greatly, and a redesign of the cooling system, to reduce drag, was put in hand. This resulted in the He 111D series which replaced the surface radiators with deeper ones under the engines and which also had improved exhausts and better streamlining. Performance was radically improved (speed by 25 mph or 40 km/h), but no series production was undertaken as DB 600 engines were in short supply and Messerschmitt Bf 109 and 110 fighters had priority. Heinkel had foreseen this shortage, however, and had initiated design studies for a series to be powered by the Junkers Jumo 210 or 211 engine. The former engine proved to be insufficiently powerful, and production He 111E aircraft, which began to appear in 1938, were powered by a pair of Jumo 211 engines.

E series aircraft were soon sent to Spain, where they enjoyed the same success as the earlier B models. One of the major disadvantages of these early models was the elliptical wing, which was difficult, and therefore expensive, to build. A new wing, with straight leading and trailing edges, was thus introduced on the He 111F series, and was retained on all later series. The He 111J was designed in the second half of 1938 as a torpedo-bomber, without internal bomb-bays, but lack of *Luftwaffe* interest meant that the few examples produced were retrofitted with bomb-bays.

Another disadvantage of the He 111 discovered by service crews was lack of visibility. In an attempt to rectify this, Heinkel redesigned the nose in 1937, eliminating the previous finely-tapered one for a shorter, fully-glazed one, faired into the fuselage contours without any breaks. To improve the pilot's visibility yet further, the nose-gunner's position was offset to starboard, giving the He 111's later series their distinctive lop-sided appearance in plan-view. The first series to feature the new nose was the He 111P, which began to enter service early in 1939. The

series, which was powered by DB 601 engines, also introduced a permanent ventral gondola with a single machine-gun in place of the earlier retractable 'dustbin', which had produced too much drag. By the time production of the He 111P series ended in the middle of 1940, combat experience with the British and French had shown that the defensive armament of three 7.92-mm machine-guns was totally inadequate, and a further three or four guns of the same calibre were added from the He 111P-4 model onwards. Some armour protection for the pilot was also added.

The most numerous He 111 series was the H model, which reverted to Junkers Jumo engines, and was built in a bewildering number of marks and sub-marks before He 111 production finally ended in 1944. Defensive armament was increased very considerably over the war years, and models to carry paratroops, torpedoes, guided bombs and even to launch *V*-1 flying bombs from the air were built. It was also intended to develop the basic He 111 as a high-altitude bomber, but the prototype of this He 111R was unsuccessful. Also built in limited numbers was the He 111Z glider tug, which consisted of two He 111H-6 fuselages, complete with empennage and one port and one starboard wing, joined by a new parallel-chord wing with a fifth engine. Remarkably, the type proved quite useful.

Throughout its life the He 111 remained a tractable, easy plane to fly, but it suffered several severe disadvantages: principal amongst these was the fact that as a suitable successor was slow to make its appearance, the He 111 was kept in service far too long. Although its range and bomb-load were adequate for the tactical tasks it was required to fulfil, the type was always underdefended, and therefore suffered heavy losses where air defence was good. Nevertheless, the He 111 was a tractable aircraft to fly, and found great favour as a torpedo-bomber. At the end of its career, the He 111 was also used as a paratroop aircraft. In all 5,656 He 111 were built.

Left: Groundcrew prepare to load a second Lufttorpedo F5b practice airborne-dropped torpedo onto the starboard PVC rack, under the wing root of an He 111H-6 bomber. The aircraft was probably one of the machines of I/KG 26, the Löwen Geschwader, which inflicted great losses on the Allied arctic convoys during the second half of 1942, operating from bases in northern Norway. The H-6 sub-mark of the He 111 was the most widely used variant of the basic type, and proved an excellent torpedo-bomber in addition to its designed task of level bombing

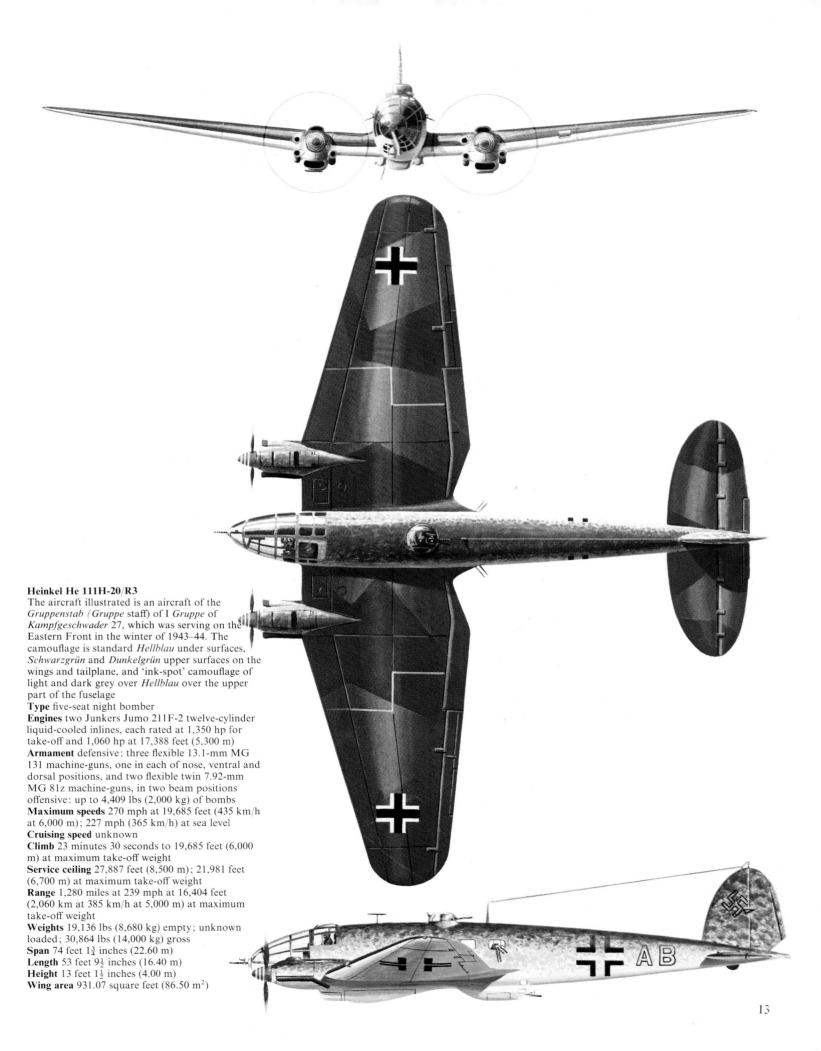

Heinkel He 111H-20/R3

The aircraft illustrated is an aircraft of the *Gruppenstab (Gruppe* staff) of I *Gruppe* of *Kampfgeschwader* 27, which was serving on the Eastern Front in the winter of 1943–44. The camouflage is standard *Hellblau* under surfaces, *Schwarzgrün* and *Dunkelgrün* upper surfaces on the wings and tailplane, and 'ink-spot' camouflage of light and dark grey over *Hellblau* over the upper part of the fuselage

Type five-seat night bomber

Engines two Junkers Jumo 211F-2 twelve-cylinder liquid-cooled inlines, each rated at 1,350 hp for take-off and 1,060 hp at 17,388 feet (5,300 m)

Armament defensive: three flexible 13.1-mm MG 131 machine-guns, one in each of nose, ventral and dorsal positions, and two flexible twin 7.92-mm MG 81z machine-guns, in two beam positions offensive: up to 4,409 lbs (2,000 kg) of bombs

Maximum speeds 270 mph at 19,685 feet (435 km/h at 6,000 m); 227 mph (365 km/h) at sea level

Cruising speed unknown

Climb 23 minutes 30 seconds to 19,685 feet (6,000 m) at maximum take-off weight

Service ceiling 27,887 feet (8,500 m); 21,981 feet (6,700 m) at maximum take-off weight

Range 1,280 miles at 239 mph at 16,404 feet (2,060 km at 385 km/h at 5,000 m) at maximum take-off weight

Weights 19,136 lbs (8,680 kg) empty; unknown loaded; 30,864 lbs (14,000 kg) gross

Span 74 feet $1\frac{3}{4}$ inches (22.60 m)

Length 53 feet $9\frac{1}{2}$ inches (16.40 m)

Height 13 feet $1\frac{1}{2}$ inches (4.00 m)

Wing area 931.07 square feet (86.50 m^2)

13

Junkers 52/3m

For all its angular ugliness, the trimotor Junkers Ju 52/3 series of bomber and transport aircraft was one of the best-loved and most useful types to serve with the *Luftwaffe*, whose personnel knew the Ju 52/3 as *Tante Ju* or Auntie Ju. The Ju 52/3, or more properly Ju 52/3m, was designed by Ernst Zindel in 1932 as a more powerful version of the single-engined Ju 52 of 1930, which was in service as a cargo aircraft with *Deutsche Lufthansa*. From the outset the new aircraft proved very successful, and Junkers terminated production of the Ju 52 in favour of this three-motor (3m) version. Intended at first only for civil transport, the Ju 52/3m was soon pressed into service by the clandestine *Luftwaffe* as an interim heavy bomber, pending deliveries of the Dornier Do 11. This was the Ju 52/3m ge model, but when problems with the Do 11 prevented that type's widespread service use, the Ju 52/3m was pressed into extended service, as the Ju 52/3m g3e with improved bomb-release gear and radio. Up to 3,307 lbs (1,500 kg) of bombs could be carried. Defensive armament consisted of only two 7.92-mm machine-guns, one in an open dorsal position and one in a retractable ventral 'dustbin'.

The Ju 52/3m went to war in August 1936, first ferrying Franco's troops from Morocco to metropolitan Spain, and then performing a variety of bombing missions. In Spain the Ju 52/3m g3e was soon joined by the Ju 52/3m g4e, which was basically similar apart from having a

tailwheel rather than a skid. With the arrival of more modern bombers, the Ju 52/3m aircraft were relegated to their original transport role. In Germany they were finished as proper transport or operational training aircraft for multi-engined aircraft pilots and navigators. The next model to appear was the Ju 52/3m g5e, with superior flying equipment and provision for an interchangeable float, ski, or wheel undercarriage. Basically similar was the Ju 52/3m g6e, which was intended only for land operations, with simplified radio equipment.

The Ju 52/3m was also intended for use by airborne forces, and the type was used operationally in this role, and as a glider tug, over Denmark, Norway, Holland and Belgium. Losses were quite heavy, but production was at full tempo, and all losses had been made good by the end of 1940. Another task undertaken by the Ju 52/3m was that of minesweeping. For this the aircraft was fitted with a great dural hoop under the fuselage and wings, energized by an auxiliary motor in the fuselage, to set off magnetic mines.

The Ju 52/3m g5e and g6e had dispensed with the ventral 'dustbin' for two lateral 7.92-mm machine-guns, and this armament was supplemented in the Ju 52/3m g7e with a further 7.92-mm machine-gun (optional) in a forward dorsal position. The starboard loading door was also enlarged. A loading hatch in the fuselage roof was added on the Ju 52/3m g8e, which also had a 13.1-mm rear dorsal machine-gun in place

of the earlier models' 7.92-mm weapon. The next model of the Ju 52/3m was the g9e, which appeared in 1942. This had a glider-towing attachment fitted as standard, and an improved undercarriage for heavier take-off weights. The last model, the Ju 52/3m g14e, appeared in 1943 with armour protection and improved defensive armament. Production ceased in mid-1944 after 3,225 examples of the Ju 52/3m had been built, 2,804 during the war.

The utility of the Ju 52/3m to the German cause can never be overestimated. The type served as a bomber in Spain, transport and airborne troops aircraft in Denmark, Norway, Holland, Belgium, France, Greece, Crete and Russia, and in a multitude of transport, training and liaison tasks in Germany herself. Unfortunately for Germany, whenever a special need for such aircraft arose, as for the invasion of Crete or the Demyansk and Stalingrad airlifts, the necessary *Tante Ju* aircraft, together with their experienced crews, were taken from their training duties and used in combat. Their destruction not only meant the loss of the aircraft and men, but also affected the training of future crews.

Below: Apparent confusion on a German airfield in North Africa as Ju 52/3m transports are unloaded of their cargoes of fuel after the flight from Italy. In the foreground are a pair of Messerschmitt Bf 110 fighters

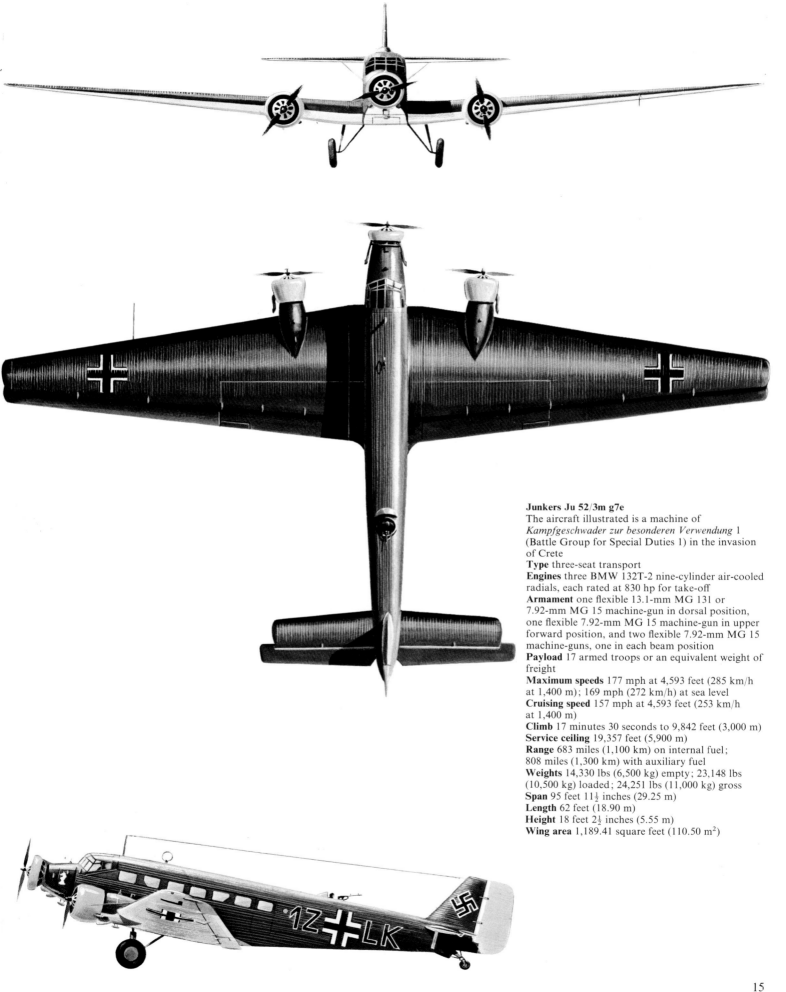

Junkers Ju 52/3m g7e
The aircraft illustrated is a machine of
Kampfgeschwader zur besonderen Verwendung 1
(Battle Group for Special Duties 1) in the invasion
of Crete
Type three-seat transport
Engines three BMW 132T-2 nine-cylinder air-cooled
radials, each rated at 830 hp for take-off
Armament one flexible 13.1-mm MG 131 or
7.92-mm MG 15 machine-gun in dorsal position,
one flexible 7.92-mm MG 15 machine-gun in upper
forward position, and two flexible 7.92-mm MG 15
machine-guns, one in each beam position
Payload 17 armed troops or an equivalent weight of
freight
Maximum speeds 177 mph at 4,593 feet (285 km/h
at 1,400 m); 169 mph (272 km/h) at sea level
Cruising speed 157 mph at 4,593 feet (253 km/h
at 1,400 m)
Climb 17 minutes 30 seconds to 9,842 feet (3,000 m)
Service ceiling 19,357 feet (5,900 m)
Range 683 miles (1,100 km) on internal fuel;
808 miles (1,300 km) with auxiliary fuel
Weights 14,330 lbs (6,500 kg) empty; 23,148 lbs
(10,500 kg) loaded; 24,251 lbs (11,000 kg) gross
Span 95 feet 11½ inches (29.25 m)
Length 62 feet (18.90 m)
Height 18 feet 2½ inches (5.55 m)
Wing area 1,189.41 square feet (110.50 m²)

15

Junkers 87

Rightly or wrongly, the Junkers Ju 87 has become synonymous with German blitzkrieg warfare under its nickname of *Stuka*. (This is an abbreviation of the German word for dive-bomber – *Sturzkampfflugzeug*.) And such has been the *Stuka*'s notoriety that a great body of legend has grown up around the aircraft itself, at times making it difficult to assess the *Stuka* correctly. For example, the aircraft has been described as 'cumbersome', because it was relatively simple for Allied fighters to shoot it down; however this is scarcely surprising as the *Stuka* was built not as a fighter but as a large, single-engined bomber. The fault implicit in the epithet 'cumbersome' belongs not to the aircraft, which was light and positive to handle and fully aerobatic, but to the false tactical doctrines of German commanders who sent in these dive-bombers against targets well-defended by good fighters, without an adequate escort of their own.

The Ju 87 stemmed directly from a visit made by Ernst Udet to the United States, where he had seen remarkable results in dive-bombing demonstrations. Designed by Hermann Pohlmann, the Ju 87 *V*1 flew for the first time in 1935. This initial prototype differed quite radically from most of its successors in several respects, having a Rolls-Royce Kestrel engine, twin vertical tail surfaces mounted at the ends of the tailplane, and a 'trousered' rather than 'spatted' undercarriage. The *V*2 had a single vertical tail surface.

The Ju 87 nearly came to a premature end in June 1936, when the head of the *Reichsluftfahrtministerium*'s technical department decided that development work should be discontinued. The history of World War II might well have been radically different had not Ernst Udet taken over the office the day after the order was issued and rescinded it. Thereafter development work went ahead swiftly. The Ju *V*3, which was flying by this time, was engined with the Junkers Jumo

that was to power the whole series. By the middle of 1936 the basic design of the Ju 87 had been fixed, only the later 'spatting' of the undercarriage altering the basic outline.

The first production Ju 87A series aircraft entered service in the early months of 1937, a few of the new dive-bombers being sent to Spain to test the aircraft operationally.

When the more powerful Jumo 211 engine appeared in 1937, Junkers took the chance to improve the Ju 87 by fitting the new engine in place of the previous Jumo 210. This necessitated a major redesign of the fuselage and vertical tail surfaces, with the result that the nose, cockpit enclosure and rear fuselage took on an appearance less streamlined than on the Ju 87A series. The undercarriage was also redesigned, the 'trousers' braced to the fuselage being replaced by cantilever 'spatted' units, which were far easier to maintain. By October 1938, some early Ju 87B-1 models had been sent to Spain, where they enjoyed considerable success. Maximum bomb-load was 2,205 lbs (1,000 kg), twice that of the Ju 87A. The Ju 87B-2 had several equipment refinements.

In the years before the war, Germany had started to build an aircraft-carrier, the *Graf Zeppelin*, and as part of its complement it was intended that it should have some navalized Ju 87 dive-bombers. The Ju 87C was derived from the 87B for this purpose, with catapult spools, flotation gear, folding wings and a jettisonable undercarriage. Only a few pre-production aircraft were built before the abandonment of the *Graf Zeppelin* project. Another contemporary of the Ju 87B series was the R series, which was basically similar, but had a reduced offensive load and increased fuel tankage for long-range anti-shipping strikes.

The next series to appear was the Ju 87D, intended to make use of the latest model of the

Jumo 211, the 211J. The nose contours were cleaned up considerably, and the cockpit canopy was streamlined more efficiently. Fixed armament was left at two 7.92-mm machine-guns, but the gunner was now given two weapons of the same calibre instead of the previous one. Bomb-load was raised to a maximum of nearly 4,000 lbs (1,814 kg). The Ju 87D-1 began to enter service in the spring of 1942. The Ju 87D series was built in large numbers and in a number of sub-marks.

The Ju 87F and Ju 187 were projected versions of the basic design to bring it up to date, but no examples of either design were built. In parallel with the Ju 87D series, Junkers built the Ju 87H, which was a dual-control trainer to enable fighter and bomber pilots to be taught to fly the *Stuka*. The final version of the *Stuka* was the Ju 87G series, of which only the Ju 87G-1 was built. This was a specialized 'tank-busting' aircraft, with a pair of 3.7-cm BK 3.7 cannon slung under the wings in pods with their ammunition. The weapon proved very successful, especially in the hands of *Stuka* aces such as Hans-Ulrich Rudel. Production of the Ju 87 ended in the summer of 1944 after 5,700 had been built, 4,881 during the war.

The *Stuka* was a very potent weapon when used against raw troops in circumstances of little air opposition; these conditions were to be found in the German campaigns against Poland, Belgium, Holland and France in 1939–40, and against Russia in 1941–43. But against competent fighter opposition, however, the *Stuka* was a death trap. All in all, though, the *Stuka* served the German cause very well.

Below: A Kette (flight) of Ju 87B Stukas in flight. Each aircraft appears to be carrying only four 110-lb (50-kg) bombs, two under each outer wing panel. A 1,102-lb (500-kg) bomb could also be carried on the crutch under the fuselage

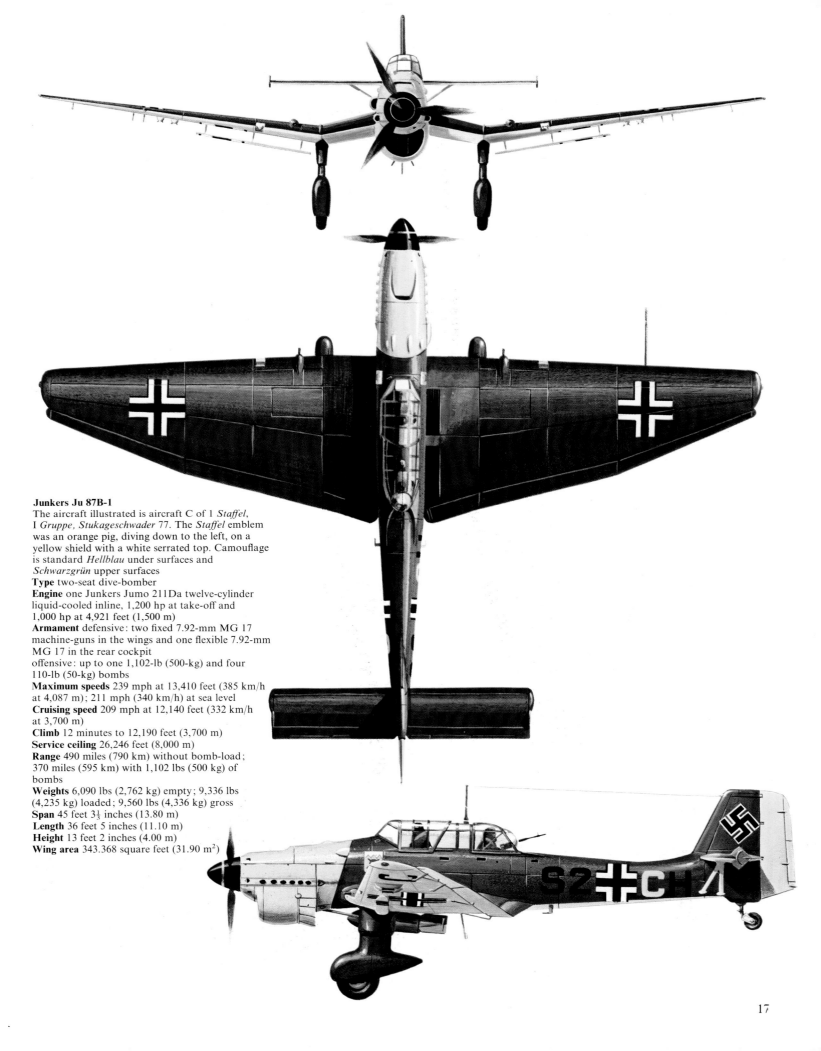

Junkers Ju 87B-1
The aircraft illustrated is aircraft C of 1 *Staffel*,
I *Gruppe, Stukageschwader* 77. The *Staffel* emblem
was an orange pig, diving down to the left, on a
yellow shield with a white serrated top. Camouflage
is standard *Hellblau* under surfaces and
Schwarzgrün upper surfaces
Type two-seat dive-bomber
Engine one Junkers Jumo 211Da twelve-cylinder
liquid-cooled inline, 1,200 hp at take-off and
1,000 hp at 4,921 feet (1,500 m)
Armament defensive: two fixed 7.92-mm MG 17
machine-guns in the wings and one flexible 7.92-mm
MG 17 in the rear cockpit
offensive: up to one 1,102-lb (500-kg) and four
110-lb (50-kg) bombs
Maximum speeds 239 mph at 13,410 feet (385 km/h
at 4,087 m); 211 mph (340 km/h) at sea level
Cruising speed 209 mph at 12,140 feet (332 km/h
at 3,700 m)
Climb 12 minutes to 12,190 feet (3,700 m)
Service ceiling 26,246 feet (8,000 m)
Range 490 miles (790 km) without bomb-load;
370 miles (595 km) with 1,102 lbs (500 kg) of
bombs
Weights 6,090 lbs (2,762 kg) empty; 9,336 lbs
(4,235 kg) loaded; 9,560 lbs (4,336 kg) gross
Span 45 feet 3⅓ inches (13.80 m)
Length 36 feet 5 inches (11.10 m)
Height 13 feet 2 inches (4.00 m)
Wing area 343.368 square feet (31.90 m²)

Junkers 88

The Junkers Ju 88 was Germany's most versatile aircraft of World War II, serving the *Luftwaffe* as a level bomber, dive-bomber, reconnaissance machine, ground-attack aircraft, trainer, day and night fighter, minelayer and torpedo-bomber.

Despite the fact that the Ju 88 was employed operationally in a multitude of tasks, it was designed to a specification calling for a *Schnellbomber* or fast bomber, as was the de Havilland Mosquito, Britain's equivalent of the remarkable Ju 88. The specification was issued in the spring of 1935, and the Ju 88 flew for the first time in December 1936. The first two prototypes could not meet the requirements of the specification with their DB 600 engines, but the Ju 88 *V*3, with two DB 601 motors, exceeded them handsomely. The authorities were delighted, but then informed Junkers that the design would have to be modified to enable the machine to undertake dive-bombing missions. This led to the Ju 88 *V*5 which had a strengthened airframe, a fully-glazed nose in place of the previous prototypes' conventional nose, and a ventral gondola with an additional machine-gun to double the type's defensive armament. Several world records were established by the Ju 88 *V*5, and by now the *Reichsluftfahrtministerium* had decided that the Ju 88 was to be the *Luftwaffe*'s next medium bomber.

Production got under way early in 1939, and the type entered service in August of the same year. The Ju 88A was destined to become the main bomber variant, and the series went through a long list of marks. In common with other combat aircraft, there was a constant growth in weight, the result of increased bomb-loads and enhanced offensive armament, with the need for more powerful engines and greater fuel capacity. The basic engine had been changed in the Ju 88 *V*5 to the Junkers Jumo 211, which powered subsequent bomber marks up to the Ju 88S, which had BMW 801 radials. The chief Ju 88A series marks were the A-4, with a wing span increased by 5 feet 4¼ inches (1.63 m), a mixed cannon/machine-gun defensive armament, and nearly twice the offensive load at 4,410 lbs (2,000

kg); the A-13, which was a ground-attack variant with a forward-firing armament of 16 7.92-mm machine-guns; the A-14, an updated version of the A-4 with better protection and balloon-cable cutters; and the A-17 torpedo-bomber with two underslung torpedoes.

The Ju 88B and 88E were planned in parallel with the Ju 88A series, with Jumo 213 engines and a larger, but better streamlined, fully-glazed nose. These did not enter widespread production. Right from the beginning of the Ju 88 programme, the *RLM* had seen the type's possibilities as a heavy fighter, and a specific fighter version, the Ju 88C, was developed to meet this need. However, as bomber production took priority over that of fighters, it was not until 1943 that Ju 88 fighters began to reach the front in any number.

The first of these models, the Ju 88C-1, was powered by two BMW 801 radials, but as this engine had a priority allocation to Focke-Wulf for the Fw 190, the Ju 88C-1 was abandoned in favour of the Jumo 211-powered Ju 88C-2. The first fighter model to go into production on a large scale was the Ju 88C-6, from mid-1942 onwards. Like all C models, this had a solid nose, with an armament of three fixed 20-mm cannon and three fixed 7.92-mm machine-guns. The Ju 88C-6b was the first Ju 88 model to be fitted with radar for night fighting, and this entered production late in 1942. The next model, the Ju 88C-6c, had the extraordinary, but very successful, *schräge Musik* (Jazz music) installation: two 20-mm cannon in the fuselage, arranged to fire obliquely forward and upwards, to hit the bellies of bombers above. The Ju 88R series was the BMW 801-powered version of the night-fighting Ju 88C series aircraft. The next model to appear was the Ju 88D, a highly successful, long-range, reconnaissance machine.

The aircraft of the Ju 88G night-fighter series, derived from the interim Ju 88R, were more numerous. The first of the new series, the Ju 88G-1 appeared in the spring of 1944, and was soon followed by improved versions, the best being the Ju 88G-7b with four 20-mm cannon in the nose, two 20-mm cannon in the *schräge Musik*

installation, and a maximum speed of over 400 mph (644 km/h). The Ju 88H series was introduced in 1942 as a very long-range reconnaissance series, with a lengthened fuselage to hold extra fuel. Maximum range was 3,200 miles (5,150 km).

The Ju 88P series, also dating from 1942, was designed to counter the enormous Russian superiority in tanks with a powerful 'tank-busting' aircraft. Models in this series were fitted with a large ventral gondola housing one or more anti-tank gun: two 3.7-cm weapons in the Ju 88P-2 and P-3, a 5-cm weapon in the P-4 and a 7.5-cm weapon in the P-1. The final bomber variant of the basic design was the Ju 88S, which was powered by BMW 801 radials, had a top speed of 379 mph (610 km/h) and an offensive load of 4,410 lbs (2,000 kg). The Ju 88T series bore the same relation to the S series as the D to the A.

The most remarkable Ju 88 aircraft were those involved in the *Mistel* operations. In these, a Ju 88 loaded with explosives was flown to its target by the pilot of a fighter mounted above the fuselage on struts. When the explosive-laden Ju 88 was diving straight at the target, the pilot broke away in his fighter leaving the Ju 88 to plunge into the target. Only a few operations had been carried out by the end of the war, but these proved quite successful.

The Ju 88 was a quite extraordinary plane, very versatile, but also very good at its many tasks. The basic design was very sound, and proved itself to have enormous development potential, as was shown by the success of the Ju 188 and 288, which were built only in limited numbers compared with the Ju 88's 15,000.

Below: A Mistel (Mistletoe) Schulung 1 (Training 1) combination of a Ju 88A-4 and Bf 109F. The operational version of this remarkable weapon, named Beethoven, featured a 8,377-lb (3,800-kg) hollow-charge warhead in place of the crew compartment of the Ju 88, which was directed onto its target by the pick-a-back fighter, which in turn released itself at the last moment

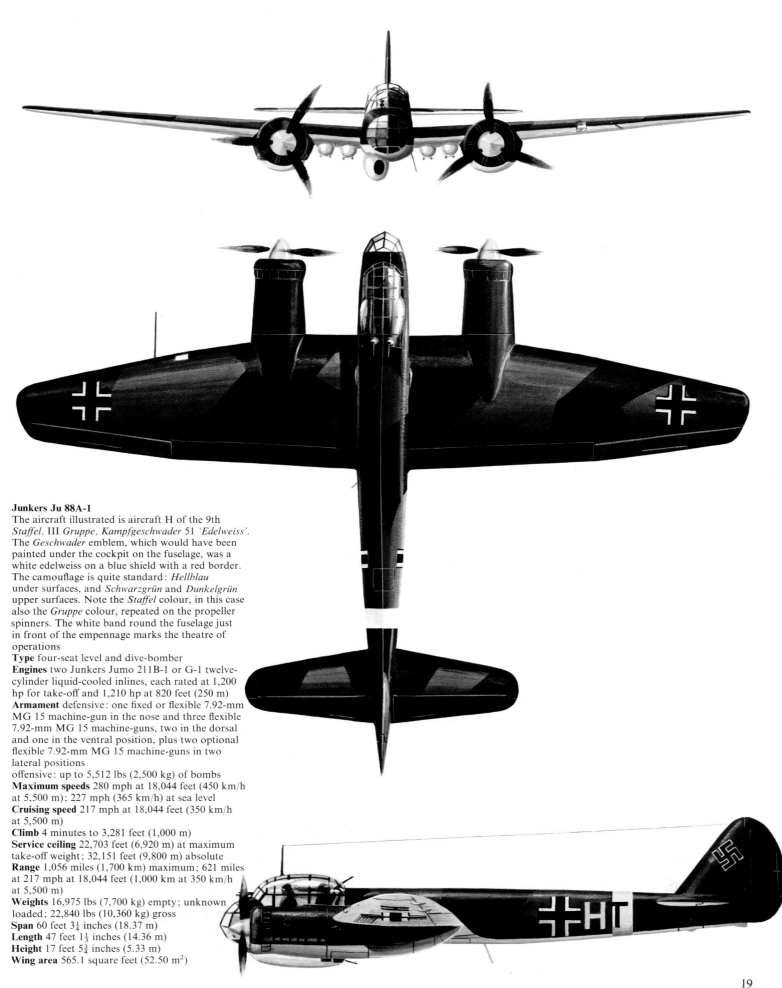

Junkers Ju 88A-1

The aircraft illustrated is aircraft H of the 9th *Staffel, III Gruppe, Kampfgeschwader* 51 *'Edelweiss'.* The *Geschwader* emblem, which would have been painted under the cockpit on the fuselage, was a white edelweiss on a blue shield with a red border. The camouflage is quite standard: *Hellblau* under surfaces, and *Schwarzgrün* and *Dunkelgrün* upper surfaces. Note the *Staffel* colour, in this case also the *Gruppe* colour, repeated on the propeller spinners. The white band round the fuselage just in front of the empennage marks the theatre of operations

Type four-seat level and dive-bomber

Engines two Junkers Jumo 211B-1 or G-1 twelve-cylinder liquid-cooled inlines, each rated at 1,200 hp for take-off and 1,210 hp at 820 feet (250 m)

Armament defensive: one fixed or flexible 7.92-mm MG 15 machine-gun in the nose and three flexible 7.92-mm MG 15 machine-guns, two in the dorsal and one in the ventral position, plus two optional flexible 7.92-mm MG 15 machine-guns in two lateral positions

offensive: up to 5,512 lbs (2,500 kg) of bombs

Maximum speeds 280 mph at 18,044 feet (450 km/h at 5,500 m); 227 mph (365 km/h) at sea level

Cruising speed 217 mph at 18,044 feet (350 km/h at 5,500 m)

Climb 4 minutes to 3,281 feet (1,000 m)

Service ceiling 22,703 feet (6,920 m) at maximum take-off weight; 32,151 feet (9,800 m) absolute

Range 1,056 miles (1,700 km) maximum; 621 miles at 217 mph at 18,044 feet (1,000 km at 350 km/h at 5,500 m)

Weights 16,975 lbs (7,700 kg) empty; unknown loaded; 22,840 lbs (10,360 kg) gross

Span 60 feet 3¼ inches (18.37 m)

Length 47 feet 1⅓ inches (14.36 m)

Height 17 feet 5¾ inches (5.33 m)

Wing area 565.1 square feet (52.50 m²)

Messerschmitt 109

The Messerschmitt Bf 109 was Germany's most celebrated fighter of World War II, and served in ever more advanced forms with the *Luftwaffe* from early in 1937 to the end of hostilities. At the time of its introduction it marked the absolute in single-seat fighter design, but yet was not derived, as were so many other equivalent aircraft, from a long line of other machines. It is worth noting here that although the fighter is usually designated Me 109, this is incorrect. Although Willi Messerschmitt bought the bankrupt Bayerische Flugzeugwerke (Bf) or Bavarian Aircraft Works in 1932, two years before design work on the Bf 109 started, the designation Bf was used up to design number 162.

The *Luftwaffe* in 1934 issued a specification and contracts for prototype construction for a new single-engined fighter to several companies, but not to Messerschmitt. This was partially the result of the personal enmity between Messerschmitt and Erhard Milch, the German Secretary of Aviation. However, the encouraging results obtained with the Bf 108 late in 1934 meant that the authorities could no longer ignore the Messerschmitt works in contracts concerning high-speed aircraft, and the Bavarian concern was added to the list of constructors for the new design competition.

The first prototype was unveiled in August of the following year. The new fighter was quite remarkable for the time, with all-metal construction, an enclosed cockpit, a retractable undercarriage, and low-set cantilever monoplane wings. A series of prototypes was produced before the *Luftwaffe* decided to accept the superlative Bf 109 as its next fighter after the competitive trials with Heinkel's contender, the He 112, late in 1936.

The first production version was the Bf 109B series, powered by a Junkers Jumo 210 engine. The first Bf 109B-1 fighters came off the production line in February 1937, and were soon sent to Spain for operational testing against the Polikarpov I-15 and I-16 fighters being flown by the Republicans. The Messerschmitt fighter soon showed itself to be superior to both. The Bf 109B-1 was soon replaced in production by the B-2, which had a variable-pitch metal propeller. These early types were quickly joined by the Bf 109C series, which had an improved engine and cooling installation, and better armament. Production models of the C series began to reach the *Luftwaffe* in the spring of 1938.

The next model to appear was the Bf 109D series, which featured a DB 600 engine and a 20-mm cannon. The new engine lifted top speed by nearly 70 mph (113 km/h), and the cannon, mounted between the cylinder banks to fire through the propeller hub, increased firepower very considerably. Deliveries of the new model began early in 1938, but trouble was soon experienced with the poor reliability of the engines. Thus few were built before the type was superseded by the Bf 109E series, which utilized the more reliable and more powerful DB 601. The new type started to reach the *Luftwaffe* in early 1938; it was destined to become the German air force's fighter mainstay until the advent of the Bf 109F in late 1940. Thus the Bf 109E was the main German fighter encountered by RAF fighters in the Battle of Britain. Compared with the Bf 109D, the E series had an armament of two or three 20-mm cannon, which gave it a distinct advantage in certain respects over current RAF fighters, which had only a machine-gun armament.

The Bf 109F series, which entered service in 1941, was the best of the whole Bf 109 family from the aerodynamic point of view, the nose contours being cleaned up considerably and the tail being redesigned to eliminate the two bracing struts that had been so much a feature of the earlier marks. It is worth noting here that the last of the types with a braced tailplane had been the Bf 109*T* (*T* for *Träger* or Carrier), a navalized version of the Bf 109E. This type had been produced in very limited quantities for Germany's projected aircraft-carrier. The armament of the Bf 109F series was, remarkably for a warplane, lighter than that of its predecessor, at one 15- or 20-mm cannon and two 7.92-mm machine-guns. Handling characteristics were superb, however, and speed was nearly 380 mph (612 km/h).

Luftwaffe pilots were unhappy about the reduction in armament on the new series, however, and the next model to appear, the Bf 109G, had a much increased firepower. The engine was also changed, the latest Daimler-Benz power unit, the DB 605, being installed. Although the weight of fire and speed had thereby been improved, it was only at the expense of the fighter's handling qualities, which declined from the beginning of the G series. This decline was further helped by the need for yet heavier armament, which resulted in the replacement of the two fuselage-mounted 7.92-mm machine-guns by a pair of 13.1-mm weapons from the Bf 109G-5 onwards. To accommodate these bulkier guns, bulged humps had to be fitted over the breeches, on each side of the fuselage in front of the cockpit. In the G series, provision was also made for the carriage of numerous different types of underwing and under-fuselage stores. These included drop-tanks, bombs, rockets, gun-packs etc.

The Bf 109H series was intended as a high-altitude fighter development of the F series, with an increased wing span and a DB 601 engine modified for high-altitude performance. In fact the Bf 109H-1 used a G-5 airframe with a DB 605 engine. No quantity production was undertaken. The last production variant of the Bf 109 was the Bf 109K, which began to appear in September 1944. This was intended to become the definitive model eliminating the need for the bewildering number of sub-marks that was bedevilling the *Luftwaffe* administrative and supply departments. A DB 605 engine boosted to over 2,000 hp was used, with this the Bf 109K-4 reached a speed of over 450 mph (724 km/h). Armament was one 30- and two 15-mm cannon. Chief distinguishing features of the K series were the revised cockpit canopy with fewer panels to improve vision, and the narrower, taller vertical tail surfaces. Not many of this last mark were built. Wartime Bf 109 production reached the vast total of 30,480 aircraft.

The Bf 109 is justly one of the most famous aircraft of World War II. Its importance was considerable, and although flying qualities had to take second place behind speed and armament from 1942 onwards, even the last marks of this redoubtable fighter had their staunch supporters. The Bf 109, despite its high wing-loading, was always manoeuvrable, capable of absorbing considerable battle damage, and always able to carry yet more in the way of weapons. The type's one real weakness lay in the outward-retracting undercarriage, which was prone to breakage, and which made taxiing difficult.

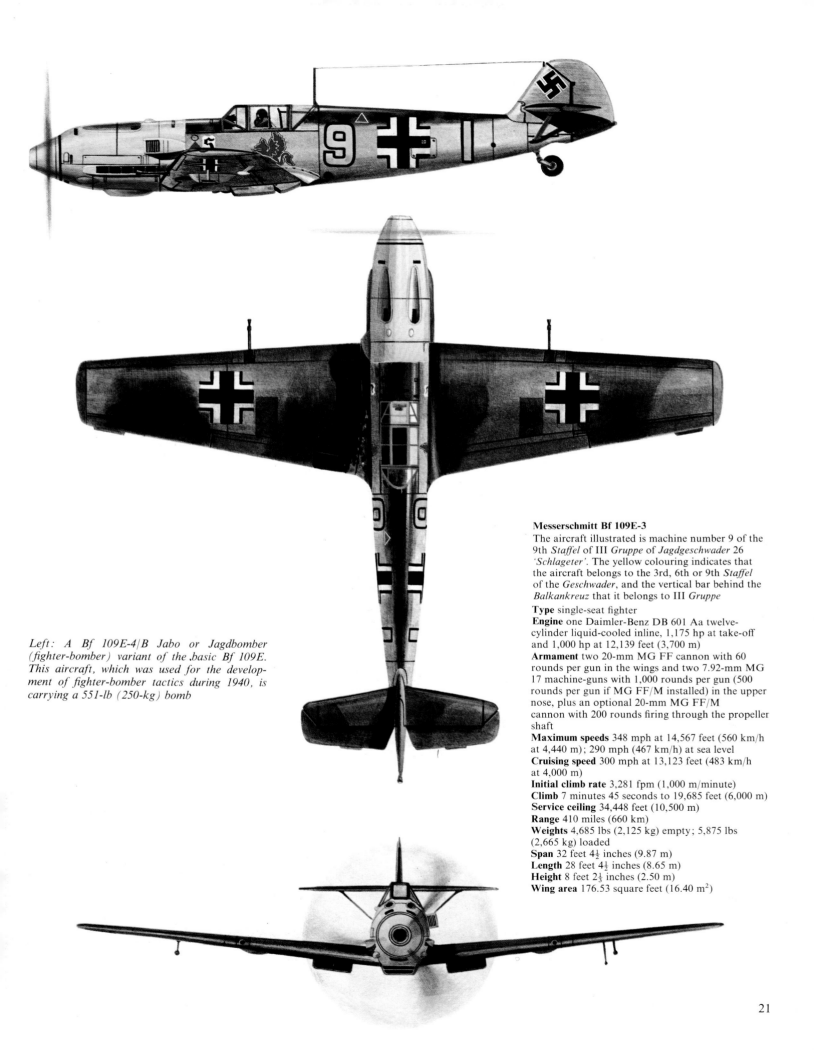

Left: A Bf 109E-4/B Jabo or Jagdbomber (fighter-bomber) variant of the ,basic Bf 109E. This aircraft, which was used for the development of fighter-bomber tactics during 1940, is carrying a 551-lb (250-kg) bomb

Messerschmitt Bf 109E-3

The aircraft illustrated is machine number 9 of the 9th *Staffel* of III *Gruppe* of *Jagdgeschwader* 26 *'Schlageter'*. The yellow colouring indicates that the aircraft belongs to the 3rd, 6th or 9th *Staffel* of the *Geschwader*, and the vertical bar behind the *Balkankreuz* that it belongs to III *Gruppe*

Type single-seat fighter

Engine one Daimler-Benz DB 601 Aa twelve-cylinder liquid-cooled inline, 1,175 hp at take-off and 1,000 hp at 12,139 feet (3,700 m)

Armament two 20-mm MG FF cannon with 60 rounds per gun in the wings and two 7.92-mm MG 17 machine-guns with 1,000 rounds per gun (500 rounds per gun if MG FF/M installed) in the upper nose, plus an optional 20-mm MG FF/M cannon with 200 rounds firing through the propeller shaft

Maximum speeds 348 mph at 14,567 feet (560 km/h at 4,440 m); 290 mph (467 km/h) at sea level

Cruising speed 300 mph at 13,123 feet (483 km/h at 4,000 m)

Initial climb rate 3,281 fpm (1,000 m/minute)

Climb 7 minutes 45 seconds to 19,685 feet (6,000 m)

Service ceiling 34,448 feet (10,500 m)

Range 410 miles (660 km)

Weights 4,685 lbs (2,125 kg) empty; 5,875 lbs (2,665 kg) loaded

Span 32 feet 4½ inches (9.87 m)

Length 28 feet 4½ inches (8.65 m)

Height 8 feet 2⅓ inches (2.50 m)

Wing area 176.53 square feet (16.40 m²)

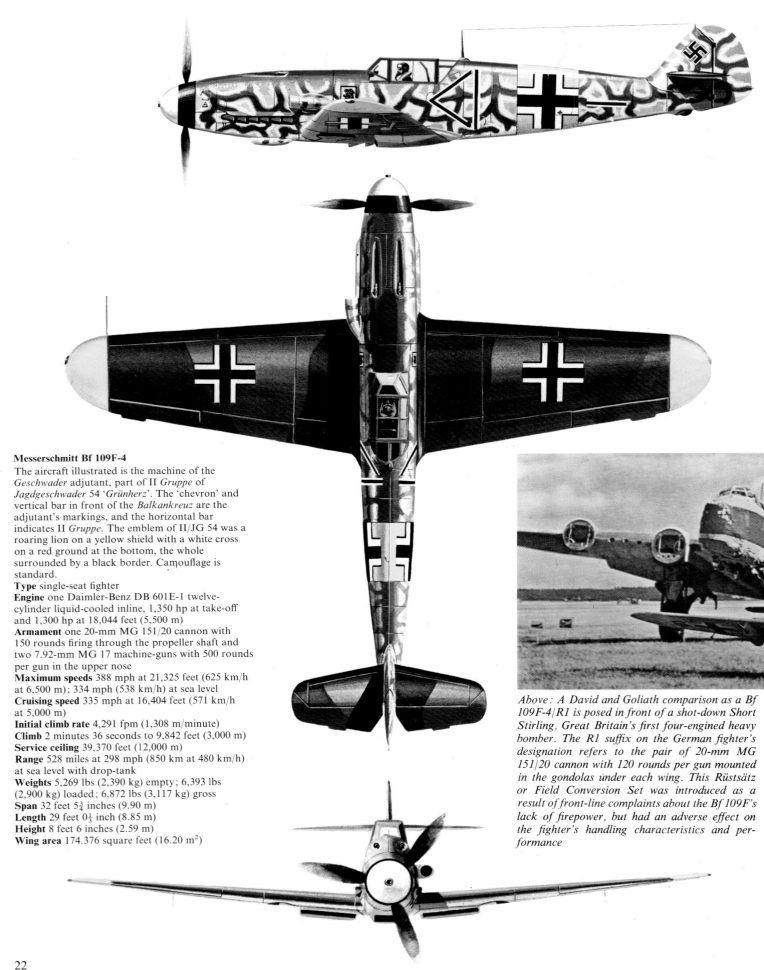

Messerschmitt Bf 109F-4

The aircraft illustrated is the machine of the *Geschwader* adjutant, part of II *Gruppe* of *Jagdgeschwader* 54 '*Grünherz*'. The 'chevron' and vertical bar in front of the *Balkankreuz* are the adjutant's markings, and the horizontal bar indicates II *Gruppe*. The emblem of II/JG 54 was a roaring lion on a yellow shield with a white cross on a red ground at the bottom, the whole surrounded by a black border. Camouflage is standard.

Type single-seat fighter

Engine one Daimler-Benz DB 601E-1 twelve-cylinder liquid-cooled inline, 1,350 hp at take-off and 1,300 hp at 18,044 feet (5,500 m)

Armament one 20-mm MG 151/20 cannon with 150 rounds firing through the propeller shaft and two 7.92-mm MG 17 machine-guns with 500 rounds per gun in the upper nose

Maximum speeds 388 mph at 21,325 feet (625 km/h at 6,500 m); 334 mph (538 km/h) at sea level

Cruising speed 335 mph at 16,404 feet (571 km/h at 5,000 m)

Initial climb rate 4,291 fpm (1,308 m/minute)

Climb 2 minutes 36 seconds to 9,842 feet (3,000 m)

Service ceiling 39,370 feet (12,000 m)

Range 528 miles at 298 mph (850 km at 480 km/h) at sea level with drop-tank

Weights 5,269 lbs (2,390 kg) empty; 6,393 lbs (2,900 kg) loaded; 6,872 lbs (3,117 kg) gross

Span 32 feet 5¾ inches (9.90 m)

Length 29 feet 0⅓ inch (8.85 m)

Height 8 feet 6 inches (2.59 m)

Wing area 174.376 square feet (16.20 m²)

Above: A David and Goliath comparison as a Bf 109F-4/R1 is posed in front of a shot-down Short Stirling, Great Britain's first four-engined heavy bomber. The R1 suffix on the German fighter's designation refers to the pair of 20-mm MG 151/20 cannon with 120 rounds per gun mounted in the gondolas under each wing. This Rüstsätz or Field Conversion Set was introduced as a result of front-line complaints about the Bf 109F's lack of firepower, but had an adverse effect on the fighter's handling characteristics and performance

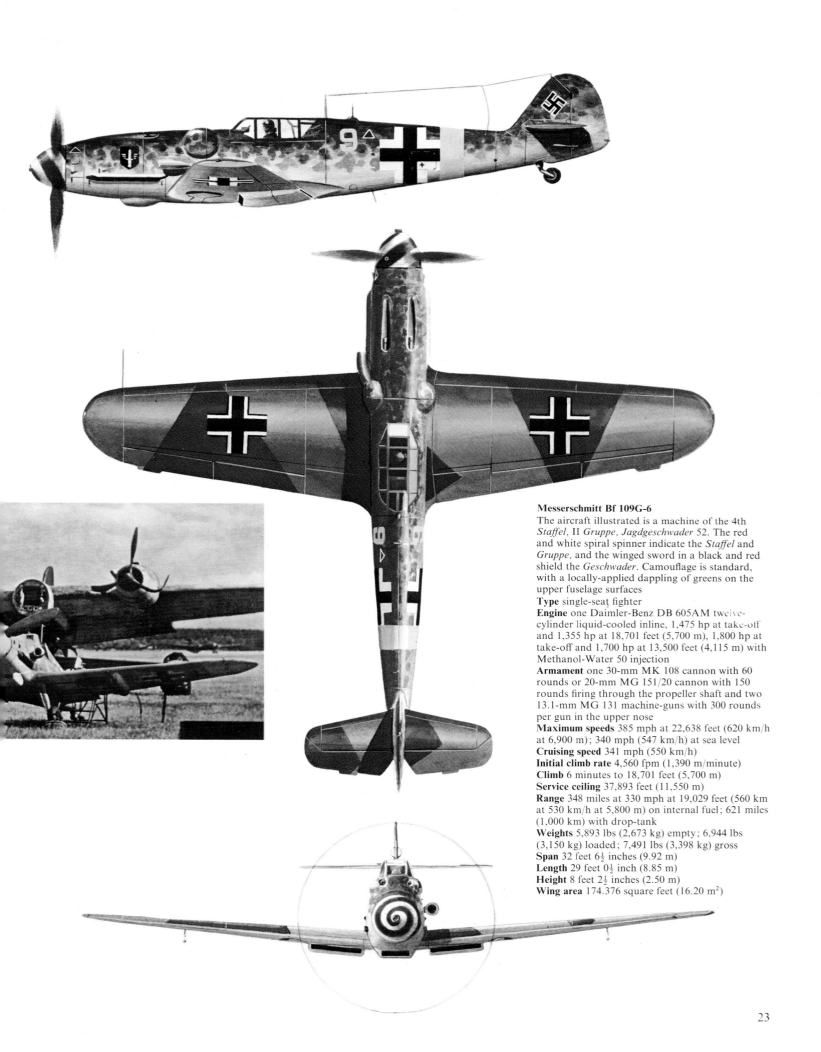

Messerschmitt Bf 109G-6

The aircraft illustrated is a machine of the 4th *Staffel*, II *Gruppe*, *Jagdgeschwader* 52. The red and white spiral spinner indicate the *Staffel* and *Gruppe*, and the winged sword in a black and red shield the *Geschwader*. Camouflage is standard, with a locally-applied dappling of greens on the upper fuselage surfaces

Type single-seat fighter

Engine one Daimler-Benz DB 605AM twelve-cylinder liquid-cooled inline, 1,475 hp at take-off and 1,355 hp at 18,701 feet (5,700 m), 1,800 hp at take-off and 1,700 hp at 13,500 feet (4,115 m) with Methanol-Water 50 injection

Armament one 30-mm MK 108 cannon with 60 rounds or 20-mm MG 151/20 cannon with 150 rounds firing through the propeller shaft and two 13.1-mm MG 131 machine-guns with 300 rounds per gun in the upper nose

Maximum speeds 385 mph at 22,638 feet (620 km/h at 6,900 m); 340 mph (547 km/h) at sea level

Cruising speed 341 mph (550 km/h)

Initial climb rate 4,560 fpm (1,390 m/minute)

Climb 6 minutes to 18,701 feet (5,700 m)

Service ceiling 37,893 feet (11,550 m)

Range 348 miles at 330 mph at 19,029 feet (560 km at 530 km/h at 5,800 m) on internal fuel; 621 miles (1,000 km) with drop-tank

Weights 5,893 lbs (2,673 kg) empty; 6,944 lbs (3,150 kg) loaded; 7,491 lbs (3,398 kg) gross

Span 32 feet 6½ inches (9.92 m)

Length 29 feet 0½ inch (8.85 m)

Height 8 feet 2½ inches (2.50 m)

Wing area 174.376 square feet (16.20 m²)

Messerschmitt 110

Like the Ju 87, the Bf 110 has had a considerable corpus of legend built up around it to the detriment of a true assessment of the real aircraft and its capabilities. Because the Bf 110 was basically a fighter, it has been compared with single-engined Allied fighters and so the assessment of the series has always been unfavourable.

The origins of the Bf 110 lay in a 1934 requirement for a twin-engined *Kampfzerstörer* or battle-destroyer, which would fulfil a basic role of clearing the way through enemy fighters for bombers, whilst still being able to undertake a variety of other tasks. After a considerable amount of political and personal wrangling within the *Luftwaffe* high command, Messerschmitt was given the order for prototype construction. Powered by two DB 600 engines, the first prototype flew in May 1936, being joined late in the year by the next two prototypes. Plans were laid for the production of a definitive Bf 110A series, but trouble with the DB 600 engine led to the abandonment of the idea. Instead the Bf 110 received two of the newer and less troublesome DB 601 engines. With these powerplants a new model, the Bf 110B series, was introduced.

The major visual differences between the A and B models were the better streamlined nose and fully enclosed retracted undercarriage of the latter. But there were production delays with the DB 601 engine, however, and the B series had to be powered by Junkers Jumo 210 motors. The first machine with the revised powerplant arrangement flew in April 1938. Thus problems with the engines had robbed the *Luftwaffe* of a chance to test their new fighter operationally in Spain. In fact performance with the Jumos was so low that machines of the B series were never considered as first-line fighters, and by the beginning of World War II had been relegated to a training role.

By the end of 1938 the troubles with production of the DB 601 had been ended, and a new series, the Bf 110C, had been introduced to take advantage of the superior power offered by the Daimler-Benz engines. Deliveries of the new model, which was over 50 mph (80 km/h) faster than its predecessor, began in January 1939. The Bf 110 saw action for the first time in the Polish campaign, in which it acquitted itself well against the inferior aircraft of the Polish air force. It also performed creditably in daylight actions against British bombers over the North Sea.

Luftwaffe confidence in the Bf 110 was by now great, and, in the spring of 1940, Messerschmitt was asked to develop the ability to perform light bombing duties to the 110's repertoire. As a result further C series aircraft were adapted for reconnaissance missions. After their severe handling by RAF fighters in the Battle of Britain, most of the C series aircraft were converted to bomber-interception and glider-towing models. The Bf 110D series was intended as a long-range model, fuel capacity being increased by either droppable or non-droppable extra tanks under the fuselage, but the model was not a success and was soon phased out of service.

Interest in the Bf 110 as a bomber had already been shown by the *Luftwaffe*, as evidenced by the Bf 110C-4/B, but now there emerged the Bf 110E series, which was intended to meet the need for a heavy fighter-bomber. The series entered service in the summer of 1941, and in the E-1/R2 variant the Bf 110 was able to deliver a bomb-load to 4,410 lbs (2,000 kg). A long-range reconnaissance model was also developed.

At the same time the Bf 110F series was introduced. This differed principally from the E series in having more powerful engines and increased protection for the crew. Apart from these differences, the Bf 110F-1 to F-3 were similar to the E-1 to E-3. However, later F series models had increased armament for the night-fighter role. The first Bf 110 model to feature radar equipment for the night-fighter role was the Bf 110F-4a. Production of the Bf 110 had been tapered off from the late summer of 1941 in expectation of the arrival of large quantities of the newer Me 210 series, but with the failure of this fighter, large-scale production of the Bf 110 was restarted early in 1942 with the Bf 110G series. This had the more powerful DB 605 engines, and the first models were intended as heavy fighter-bombers and bomber-destroyers. For this latter role a variety of weapons was tested, ranging from massed underwing rocket batteries to heavy cannon mounted in packs under the fuselage. From the Bf 110G-4 onwards, however, it was decided to concentrate on the Bf 110 as a night fighter. Numerous models were introduced, with various radar and armament installations. Bf 110 wartime production totalled 5,762 aircraft.

The fault of the Bf 110 series lay not with the aircraft itself, but with the roles for which it was designed. Needless to say, it proved impossible to produce a fighter that could undertake several tasks, including combat with first-rate single-engined fighters, with any degree of competence. After the fallacy of this idea had been more than amply demonstrated by RAF fighters in the Battle of Britain, the multi-destroyer role of the Bf 110 series was abandoned and it then emerged as a highly successful bomber destroyer. With its good load-carrying capacity, heavy armament and more than adequate performance, Bf 110 night fighters and heavy day-fighting bomber-destroyers proved to be the single greatest scourge of the Allied bombers which tore Germany apart in the closing stages of the war. If for nothing else, the Bf 110 should be remembered for this. Compared with other twin-engined fighters designed to the voguish interest in such aircraft during the late 1930s, the Bf 110 was remarkably successful. The Dutch Fokker G-1 was a good aircraft, but built only in limited numbers; the British Westland Whirlwind was plagued by engine difficulties; the Italian Industrie Meccaniche e Aeronautiche Meridonali Ro 57 failed for lack of suitably powerful indigenous engines; and the French Hanriot NC 600 was flown only in prototype form. Only the French Potez 63 series of general purpose aircraft attained great success.

Left: A Bf 110 heavy fighter on a typical North African airfield. Aircraft movements on such airfields could be detected from considerable distances as a result of the large clouds of dust thrown up. This dust also proved a great problem for engine life: unless special filters against the dust were provided, engine life could be as short as 30 hours

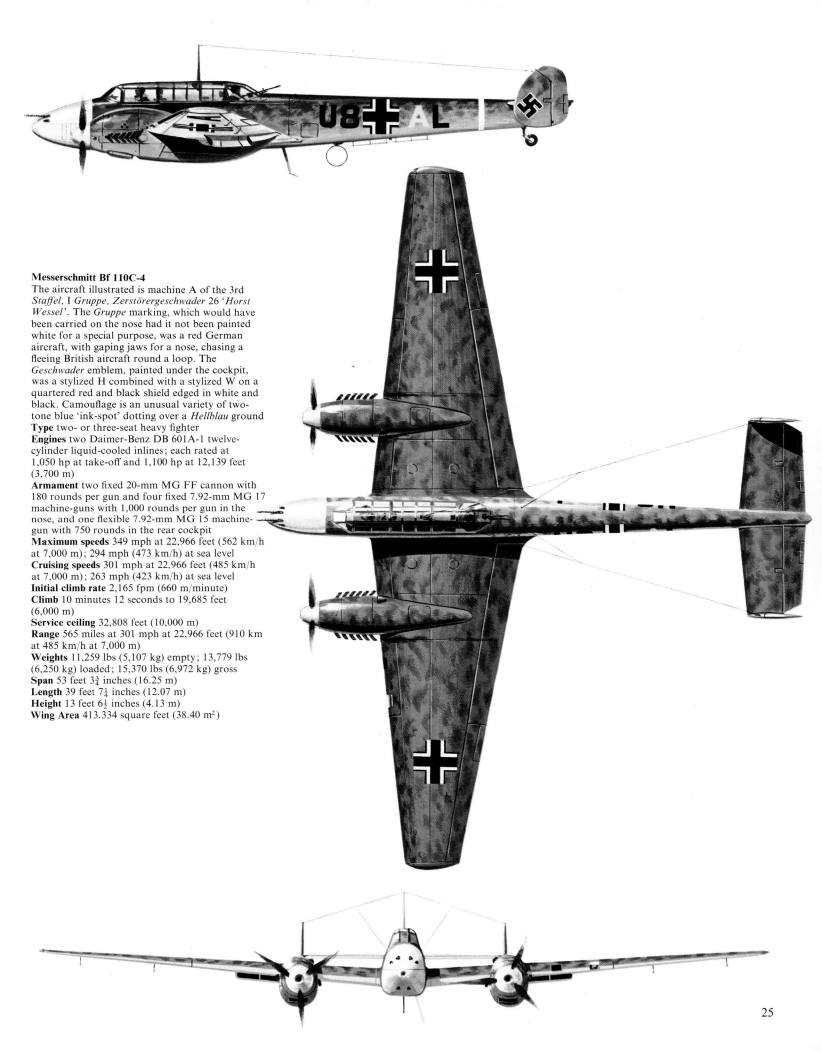

Messerschmitt Bf 110C-4
The aircraft illustrated is machine A of the 3rd
Staffel, I *Gruppe, Zerstörergeschwader* 26 '*Horst
Wessel*'. The *Gruppe* marking, which would have
been carried on the nose had it not been painted
white for a special purpose, was a red German
aircraft, with gaping jaws for a nose, chasing a
fleeing British aircraft round a loop. The
Geschwader emblem, painted under the cockpit,
was a stylized H combined with a stylized W on a
quartered red and black shield edged in white and
black. Camouflage is an unusual variety of two-
tone blue 'ink-spot' dotting over a *Hellblau* ground
Type two- or three-seat heavy fighter
Engines two Daimer-Benz DB 601A-1 twelve-
cylinder liquid-cooled inlines; each rated at
1,050 hp at take-off and 1,100 hp at 12,139 feet
(3,700 m)
Armament two fixed 20-mm MG FF cannon with
180 rounds per gun and four fixed 7.92-mm MG 17
machine-guns with 1,000 rounds per gun in the
nose, and one flexible 7.92-mm MG 15 machine-
gun with 750 rounds in the rear cockpit
Maximum speeds 349 mph at 22,966 feet (562 km/h
at 7,000 m); 294 mph (473 km/h) at sea level
Cruising speeds 301 mph at 22,966 feet (485 km/h
at 7,000 m); 263 mph (423 km/h) at sea level
Initial climb rate 2,165 fpm (660 m/minute)
Climb 10 minutes 12 seconds to 19,685 feet
(6,000 m)
Service ceiling 32,808 feet (10,000 m)
Range 565 miles at 301 mph at 22,966 feet (910 km
at 485 km/h at 7,000 m)
Weights 11,259 lbs (5,107 kg) empty; 13,779 lbs
(6,250 kg) loaded; 15,370 lbs (6,972 kg) gross
Span 53 feet 3¾ inches (16.25 m)
Length 39 feet 7¼ inches (12.07 m)
Height 13 feet 6½ inches (4.13 m)
Wing Area 413.334 square feet (38.40 m²)

Messerschmitt 163 Komet

The Messerschmitt Me 163 was perhaps the most radical military aircraft to see combat in either World War. Notable for its diminutive size, phenomenal speed, and extremely high rate of climb, the Me 163 was also a very dangerous machine to fly and to land. During the latter operation, the slightest jar could cause any fuel left in the tanks to detonate, sending the aircraft and pilot up in a ball of fire.

The origins of the Me 163 can be traced back to a period long before the war, to the work of Professor Alexander Lippisch, one of the great names in the history of aerodynamics, on small, delta-winged, tailless aircraft. In 1938 the idea was born of combining a Lippisch-type aircraft, the DFS 194, with the new liquid-fuelled rocket motor being developed by Hellmuth Walter, as the Heinkel 'Projekt X'. This motor had a high power/weight ratio, but with a thrust of under 1,000 lbs (454 kg), a small, light aircraft was essential. At the beginning of 1939 Lippisch joined the Messerschmitt concern, having found it impossible to pursue his work properly at the government-owned DFS institute, and the Heinkel project unworkable.

After a period of crisis in the middle of 1939, the success of the rocket-powered DFS 194 brought renewed official interest, and work on the Me 163, as it became, was pressed on as fast as possible, the first prototype making gliding trials in the spring of 1941. Uprated Walter engines of over 1,600 lbs (726 kg) thrust were now available, and powered trials took place in the late summer of 1941. These proved very successful, speeds of over 500 mph (805 km/h) soon being recorded.

The type entered production, with certain modifications to help low-speed handling characteristics, as the Me 163A. The few aircraft built were used mainly for armament trials and the training of pilots for the definitive Me 163B. This was in fact a very extensively redesigned aircraft, with a considerably more powerful (3,750 lbs or 1,701 kg thrust) rocket engine. By the summer of 1942, the two Me 163B prototypes were flying and proving the type to have a spectacular performance.

The first production Me 163B-1a flew in February 1944, and the type entered combat late in July of the same year. Although the type proved successful in its role as a bomber-interceptor, the tide of war had swung so far in the Allies' favour that the Me 163 could do little to stop it; especially as production of the fighter and its fuel was seriously hampered by Allied bombing, and there were few pilots skilful enough to fly the Me 163 left in Germany. A two-seat trainer was built (Me 163S), and plans had been laid for large-scale production of the much improved Me 163C series, but the war ended before any great progress could be made.

Aerodynamically, the Me 163 was a fascinating, but successful, oddity. For combat operations, however, the type suffered from two major drawbacks. Firstly, its powered endurance was very low, as the result of the high fuel consumption rate of the rocket motor, and, secondly, it lacked an undercarriage. This had been eliminated to save airframe size and weight, and the type landed on a retractable skid. This meant, however, that the aircraft often came down with a jolt sufficient to detonate the highly volatile fuel left in the tanks.

Below: One of the B-series prototypes, the Me 163 V8, which was the second pre-production Me 163B-0. Some 30 of the 70 pre-production B-series aircraft built were used for experimental purposes. The detachable take-off dolly, which was jettisoned as the aircraft climbed after take-off, and the retractable metal landing-skid are clearly visible under the fuselage

Messerschmitt Me 163B-1a Komet (Comet)
The aircraft illustrated is machine number 15 of the
2nd *Staffel, Jagdgeschwader* 400, whose emblem
was a rocket-powered flea climbing across a black
shield with a white border. Camouflage is standard
Type single-seat target interceptor fighter
Engine one Walter HWK 509A-2 rocket motor,
3,748 lbs (1,700 kg) thrust
Armament two 30-mm MK 108 cannon with 60
rounds per gun or two 20-mm MG 151/20 cannon
with 100 rounds per gun in the wing roots
Maximum speeds 596 mph (960 km/h) between
9,842 and 29,527 feet (3,000 m and 9,000 m);
515 mph (830 km/h) at sea level
Initial climb rate 16,010 fpm (4,880 m/minute)
Climb 2 minutes 36 seconds to 29,527 feet
(9,000 m)
Service ceiling 39,500 feet (12,040 m)
Powered endurance 7 minutes 30 seconds maximum;
2 minutes 30 seconds after climb at 495 mph
(800 km/h)
Weights 4,200 lbs (1,905 kg) empty; unknown
loaded; 9,502 lbs (4,310 kg) gross
Span 30 feet 7⅓ inches (9.33 m)
Length 19 feet 2⅓ inches (5.85 m)
Height 9 feet 0⅔ inch (2.75 m)
Wing area 199.132 square feet (18.50 m²)

Messerschmitt 262 Schwalbe

The Messerschmitt Me 262 was the first turbojet-powered aircraft in the world to see combat. Although the Allies had jet aircraft of their own by the end of World War II, none of those constructed or designed were as advanced aerodynamically as the superlative Messerschmitt fighter with its revolutionary 'swept' wings. This is all the more remarkable for the fact that design work on Messerschmitt's first jet aircraft started before the outbreak of war years before any comparable Allied development.

By the autumn of 1938, progress with the revolutionary new jet engines, being developed by BMW, was sufficiently encouraging to warrant the construction of an aircraft to use them. Accordingly the Messerschmitt concern was asked to develop an aircraft powered by two of the new engines, which it was hoped would be ready by the end of 1939. Messerschmitt realized that the engines would be ideal for an advanced fighter, and set to work to take advantage of all the latest developments in the field of aerodynamics.

Design work progressed smoothly, but trouble with the BMW motors meant firstly that plans to place the engines in the wing roots had to be amended to locate them actually in the wings, and finally to install a pair of Junkers Jumo 004 engines, the BMW 003s proving very slow in development. But by the time the first prototype of the Me 262 was ready for flight, the Jumo 004 programme had also run into trouble, and no engines were available. The type was first flown, therefore, with a Junkers Jumo 210 piston engine mounted in the nose. Basic flying trials were carried out satisfactorily with this engine. In November 1941, the first BMW engines were finally delivered, and were mounted under the wings; the piston engine was retained initially to provide extra power. The BMW engines proved a total failure on their first flight in March 1942 as the compressor blades in both engines sheared off. The BMW 003 had to be completely redesigned. Soon after the failure of the BMW 003 units, the first Jumo 004 engines were delivered. These were larger than the BMW motors,

and were accommodated under the wings in bigger nacelles. By this time the piston engine had also been removed. The Me 262 V3 thus became the first 262 prototype to fly on jet power alone in July 1942. After further testing of this and other prototypes, not all successful for a variety of aerodynamic and engine problems, the decision to produce the type in quantity as a fighter was taken in June 1943.

One of the chief difficulties with the prototypes had been the difficulty in getting the tail off the ground during the take-off run, but this problem was solved by the V5, which featured a fixed tricycle undercarriage, and the V6, which had a retractable unit of the same configuration. Hitler's insistence on bomb-carrying capability, and further problems with the jets, delayed the delivery of pre-production machines to the *Luftwaffe* until April 1944; production aircraft arrived in July 1944. These were Me 262A series aircraft, whose sub-types included night-fighter and fighter-bomber versions, as well as a number of fighter versions with different armament, including one with a 5-cm cannon.

The Me 262B series were two-seater aircraft, the principal variants being trainer and night-fighter models. The Me 262C series was designed as a fast-climbing interceptor, the rate of climb being boosted by rockets. For example the Me 262C-1a, with a liquid-fuelled Walter rocket in the tail, could reach an altitude of over 38,000 feet (11,583 m) in 4 minutes 30 seconds. However, none of the Me 262C series entered quantity production.

Although it was an excellent and very advanced type, the Me 262 did not have a significant impact on the course of the war. By the time of its service *début* the defeat of Germany was inevitable. The Me 262 did, however, perform very creditably, its high speed, good rate of climb and heavy firepower making it a formidable opponent for Allied bombers. Much has been made of Hitler's insistence that the aircraft should be able to carry a 2,205-lb (1,000-kg) bomb-load; but work to enable the machine to carry bombs had already been done, and any delay resulting from Hitler's

order occurred because the manufacturers and the users were reluctant to implement the order, not because of any difficulty in the work involved. The main reason for the Me 262's slow arrival in service was the trouble with production of the Jumo 004 turbojet. These troubles were never fully solved, and bedevilled service aircraft in combat. Total Me 263 production amounted to 1,294 aircraft.

The type's one major failing, as far as operations were concerned, was the low rate of acceleration bestowed by the jet engines. Most of the Me 262 aircraft shot down by Allied fighters were caught during their landing run, during which they had to approach the runway slowly, with the engines throttled down. In this landing mode they could be 'bounced' by patrolling Allied fighters: all the Me 262 pilot could do was to try to outdistance the enemy. And in this he had two problems: if he opened the throttles too swiftly, the engines would stall, and if he opened them slowly, the rate of acceleration was so slow that he was a sitting target for the Allied fighter for some time. Overall, however, the Me 262 was a superb aircraft, one that came as a very rude shock to the Allies, and one which showed how far ahead the Germans were of the Allies in overcoming the problems associated with high-speed flight.

Perhaps more interesting than the Me 262's war career, important as this was, is the very considerable effect the type (and the research into aerodynamics that made it so successful an aircraft) had on postwar thinking by the Russians and the Americans. The Me 262 was so clearly more advanced in concept than aircraft such as the Gloster Meteor and Bell P-59 Airacomet that great efforts were made to seize, assimilate and further expand on German work into high-speed aerodynamics, thus paving the way for the modern type of jet aircraft.

Below: An Me 262A captured and tested by the Allies at the end of the war. The fine, streamlined appearance of the aircraft, in particular the fuselage, is well displayed

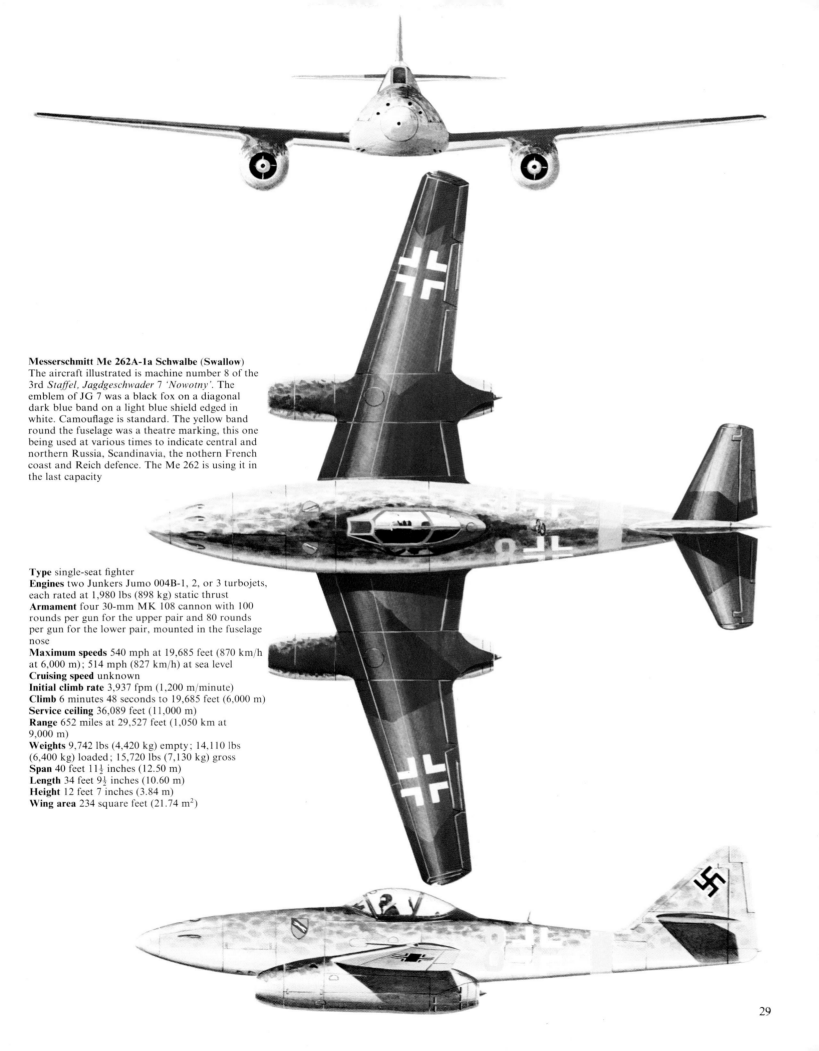

Messerschmitt Me 262A-1a Schwalbe (Swallow)
The aircraft illustrated is machine number 8 of the
3rd *Staffel, Jagdgeschwader 7 'Nowotny'.* The
emblem of JG 7 was a black fox on a diagonal
dark blue band on a light blue shield edged in
white. Camouflage is standard. The yellow band
round the fuselage was a theatre marking, this one
being used at various times to indicate central and
northern Russia, Scandinavia, the nothern French
coast and Reich defence. The Me 262 is using it in
the last capacity

Type single-seat fighter
Engines two Junkers Jumo 004B-1, 2, or 3 turbojets,
each rated at 1,980 lbs (898 kg) static thrust
Armament four 30-mm MK 108 cannon with 100
rounds per gun for the upper pair and 80 rounds
per gun for the lower pair, mounted in the fuselage
nose
Maximum speeds 540 mph at 19,685 feet (870 km/h
at 6,000 m); 514 mph (827 km/h) at sea level
Cruising speed unknown
Initial climb rate 3,937 fpm (1,200 m/minute)
Climb 6 minutes 48 seconds to 19,685 feet (6,000 m)
Service ceiling 36,089 feet (11,000 m)
Range 652 miles at 29,527 feet (1,050 km at
9,000 m)
Weights 9,742 lbs (4,420 kg) empty; 14,110 lbs
(6,400 kg) loaded; 15,720 lbs (7,130 kg) gross
Span 40 feet 11½ inches (12.50 m)
Length 34 feet 9½ inches (10.60 m)
Height 12 feet 7 inches (3.84 m)
Wing area 234 square feet (21.74 m²)

ITALY

In common with other countries that had taken part in World War I, from 1919 onwards Italy underwent a retrenchment in her world financial position. This, coupled with the feeling that World War I had been the 'war to end all wars', led the Italian government to allow the size and quality of its wartime air force to decline sadly in the early 1920s. Like other countries too, Italy tried with some success to keep abreast of the latest developments in the field of aeronautics by devoting a large portion of her military budget to racing and record-breaking aircraft. This ensured that Italian aircraft were in the forefront technologically. However, little thought was given to the revolution in the theory of air warfare that gripped the rest of the world in the late 1920s and early 1930s and the theories of General Douhet, one of the great prophets of the voguish enthusiasm for strategic bombing, were ignored in practice.

In the late 1920s and early 1930s the military aspirations of Benito Mussolini's Fascist regime resulted in the growth of the Italian air force, the *Regia Aeronautica*, into a well-equipped and moderately-sized weapon. This was soon tested in combat in the Italian invasion of Abyssinia, which began in 1935, and in the Spanish Civil War, which began in the following year. In the former campaign the *Regia Aeronautica* had little or no opposition, and performed quite well, especially in the transport and supply role. In the latter campaign, however, although it outnumbered the Republican forces considerably, the *Regia Aeronautica* did little more than hold its own. The worst aspect of the Spanish Civil War for the Italians was that their high command drew the wrong conclusions from their Spanish experiences: thus whilst other countries were developing aircraft with far greater payloads, higher speeds, increased rates of climb and enhanced ranges, the Italians were content with their open-cockpit fighters, with their extreme manoeuvrability as the result of a biplane configuration, and relatively slow medium bombers.

The results of this basic miscalculation were disastrous for Italy in World War II. Even when monoplane fighters were introduced they lacked an enclosed cockpit, adequate protection and performance and heavy armament until the generation that appeared late in 1941 with the Macchi C 202 and later C 205. Only in the field of torpedo-bombing, with the Savoia-Marchetti SM 79, did Italy show the way for other combatants of World War II.

During the course of the war Italy produced some excellent and original designs, but the country lacked the basic industrial facilities to make a large, advanced air force a practical possibility. The most important production and design failure was that of not producing a high-powered inline engine, and having therefore to rely on German sources.

The real problems with Italy's air force in World War II, apart from the difficulties of producing large numbers of advanced aircraft in a basically non-industrial country, were the lack of forethought and control by the authorities. The need for new types was not seen early

enough, with the result that Italy entered the war against foes who were using aircraft of more advanced design, and even when this need had been realized, and the right type of aircraft specified, the producers were allowed to compete with each other in an entirely haphazard fashion. It is always useful to have several different prototypes to test against each other for an order, only the best then being ordered into production. The Italians, however, often ordered two types into production, which made both manufacture and subsequent supply and modification more difficult. The *Regia Aeronautica* would have been far better supplied had the Italian air ministry been far more ruthless in the ordering of production types. As it was, the aircraft industry never achieved the capacity that it might have, and, with the severe losses

suffered by front-line units, Italy was forced to rely on German sources of supply for essential items such as engines and guns, and also for large numbers of aircraft such as the Messerschmitt Bf 109 and 110 fighters and the Junkers Ju 87 dive-bomber.

Italy was capable of producing aircraft the match for anything possessed by the Allies, but these types always came too late and in quantities too small to turn the tide: the Piaggio P 108 was a good heavy bomber, but only 163 were built; the Fiat G 55 was a superlative fighter, but only 105 were built during the war; and the Macchi C 205V *Veltro* (Greyhound) was an excellent fighter-bomber, but only 262 were produced. The story of the *Regia Aeronautica* in World War II was very much the story of what might have been, rather than what was.

Above: Savoia-Marchetti SM 79 Sparviero medium bombers of the Regia Aeronautica or Italian Air Force. Although this force played a relatively minor part in the war, the Italian aircraft industry produced several very interesting and advanced designs, including the SM 79, the best torpedo-bomber of the war

Fiat CR 32

Aircraft of the CR 32 series were the mainstay of the Italian fighter arm in the 1930s, and in many respects formed one of the high points of biplane fighter development in the tradition of World War I tactical theory. The CR 32 was derived directly from the CR 30 of 1932 by Celestino Rosatelli in 1933, and was intended as a pure interceptor type.

The CR 32 employed W-type Warren interplane bracing of the wings, thus obviating the need for wire bracing, but was otherwise conventional in design: a sturdy, compact biplane fighter powered by an inline engine and armed with two 12.7-mm machine-guns. The airframe, of metal construction with fabric covering, was quite conventional for the early 1930s, but the armament was relatively heavy, most contemporary fighters being armed with two 7.7-mm machine-guns.

Despite this, in 1935 there appeared the CR 32*bis*, armed with two 7.7-mm machine-guns in the lower wings, inboard of the interplane struts, in addition to the two 12.7-mm guns. Provision was also made for two 110- (50-kg) or one 220-lb (100-kg) bomb on a rack under the fuselage. Aircraft of this type were the first Italian fighters to arrive in Spain in 1936.

At about the same time, modifications to the undercarriage resulted in the CR 32*ter*, which was built only in limited numbers. The type was, however, exported to Paraguay, Venezuela, China and Hungary in the *bis* and *ter* forms.

The final Italian production version was the CR 32*quater*, which appeared late in 1936. This reverted to the armament of the original version, although numerous CR 32*quaters* were fitted with rudimentary night-fighting aids, although not radar of course. Production of the CR 32

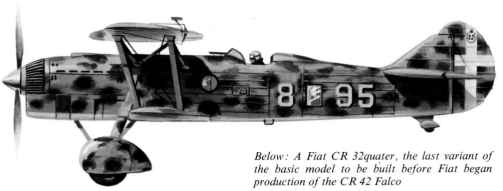

Below: A Fiat CR 32quater, the last variant of the basic model to be built before Fiat began production of the CR 42 Falco

Fiat CR 32quater
The aircraft illustrated is a machine of the 95th *Squadriglia*, whose emblem was three white arrows across a blue *fasces* on a yellow ground. The insigne of the white cross on the rudder is the arms of the house of Savoy, the Italian royal house, and the emblem forward of the cockpit is a representation of the Fascist *fasces*. Camouflage is that designed for the Spanish Civil War and retained for North Africa: a mid-green base with light brown patches sprayed over on the upper surfaces, and mid-stone on the under surfaces

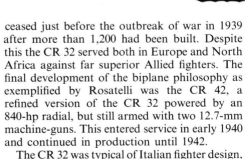

ceased just before the outbreak of war in 1939 after more than 1,200 had been built. Despite this the CR 32 served both in Europe and North Africa against far superior Allied fighters. The final development of the biplane philosophy as exemplified by Rosatelli was the CR 42, a refined version of the CR 32 powered by an 840-hp radial, but still armed with two 12.7-mm machine-guns. This entered service in early 1940 and continued in production until 1942.

The CR 32 was typical of Italian fighter design, and its continued production, up to 1939, puts Italian fighter design in its correct perspective. As the CR 32, with its superb manoeuvrability, had performed adequately against inferior opposition (such as Russian I-15s) in Spain, it was kept in production during the time it might be expected to meet in combat Allied aircraft more than 100 mph faster and with firepower at least six times as powerful.

Type single-seat fighter
Engine one Fiat A 30 RA *bis* twelve-cylinder liquid-cooled inline, 600 hp at 9,842 feet (3,000 m)
Armament two 12.7-mm Breda-SAFAT machine-guns in the upper nose with 375 rounds per gun, plus twelve 4.4-lb (2.00-kg) anti-personnel bombs
Maximum speeds 220 mph at 9,842 feet (355 km/h at 3,000 m); 206 mph (322 km/h) at sea level
Cruising speed 196 mph at 15,748 feet (315 km/h at 4,800 m)
Initial climb rate 2,198 fpm (670 m/minute)
Climb 14 minutes 25 seconds to 19,685 feet (6,000 m)
Service ceiling 25,262 feet (7,700 m)
Range 485 miles at 196 mph at 15,748 feet (780 km at 315 km/h at 4,800 m)
Weights 3,208 lbs (1,455 kg) empty; 4,222 lbs loaded
Span 31 feet 2 inches (9.50 m)
Length 24 feet 3½ inches (7.40 m)
Height 8 feet 7½ inches (2.63 m)
Wing area 237.88 square feet (22.10 m²)

Fiat G 55 Centauro

The Fiat G 55 was undoubtedly Italy's best fighter of the war, and in many ways exemplifies all that was good in the basic design philosophy of the Italian aircraft industry. As has been noted in the introduction, Italian aircraft were always aerodynamically excellent, their major failings being lack of armament and powerful engines.

The origins of the G 55 lay in the G 50 *Freccia* (Arrow), which had entered service with the *Regia Aeronautica* in 1938. This was the first metal monoplane fighter to fly in Italy, and at the time when fighters of the other Western powers were armed with a mixed machine-gun/cannon or multi machine-gun armament, and capable of speeds in the order of 350 mph (563 km/h), the Italian fighter was armed with two machine-guns and was capable of under 300 mph (483 km/h) on its 840-hp radial engine. Incredibly, after 45 machines had been produced, at service pilots' insistence the canopy enclosing the cockpit was removed. The *Freccia*'s only saving grace was its superb manoeuvrability.

War experience soon showed Italian pilots the errors of their ways, and demands for better performance and protection were soon heard. In the case of *Freccia* development, the results of these service demands was the *Centauro*. Although this was extensively redesigned, it used many *Freccia* components, and had the same aerodynamic qualities. Performance was improved by installing an Italian-built Daimler-Benz DB 605 engine in a new finely-contoured fuselage, adequate armour protection was added, and armament was improved by fitting German cannon. The combination of German power and armament and Italian aerodynamic flair resulted in a superlative fighter. The first model, the G 55/0, was armed with one 20-mm cannon and

Below: A Fiat G 55 Centauro, perhaps Italy's best fighter of the war

Fiat G 55 Centauro (Centaur)
The aircraft illustrated is a machine of the *Aviazione della Repubblica Sociale Italiana*. Note the revised *fasces* marking on the wings, with two instead of the earlier three rod and axe bundles on each. The fuselage and tail markings also reverted to the pre-war green, white and red stripes, which had been abandoned in favour of a white cross in June 1940 to avoid confusion with the French

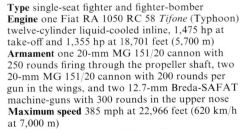

four 12.7-mm machine-guns, but the second model, the G 55/I, featured three cannon and two machine-guns. Other versions, which did not enter service, were the G 55/II with five 20-mm cannon, and the G 55/S with a torpedo. For this last model the radiator had to be removed from under the fuselage and two smaller units were placed under each wing.

The first *Centauro* flew in April 1942, but production was slow with initial service deliveries starting only in August 1943. Italy capitulated to the Allies on September 9, but as production of the *Centauro* was located in the north, deliveries of the fighter to the *Aviazione della Repubblica Sociale Italiana* were able to continue. This force was the air arm of the new Fascist state declared in German-held Italy after the rescue of Mussolini. With the worsening situation for the Axis, however, deliveries of the engine were very slow, and only 105 *Centauros* were delivered.

Type single-seat fighter and fighter-bomber
Engine one Fiat RA 1050 RC 58 *Tifone* (Typhoon) twelve-cylinder liquid-cooled inline, 1,475 hp at take-off and 1,355 hp at 18,701 feet (5,700 m)
Armament one 20-mm MG 151/20 cannon with 250 rounds firing through the propeller shaft, two 20-mm MG 151/20 cannon with 200 rounds per gun in the wings, and two 12.7-mm Breda-SAFAT machine-guns with 300 rounds in the upper nose
Maximum speed 385 mph at 22,966 feet (620 km/h at 7,000 m)
Cruising speed 348 mph (560 km/h)
Initial climb rate unknown
Climb 7 minutes 12 seconds to 19,685 feet (6,000 m)
Range 746 miles (1,200 km) on internal fuel; 1,025 miles (1,650 km) with drop-tanks
Weights 5,952 lbs (2,700 kg) empty; 8,179 lbs (3,710 kg) loaded
Span 38 feet 10½ inches (11.85 m)
Length 30 feet 8¾ inches (9.37 m)
Height 10 feet 3¼ inches (3.13 m)
Wing area 227.226 square feet (21.11 m²)

Savoia-Marchetti SM 79

The Savoia-Marchetti SM 79 was Italy's best medium bomber of the World War II period, and is considered by most authorities to have been unbeaten as a land-based torpedo-bomber during the whole of its service. Although it appeared superficially ungainly, the aircraft was in fact quite clean, adequately defended and well-powered.

The SM 79 could trace its origins back to the SM 73 commercial airliner and transport of the early 1930s. From this was developed the SM 81 *Pipistrello* (Bat), a trimotor monoplane bomber with a fixed undercarriage. For its time the *Pipistrello* was a good aircraft, and served with success in Abyssinia and Spain. A few were still in use as bombers when Italy entered the war in June 1940, but these were soon relegated to transport and paratroop-dropping roles as they were no match for Allied fighters. Despite its earlier sequence number, the SM 79 was in fact derived from the SM 81, and appeared in 1934 as a civilian transport aircraft. It had nearly half as much power again as the SM 81, and, with its retractable undercarriage, a very respectable performance. The *Regia Aeronautica* soon developed an interest in the new type as a bomber.

The first production version for military use was the SM 79-I, which was intended only as a medium bomber. Power was provided by three Alfa Romeo 126 radials of 780 hp each, and a bomb-load of 2,756 lbs (1,250 kg) could be carried 1,180 miles (1,899 km). The new bomber was tested operationally in the Spanish Civil War, and proved to be very successful. With a top speed of nearly 270 mph (435 km), it was difficult for many Republican fighters to catch. Indeed, Fiat CR 32 fighters could not keep up with it, and Fiat G 50 fighters were only a little faster.

The Italian air force had always been interested in the use of air-launched torpedoes against shipping in the Mediterranean, and led the world in the development of such weapons, aircraft to launch them, and tactical theories of employment in the period from the end of World War I to the end of World War II. Trials were carried out with the SM 79 as a launching aircraft in 1937, and by the summer of 1939 a new model, the SM 79-II, was in production as a torpedo-bomber. This could deliver two torpedoes, and proved an extremely efficient weapon in World War II.

After the capitulation of Italy, a few SM 79-IIIs were built for use by the *Aviazione della Repubblica Sociale Italiana*. This model was a cleaned-up version of the SM 79-II, with the ventral gondola removed and the forward-firing machine-gun replaced by a 20-mm cannon. Another version, the SM 79B, was produced before the war for export. This model had only two engines, the place of the fuselage-mounted engine being taken by a well-streamlined and glazed nose section. The fin and rudder were also modified. This variant achieved some commercial success with sales to countries in the Balkans. Production totalled 1,330 aircraft.

Left: US personnel inspect an SM 79 which had been flown to Sicily by an Italian instructor with six pupils on board after the Italian surrender in September 1943. Note the 12.7-mm machine-gun for rear defence mounted just to the rear of the cockpit
Below: Two SM 79 bombers (for obvious reasons the type was nicknamed il Gobbo or the hunchback) of the 10th Squadriglia in flight

Savoia-Marchetti SM 79-II Sparviero (Hawk)
The aircraft illustrated is a machine of the 192nd
Squadriglia. Note the triple *fasces* on the wing
markings, and the white cross on the rudder. The
marking at the top of the cross is a representation
of the arms of the House of Savoy, the Italian
royal family. Note also the *fasces* on a blue circle
on the fuselage engine's cowling. This was standard
fuselage marking for the *Regia Aeronautica*.
Camouflage is that for semi-desert conditions

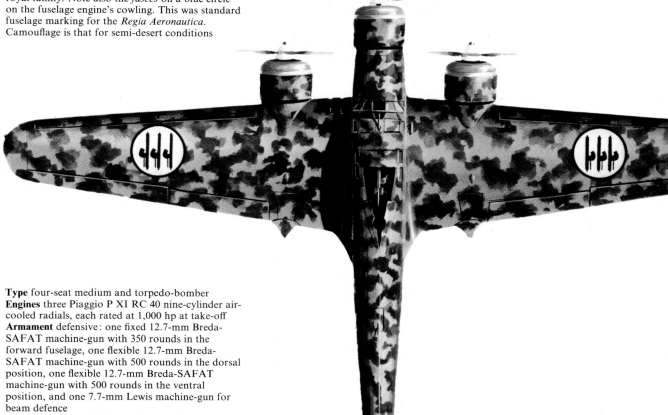

Type four-seat medium and torpedo-bomber
Engines three Piaggio P XI RC 40 nine-cylinder air-
cooled radials, each rated at 1,000 hp at take-off
Armament defensive: one fixed 12.7-mm Breda-
SAFAT machine-gun with 350 rounds in the
forward fuselage, one flexible 12.7-mm Breda-
SAFAT machine-gun with 500 rounds in the dorsal
position, one flexible 12.7-mm Breda-SAFAT
machine-gun with 500 rounds in the ventral
position, and one 7.7-mm Lewis machine-gun for
beam defence
offensive: up to 2,756 lbs (1,250 kg) of bombs
or two 17.7-inch (45-cm) torpedoes
Maximum speeds 267 mph at 13,123 feet (430 km/h
at 4,000 m); 224 mph (360 km/h) at sea level
Cruising speed 230 mph at 19,685 feet (370 km/h
at 6,000 m)
Climb 19 minutes 45 seconds to 16,404 feet
(5,000 m)
Service ceiling 22,966 feet (7,000 m)
Range 1,243 miles (2,000 km)
Weights 16,755 lbs (7,600 kg) empty; 24,912 lbs
(11,300 kg) loaded
Span 69 feet 6¾ inches (21.20 m)
Length 53 feet 1¼ inches (16.20 m)
Height 13 feet 5½ inches (4.10 m)
Wing area 656.6 square feet (61.00 m²)

JAPAN

Although Japan introduced military aviation in 1909, she was very reliant on imported aircraft of Western origins until late in the 1920s. The Japanese had, however, carefully absorbed the design and production techniques used abroad, and in the 1920s began to build up their own formidable aircraft industry. Not loath to learn from their foreign contemporaries, as were so many Western countries, the Japanese also continued to import non-Japanese types so that they could keep abreast of the latest developments and production ideas. Ironically, this constant import of Western designs, and the subsequent appearance of similar design features on Japanese aircraft, led the Western world to the safe, but entirely erroneous assumption that the Japanese were, and could only be, excellent imitators of more advanced Western ideas.

Yet by the mid-1930s the Japanese were producing for their separate Army and Navy air forces some good indigenous designs, characterized by their extreme manoeuvrability and great range. These types were tested operationally in China, but despite the dire warnings of men such as Claire Chennault, the West steadfastly refused to believe that 'mere Orientals' could produce designs of their own to match the best that the West could turn out.

This fallacy on the part of the Allies, as they were to become in World War II, was absolutely shattered in the first few months of the Japanese onslaught in the Pacific and South-east Asia. Japanese bombers, escorted by fighters, roamed over ranges that could not be matched by their Allied opponents until 1944, completely outflying the Allied fighters deployed in the area. Even when the latest British and American fighters were dispatched to fight the Japanese, the latter's fighters still showed a slight edge up to the start of 1943.

Like the Italians, however, the Japanese drew one major, and totally incorrect, conclusion from their operational experiences before World War II. They assumed that the aircraft they already possessed, designed for and tested in the war with China, would be sufficient to overwhelm the Allies. Japan gambled on a swift war, and when the error of this assessment was shown up by the Allied counter-offensive of 1943 onwards, she had nothing with which to oppose them. In the natural course of aeronautical development new types had appeared but no great priority had been allocated to get them into service quickly. The Japanese reacted quickly, but it takes time to get new aircraft into operation, and time was one commodity that Japan did not possess. Production was hampered, too, by the need to import vital materials, especially oil, from abroad and, as increasingly large numbers

of merchant ships were destroyed by US submarines, the Japanese armaments industry was slowly throttled.

Again like the Italians, the Japanese had realized insufficiently that new designs must possess not only enhanced performance but improved armament. Thus Japanese aircraft could normally outfly similar Allied aircraft, even at the end of the war, but could not inflict

or receive the same amount of battle damage. Firepower that would only damage an Allied aircraft would almost certainly destroy an equivalent Japanese aircraft, which lacked pilot and fuel protection in an effort to preserve handling qualities by saving weight and size. Only the last generation of Japanese aircraft was a match for Allied types, and these came too late and were too few to halt the Allies.

Japanese fighters could not stop the Allied bombers from 1943 or halt the Allied sea and land advances. To obtain the ranges necessary to operate over the Pacific with a relatively small aircraft, protection and payload had been sacrificed to fuel, and types that the Japanese considered heavy bombers were the inferior equivalent of Allied medium bombers.

Japan was also deficient in pilots as well as

aircraft. Although these former had been the equal of any in the world in 1941, continued combat quickly thinned their ranks, and the newer pilots lacked the training and skill of their predecessors. Japan had gambled with her attack on the Western industrialized democracies in 1941, but her gamble failed. The price that she had to pay for her miscalculation was the almost total destruction of her cities and her factories by American bombers, which roamed the Japanese skies almost unmolested, the few fighters left being stranded on the ground, with their inferior pilots, by the absence of fuel.

(The name in single inverted commas after the Japanese name or designation for an aircraft is the Allied code-name for the type, fighters being given boys' names, and other types, except trainers, girls' names.)

Left: A flight of Yokosuka D4Y Suisei (Comet) carrier dive-bombers, code-named Judy by the Allies, over Mount Fuji. The Suisei was mass produced in both radial- and inline-engined forms, and was the fastest carrier-borne dive-bomber of the war with a maximum speed of some 360 mph at 17,224 feet 580 km/h at 5,250 metres

Aichi D3A 'Val'

The Aichi D3A series was Japan's most celebrated naval dive-bomber of the war, and was the most successful Axis aircraft against Allied warships in the whole of World War II. The type was the last Japanese carrier aircraft to be fitted with a fixed undercarriage, but despite its apparent obsolescence, it performed with stunning success in the first year of the war. To a certain extent the D3A can be considered the Japanese navy's equivalent of the British navy's Fairey Swordfish.

The requirement for a monoplane dive-bomber to replace the biplane Aichi D1A was issued in 1936, and Aichi, Mitsubishi and Nakajima all tendered designs. Only the Aichi and Nakajima designs received prototype contracts, however. The Aichi aircraft, designed by Tokuhishiro Goake, drew many of its features, including the elliptical wing, from contemporary designs by Heinkel, especially the He 70 high-speed monoplane. A fixed undercarriage was used as it was felt that its simplicity and lightness would compensate for the increased drag. The initial prototype, powered by a Nakajima Hikari of 710 hp, was ready by the end of 1937, and trials began early in 1938. Although the aircraft proved to be very strong, it was also underpowered, and difficult to steer. The dive brakes, moreover, proved particularly troublesome. These problems were largely overcome in the second prototype, which had an 840-hp Mitsubishi Kinsei radial, a larger fin and rudder, and strengthened dive brakes. The wings were also enlarged by 21½ square feet (2 m²) to help in tight turns. The D3A was generally superior to the Nakajima D3N, and was ordered into production as the Navy Type 99 Carrier Bomber Model 11, with the company designation D3A1, in December 1939.

As the type went into production, further improvements were made, thereby increasing the weight and necessitating the instalment of the 1,000-hp Kinsei 43 engine. The wings were slightly smaller than those of the second prototype, and the last vestiges of the directional problems encountered with the first prototype were solved by the provision of a dorsal extension to the fin. Although the D3A1 performed satisfactory carrier trials on board the *Akagi* and *Kaga* in 1940, the type saw its first action operating from land bases against the Chinese later that year.

At Pearl Harbor, 126 D3A1 aircraft were involved, and thereafter the type had a spectacular career in the Pacific and Indian oceans. Losses in the Solomons campaign of late 1942 and early 1943 were very heavy, however, and the D3A1 was increasingly relegated to land-based units of the Imperial Japanese Naval Air Force. Realizing that its type was becoming obsolete, Aichi introduced the more powerful D3A2 in June 1942. This had a 1,300-hp Kinsei 54 radial engine, which boosted top speed by nearly 30 mph (48 km/h) to 267 mph (430 km/h). The new model was accepted for service as the Navy Type 99 Carrier Bomber Model 22. Externally, the later model could be distinguished by its revised cockpit canopy and the provision of a small propeller spinner. The D3A was by now obsolete, however, and was increasingly

replaced by the Yokosuka D4Y *Suisei* on the aircraft-carrier. Land-based units continued to use the D3A, but losses were very heavy, despite the type's remarkable agility, which enabled it to dogfight with American fighters. The D3A's service career ended as a *kamikaze* aircraft. In this role its losses were appallingly heavy, out of all proportion to any tasks it could have fulfilled. Production reached a total of 1,495 aircraft.

Above: An Aichi D3A1 'Val' carrier dive-bomber of the type that proved so successful in the Japanese surprise attack on Pearl Harbor
Below: The improved D3A2 model, which could be told from the D3A1 by its spinner, appeared in June 1942. Note the 551-lb (250-kg) bomb on the crutch under the fuselage. The crutch was used to swing the bomb out clear of the propeller as the aircraft dived on its target

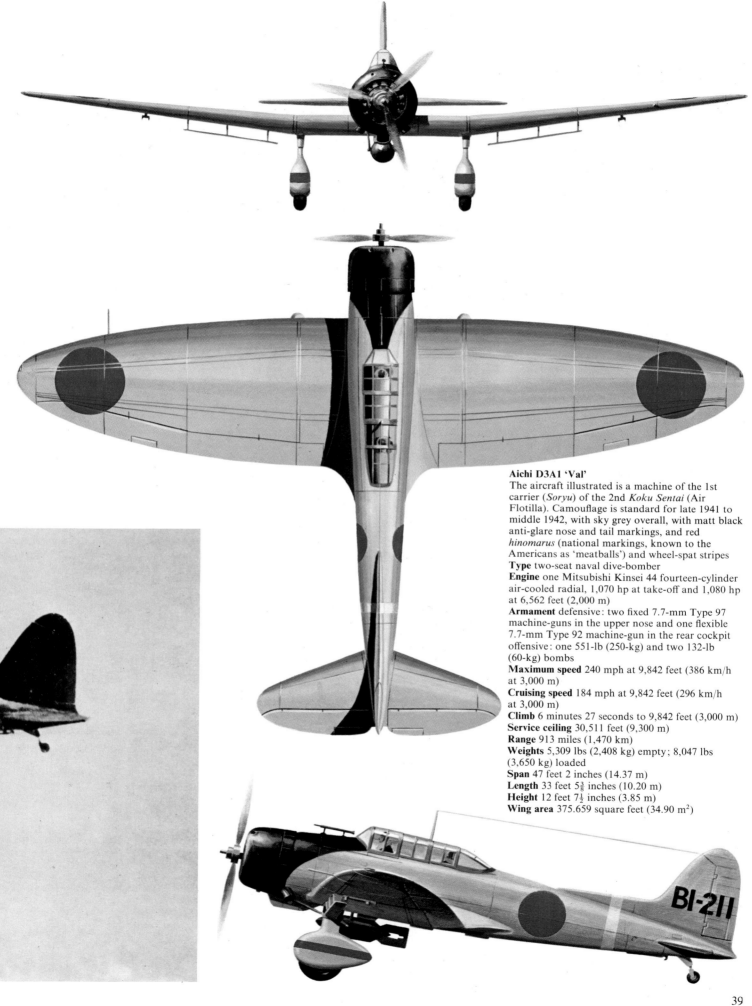

Aichi D3A1 'Val'
The aircraft illustrated is a machine of the 1st
carrier (*Soryu*) of the 2nd *Koku Sentai* (Air
Flotilla). Camouflage is standard for late 1941 to
middle 1942, with sky grey overall, with matt black
anti-glare nose and tail markings, and red
hinomarus (national markings, known to the
Americans as 'meatballs') and wheel-spat stripes
Type two-seat naval dive-bomber
Engine one Mitsubishi Kinsei 44 fourteen-cylinder
air-cooled radial, 1,070 hp at take-off and 1,080 hp
at 6,562 feet (2,000 m)
Armament defensive: two fixed 7.7-mm Type 97
machine-guns in the upper nose and one flexible
7.7-mm Type 92 machine-gun in the rear cockpit
offensive: one 551-lb (250-kg) and two 132-lb
(60-kg) bombs
Maximum speed 240 mph at 9,842 feet (386 km/h
at 3,000 m)
Cruising speed 184 mph at 9,842 feet (296 km/h
at 3,000 m)
Climb 6 minutes 27 seconds to 9,842 feet (3,000 m)
Service ceiling 30,511 feet (9,300 m)
Range 913 miles (1,470 km)
Weights 5,309 lbs (2,408 kg) empty; 8,047 lbs
(3,650 kg) loaded
Span 47 feet 2 inches (14.37 m)
Length 33 feet $5\frac{3}{8}$ inches (10.20 m)
Height 12 feet $7\frac{1}{2}$ inches (3.85 m)
Wing area 375.659 square feet (34.90 m²)

Kawasaki Ki-45 Toryu

The Kawasaki Ki-45 was one of the best night-fighters to see service with the Imperial Japanese Army Air Force in World War II, but its introduction to combat was seriously delayed by technical difficulties. The army requirement for a long-range, twin-engined heavy fighter, which was issued early in 1937, was the direct result of European ideas on such aircraft. Although three companies started design work, only the Kawasaki Ki-38 reached the mock-up stage. As the army was uncertain what the performance parameters of such an aircraft should be, however, further work was shelved until a proper specification could be formulated.

The specification was finally issued at the end of the year, and Kawasaki started development work on the Ki-45, based on the Ki-38, to meet it. The prototype was completed by January 1939, but trouble with the licence-built Bristol Mercury radial engines, and the excessive drag of their nacelles, meant that performance was well below that specified. Improvements were effected on the second prototype, but even this was not sufficient to raise speed to the 300 mph (483 km/h) mark, whereas the specified target was 335 mph (539 km/h). As a result of these problems, further development work was halted late in 1939. In an effort to solve the engine problems with the Ki-45, Kawasaki was told to replace the unsuccessful Nakajima Na-20b engines with Nakajima Ha-25 units. Despite being 160 hp more powerful, the Ha-25 had a smaller diameter than the Ha-20b, and the improved prototype could use smaller nacelles, which reduced drag and raised top speed by 25 mph (40 km/h). At the same time, the design team of Takeo Doi had revised the aircraft with a view to easing production, and the prototype of this Ki-45 proved so successful that at last the type was ordered into production late in 1941, with the army designation Army Type 2 Two-seat Fighter Model A and company designation Ki-45 KAIa.

Service deliveries began in August 1942, the first units to take the new fighter into combat being those in Burma and China. The type was an immediate success, principally for its protection and heavy armament: two forward-firing 12.7-mm machine-guns in the Model A. In the Model B, or Ki-45 KAIb, this was raised to one 37-mm and one 20-mm cannon, which made the *Toryu* especially potent against torpedo-boats and bombers.

Success with a field modification, the fitting of two 12.7-mm machine-guns just behind the cockpit to fire obliquely upwards and forwards, in the manner of the German *schräge Musik*, prompted the army to develop the idea adequately. Thus the Ki-45 KAIc featured an improved 37-mm cannon and two upward-firing 20-mm cannon. No other nose armament was fitted as this space was reserved for the radar that was intended to complete this night-fighter design. The radar only reached prototype form, however, and Japanese night-fighter crews had to rely on visual sightings of the American B-29 bombers raiding Japan.

Various other models with revised powerplant and armament arrangements were proposed, including an anti-shipping strike aircraft with a 75-mm gun, but these came to nothing. There were, however, a considerable number of field

modifications of the armament. Further development of the basic design resulted in the very promising Ki-96 single-seat heavy fighter. The Ki-45 proved a very useful and versatile machine, and for the Japanese it was unfortunate that the engine problems delayed its introduction for so long, and that the lack of suitable radar equipment curtailed its career as a night-fighter. A total of 1,370 Ki-45 aircraft was built.

Below: A Kawasaki Ki-45 KAI Toryu (Dragon Killer), code-named Nick by the Allies, in flight. Note the muzzles of the two 20-mm Ho-5 cannon in a 'schrage Musik' installation poking up through the roof of the fuselage just in front of the radio mast and behind the pilot's cockpit. No rear-firing defensive armament, normally a 7.92-mm Type 98 machine-gun, is fitted

Bottom: An Army Type 2 Two-Seat Fighter Model A, designated Ki-45 KAIa by the manufacturers, on a Japanese airfield. This was the first production model, and was taken into action for the first time by the 21st Sentai (Group) in Burma during October 1942 and by the 16th Sentai in China during November of the same year. The type was unusual amongst Japanese aircraft of the time in having the heavy forward-firing armament of one 20- and one 12.7-mm gun, later 37- and 20-mm weapons

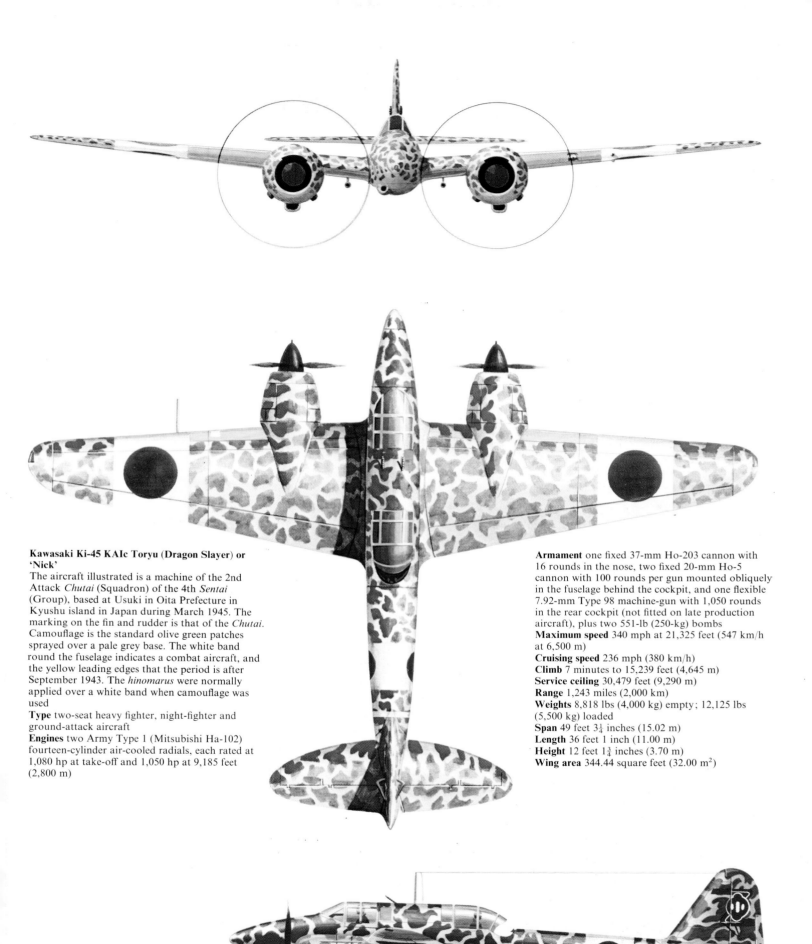

Kawasaki Ki-45 KAIc Toryu (Dragon Slayer) or 'Nick'

The aircraft illustrated is a machine of the 2nd Attack *Chutai* (Squadron) of the 4th *Sentai* (Group), based at Usuki in Oita Prefecture in Kyushu island in Japan during March 1945. The marking on the fin and rudder is that of the *Chutai*. Camouflage is the standard olive green patches sprayed over a pale grey base. The white band round the fuselage indicates a combat aircraft, and the yellow leading edges that the period is after September 1943. The *hinomarus* were normally applied over a white band when camouflage was used

Type two-seat heavy fighter, night-fighter and ground-attack aircraft

Engines two Army Type 1 (Mitsubishi Ha-102) fourteen-cylinder air-cooled radials, each rated at 1,080 hp at take-off and 1,050 hp at 9,185 feet (2,800 m)

Armament one fixed 37-mm Ho-203 cannon with 16 rounds in the nose, two fixed 20-mm Ho-5 cannon with 100 rounds per gun mounted obliquely in the fuselage behind the cockpit, and one flexible 7.92-mm Type 98 machine-gun with 1,050 rounds in the rear cockpit (not fitted on late production aircraft), plus two 551-lb (250-kg) bombs

Maximum speed 340 mph at 21,325 feet (547 km/h at 6,500 m)

Cruising speed 236 mph (380 km/h)

Climb 7 minutes to 15,239 feet (4,645 m)

Service ceiling 30,479 feet (9,290 m)

Range 1,243 miles (2,000 km)

Weights 8,818 lbs (4,000 kg) empty; 12,125 lbs (5,500 kg) loaded

Span 49 feet 3¼ inches (15.02 m)

Length 36 feet 1 inch (11.00 m)

Height 12 feet 1¾ inches (3.70 m)

Wing area 344.44 square feet (32.00 m²)

Kawasaki Ki-61 Hien

The Kawasaki Ki-61 was the only major Japanese warplane of World War II to be powered by an inline engine. This was the superlative Daimler-Benz DB 601, revised and lightened for Japanese production purposes as the Kawasaki Ha-40. Although it was as powerful as the German original, the Japanese engine was far less reliable, and this was to plague the service career of the Ki-61.

Kawasaki's interest in inline engines started in the 1920s, when the firm had enjoyed the services of Dr Richard Vogt, later the chief designer of Blohm und Voss aircraft. Concomitant with this interest in inline engines was the design of aircraft to use the engines. Thus Kawasaki approached the army authorities with ideas for fighters similar to those that were proving so successful in Europe. In February 1940, while development work with the new Ha-40 was still proceeding, the army ordered Kawasaki to investigate the possibilities of a heavy fighter and a light fighter to use the Ha-40. These emerged as the Ki-60 and the Ki-61 respectively. The former was quite successful, but the type was abandoned late in 1941.

The Ki-61, designed by Takeo Doi and Shin Owada, first flew in December 1941, and soon proved itself an excellent design. Although handling characteristics were inferior to those of contemporary Japanese designs, the new fighter received considerable praise for its high speed – especially in a dive – protection for pilot and fuel, and heavy armament. This comprised up to four 12.7-mm machine-guns, twice as much hitting power as other army fighters. Late in 1942 the Ki-61 was tested against a Curtiss P-40E and a Messerschmitt Bf 109E, and was considered to be a better machine than both of the Western aircraft. As with other Japanese aircraft, it could outfly the two Western fighters; more importantly, perhaps, it was also superior in those aspects that had always been the forte of Western designs – speed, protection and strength.

The army accepted the Ki-61 for service as the Army Type 3 Fighter Model 1 late in 1942. Deliveries of production fighters began in February 1943, the first examples being of the Model 1B (four 12.7-mm machine-guns) variety. The new fighter first went into combat over New Guinea in April 1943, and immediately demonstrated its superiority over the Nakajima Ki-43 and Allied fighters in the area. The one weak point in the Ki-61's make-up was the unreliability of its engine.

These first production machines had the company designation Ki-61-Ia and Ib and to improve hitting power, 388 of these models were converted on the production line to accommodate two 20-mm Mauser MG 151/20 cannon, one in each wing. With the introduction of the Japanese-designed Ho-5 20-mm cannon, Kawasaki developed the Ki-61-I KAIc, with two Ho-5 cannon replacing the two 12.7-mm machine-guns in the fuselage, a slightly longer fuselage, and strengthened wings to allow the carriage of underwing stores and permit higher diving speeds. The last Ki-61-I variant was the Ki-61-I KAId, which was armed with two 30-mm Ho-105 cannon in

the wings and two 12.7-mm machine-guns in the fuselage. The Ki-61-I KAI series was in production from January 1944 to January 1945, and the first American aircraft to be able to best the type was the North American P-51 Mustang, which began to operate over Japan only in late spring of 1945.

As the Ha-40 engine went into production, Kawasaki turned to the development of an improved version with superior high-altitude performance. This eventually emerged as the Ha-140, and, to make full use of the new engine, Takeo Doi revised the Ki-61. The first of the new type, designated Ki-61-II by the producers, had larger wings and an improved cockpit canopy. Flight trials, which started in December 1943, proved unsatisfactory at altitude, and only eight Ki-61-II fighters were built before another version, the Ki-61-II KAI, was introduced. This had a longer fuselage together with the wings of the original Ki-61-I model, and proved an excellent fighter when its engine could be coaxed into reliable life. The type was built in limited numbers as the Army Type 3 Fighter Model 2, in two versions: the Model 2A (two 20-mm cannon in the fuselage and two 12.7-mm machine-guns in the wings) and the Model 2B (four 20-mm cannon).

The Ki-61-II KAI proved efficient against the

Top: A Ki-61-I fighter in flight. The clean lines of cowling round the inline engine are very apparent
Above: The belly of a captured Kawasaki Ki-61-I KAIc is examined by three Americans. The Hien (Swallow), or Tony as it was known to the Allies, was the only Japanese inline-engined fighter to enter widespread service, and was at first thought by the Allies to be a licence-built version of the Messerschmitt Bf 109. In fact, early attempts to improve firepower led to the use of German MG 151 cannon in the wings of 388 Ki-61-Is.

B-29 formations bombing Japan, but only when the engine was behaving properly, which was an infrequent occurrence. Problems with the engine grew steadily worse as skilled workers were drafted into the army, and finally the factory producing the Ha-140 was destroyed by American bombing in January 1945. Before this date the engine problems had led to the development of the Kawasaki Ki-100, which featured the Ki-61 airframe married to a Mitsubishi Ha-112-II radial. This was in every respect a superlative fighter. Only 3,078 Ki-61 fighters were built, and it is interesting to speculate what affect on the war the type might have made if its engine's performance had matched that of the airframe, and had production been smoother and on a larger scale.

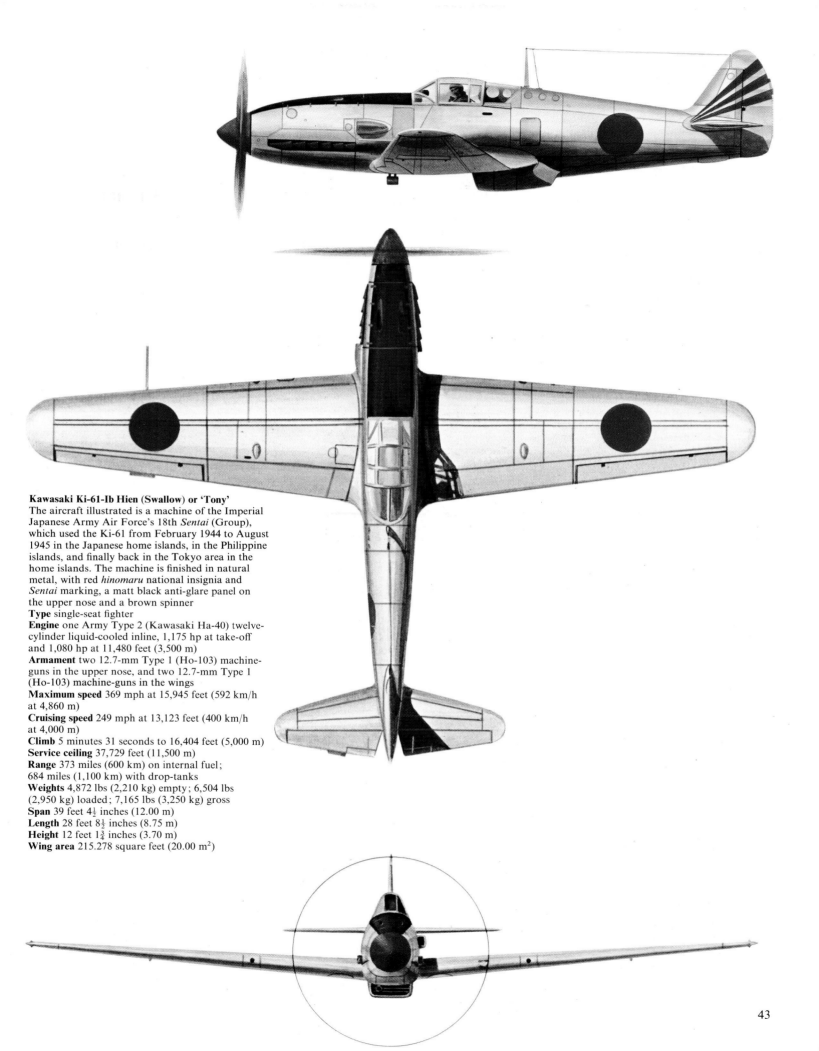

Kawasaki Ki-61-Ib Hien (Swallow) or 'Tony'
The aircraft illustrated is a machine of the Imperial
Japanese Army Air Force's 18th *Sentai* (Group),
which used the Ki-61 from February 1944 to August
1945 in the Japanese home islands, in the Philippine
islands, and finally back in the Tokyo area in the
home islands. The machine is finished in natural
metal, with red *hinomaru* national insignia and
Sentai marking, a matt black anti-glare panel on
the upper nose and a brown spinner
Type single-seat fighter
Engine one Army Type 2 (Kawasaki Ha-40) twelve-
cylinder liquid-cooled inline, 1,175 hp at take-off
and 1,080 hp at 11,480 feet (3,500 m)
Armament two 12.7-mm Type 1 (Ho-103) machine-
guns in the upper nose, and two 12.7-mm Type 1
(Ho-103) machine-guns in the wings
Maximum speed 369 mph at 15,945 feet (592 km/h
at 4,860 m)
Cruising speed 249 mph at 13,123 feet (400 km/h
at 4,000 m)
Climb 5 minutes 31 seconds to 16,404 feet (5,000 m)
Service ceiling 37,729 feet (11,500 m)
Range 373 miles (600 km) on internal fuel;
684 miles (1,100 km) with drop-tanks
Weights 4,872 lbs (2,210 kg) empty; 6,504 lbs
(2,950 kg) loaded; 7,165 lbs (3,250 kg) gross
Span 39 feet 4½ inches (12.00 m)
Length 28 feet 8½ inches (8.75 m)
Height 12 feet 1¾ inches (3.70 m)
Wing area 215.278 square feet (20.00 m²)

Mitsubishi A6M Reisen

The Mitsubishi A6M series of fighters is deservedly the most celebrated aircraft used by the Japanese armed forces in World War II. At a time when other naval fighters were slow, clumsy machines, in every way inferior to their land-based counterparts, the A6M could outfly almost all land-based fighters, had an enormous range, and was possessed of a heavy armament. The type operated from land bases as well as from aircraft-carriers, and was used in almost every major action in which the Imperial Japanese Navy was involved.

The origins of the A6M lay in a 1937 requirement for a fighter to replace the Mitsubishi A5M, which had just entered service. The A5M was a monoplane, but had an open cockpit and a fixed, 'spatted' undercarriage. The revised requirement issued by the navy later in 1937, which reflected the lessons of combat gained over China, meant that the new fighter would have to be a very advanced design. The Mitsubishi team, led by Jiro Horikoshi, produced an excellent all-metal machine, carefully streamlined and with a fully glazed, all-round vision cockpit canopy. This last was quite remarkable for 1938. The first prototype, powered by a 780-hp Mitsubishi Zuisei radial, first flew in April 1939, and proved to be a delightful aircraft, fulfilling or exceeding all the specifications except that of speed. To rectify this failing, Mitsubishi was instructed to replace the Zuisei engine with the 940-hp Nakajima Sakae. The third prototype was fitted with the new engine, and with it the type's designation was changed from A6M1 to A6M2. The new powerplant also raised speed to well over the specified minimum. The Mitsubishi A6M2 was ordered into production as the Navy Type 0 (Zero) Carrier Fighter Model 11 in July 1940. Pre-production models were already in service in China, where their record was extremely impressive.

Several minor modifications were incorporated in production aircraft but only the provision of folding wingtips for carrier use resulted in a different designation, the Model 21. The Japanese navy had 328 operational A6M2 fighters in December 1941, and these spearheaded the incredible run of Japanese successes in the Pacific and South-east Asia up to the middle of 1942. By this time the latest A6M model, the A6M3, was beginning to reach service units as the Model 32. This new model had a 1,130-hp Sakae 21 engine, greater cannon ammunition capacity, and, in later aircraft, wings shortened by the removal of the folding tips. The span now became 36 feet 1 inch (11 m). With these modifications speed was improved by 7 mph (11 km/h) at altitude although handling characteristics were very slightly impaired.

The A6M3 was the first of the A6M series to suffer severe losses at the hands of the Americans. This occurred in the fighting over Guadalcanal. The Sakae 21 was larger than the Sakae 12, which resulted in a reduced fuselage tankage capacity, and also had a higher fuel consumption, with the result that maximum range was reduced to 1,477 miles (2,377 km). As the A6M3s had to operate from airfields over 550 miles (885 km) from Guadalcanal, combat endurance was very

limited, damaged machines had a long haul back home, and casualties rose sharply. In an effort to restore the earlier range, Mitsubishi introduced the Model 22 or 22A, depending on the cannon fitted. This had provision for under-wing drop-tanks, and the longer wings of the Model 21. Range was restored to 1,930 miles (3,106 km), however, the A6M was now beginning to be equalled by the latest Allied fighters, and as a newer model was on its way, production of the Model 22 was very limited.

The next model to appear was designed to be able to hold its own with American fighters at medium and high altitudes. This was A6M4, with a turbo-supercharged Sakae, but it proved a failure as a result of problems with the supercharger. Thus the navy had to make do with the next model, the A6M5, pending the introduction of an A6M replacement.

The A6M5, or Model 52, had shorter wings again, with rounded tips, and individual exhausts, the thrust augmentation lifting speed to 351 mph (565 km/h). The wings were also covered with thicker skinning, which permitted higher diving speeds. Previously, Allied types had been able to escape the A6M by using their superior dive characteristics. This was now largely halted. The weakness of the A6M5 lay not in performance, however, but in protection, for even a short burst from six 0.50-inch (12.7-mm) machine-guns could cause the A6M5 to break up. Thus in March deliveries of the A6M5a began. This had thicker skinning again on the wings, and belt-fed instead of drum-fed cannon in the wings. This Model 52A was quickly superseded, however, by the Model 52B, or A6M5b, which had an armoured glass windscreen and fire extinguishers for the fuel tanks. One of the fuselage 7.7-mm machine-guns was also replaced by a 13.2-mm weapon. But the A6M series was now obsolete, and even the latest A6M5 fighters suffered almost total annihilation in the 'Great Marianas Turkey Shoot' in the Battle of the Philippine Sea in June 1944.

Production of an A6M replacement had still not made any headway, and so further development of the A6M had to be undertaken. Although the designers wished to replace the Sakae engine with the Mitsubishi Kinsei, the navy forbade this. Pending the arrival of the Sakae 31 with methanol-water fuel injection, the

Sakae 21 was retained in the A6M5c (Model 520). This had additional fuel tankage, armour protection for the pilot, and an additional pair of 13.2-mm Type 3 machine-guns in the wings, which had yet thicker skinning. Combat units often extemporized a rack to carry a 551-lb (250-kg) bomb instead of the drop-tank under the fuselage. Further official development of the idea to produce a dive-bomber for light carriers resulted in the A6M7 or Model 63.

The navy finally realized that the only way in which the necessary performance could be achieved was to allow the A6M to use the Kinsei engine. The need was borne home by the failure of the A6M6c (Model 53C), which had a top speed of only 346 mph (557 km/h) despite the methanol-water boosted Sakae 31. To accommodate the 1,560-hp Kinsei 62 the fuselage of the A6M had to be revised, and the first of the new type, designated A6M8, appeared in April 1945. Performance was promising, but no production Model 64 fighters were built before the end of the war.

Although the A6M had been pre-eminent amongst naval fighters in 1941, it was obsolete by 1943. Although its performance was still only a little inferior to that of the latest Allied fighters, it lacked protection for the pilot and fuel. The structure, moreover, was too light to take the combat damage caused by the firepower of Allied fighters in the closing stages of the war. But failure of the navy to develop a replacement in time meant that production of the A6M had to continue to the end of the war and in all 11,291 were built. Many of the earlier models were expended as *kamikaze* aircraft in the Philippines, Iwo Jima and Okinawa campaigns.

The importance of the A6M early in the war was as much psychological as physical: the 'Zero' shocked the Allies, who expected only second-rate *matériel*, copied from the West, to be used by the Japanese.

Below: One of a series of American recognition photographs of the Mitsubishi A6M5 Reisen Zero Fighter), known to the Imperial Japanese Navy as the Navy Type 0 Carrier Fighter Model 52 and to the Allies as the Zeke 52. Note the individual ejector exhaust stubs, which provided some thrust, boosting top speed by 13 mph (21 km/h) compared with the A6M3

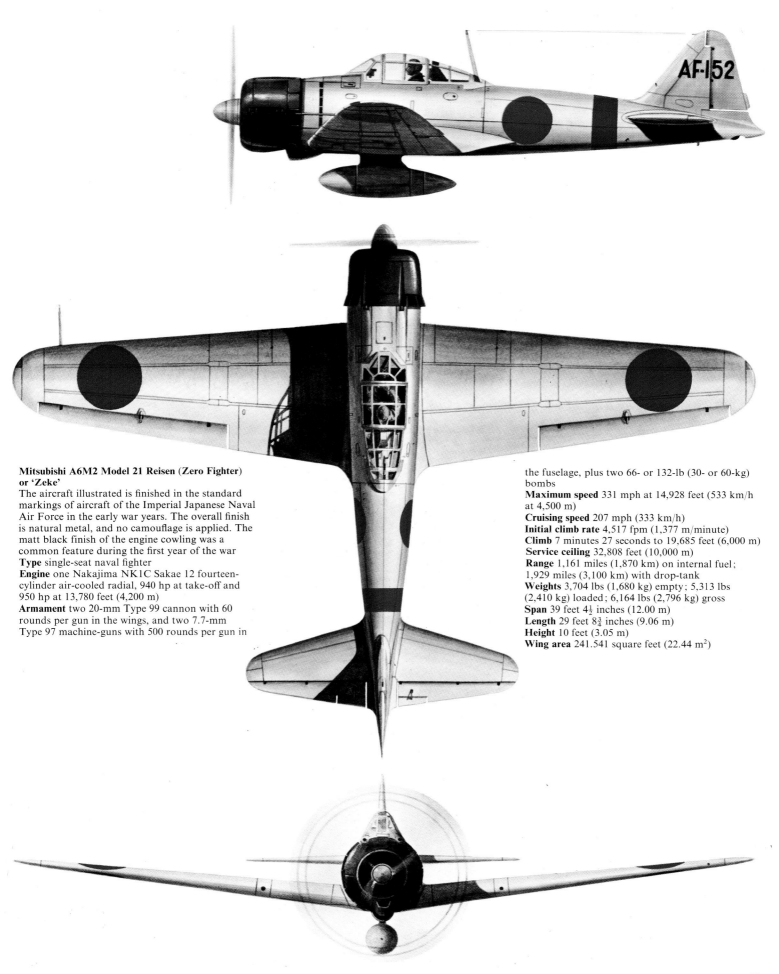

Mitsubishi A6M2 Model 21 Reisen (Zero Fighter) or 'Zeke'

The aircraft illustrated is finished in the standard markings of aircraft of the Imperial Japanese Naval Air Force in the early war years. The overall finish is natural metal, and no camouflage is applied. The matt black finish of the engine cowling was a common feature during the first year of the war

Type single-seat naval fighter

Engine one Nakajima NK1C Sakae 12 fourteen-cylinder air-cooled radial, 940 hp at take-off and 950 hp at 13,780 feet (4,200 m)

Armament two 20-mm Type 99 cannon with 60 rounds per gun in the wings, and two 7.7-mm Type 97 machine-guns with 500 rounds per gun in the fuselage, plus two 66- or 132-lb (30- or 60-kg) bombs

Maximum speed 331 mph at 14,928 feet (533 km/h at 4,500 m)

Cruising speed 207 mph (333 km/h)

Initial climb rate 4,517 fpm (1,377 m/minute)

Climb 7 minutes 27 seconds to 19,685 feet (6,000 m)

Service ceiling 32,808 feet (10,000 m)

Range 1,161 miles (1,870 km) on internal fuel; 1,929 miles (3,100 km) with drop-tank

Weights 3,704 lbs (1,680 kg) empty; 5,313 lbs (2,410 kg) loaded; 6,164 lbs (2,796 kg) gross

Span 39 feet 4½ inches (12.00 m)

Length 29 feet 8¾ inches (9.06 m)

Height 10 feet (3.05 m)

Wing area 241.541 square feet (22.44 m²)

Mitsubishi G4M & Yokosuka MXY7

The Mitsubishi G4M series of bombers was the best, and most famous, type of attack bomber flown by the Imperial Japanese Naval Air Force from its land bases throughout the Eastern theatre of war in World War II. Although its payload was light and its protection for crew and fuel appallingly bad, its performance, especially in range, was spectacular. Together with the same company's A6M fighter, the G4M spearheaded the fast, far-ranging air strikes that opened the way for Japanese advances in the Pacific and South-east Asia in 1941 and 1942.

Design work on the G4M began in 1937, when the navy issued a requirement for a naval attack bomber to replace the Mitsubishi G3M, which had just entered service with units in China. The new type was to be powered by a pair of 1,000-hp engines, and have a range of nearly 3,000 miles (4,828 km) and a speed of nearly 250 mph (402 km/h). The Mitsubishi team, led by Kiro Honjo, soon realized that the performance requirements could not be met with so little power, and instead concentrated their efforts on a clean monoplane with two 1,500-hp Mitsubishi Kasei radials. One of the major failings of the G3M was its lack of adequate defensive armament, and this was rectified in the G4M by the provision of five 7.7-mm machine-guns and one 20-mm cannon. Although a considerable volume of fuel could be carried, to achieve the necessary range the Mitsubishi team decided to abandon any ideas of fuel and crew protection to save weight. This was to have disastrous consequences in combat.

The first prototype flew in October 1939, and quickly showed itself to have excellent performance, well above that demanded. The type was put into production almost immediately, but only as the Mitsubishi G6M1 escort fighter, not in its intended role as a bomber. This occurred because of the losses being suffered over China by the G3M. Thus the G4M was modified to serve as the G6M1 fighter. The nose and tail guns were retained, the dorsal gun was eliminated, the two beam guns were replaced by a 20-mm cannon, and a ventral gondola with

another pair of 20-mm cannon replaced the bomb-bay and doors. Only 30 of these aircraft were built, however, and even these did not prove very successful.

Production of the G4M1, or Navy Type 1 Attack Bomber Model 11, finally began in 1940, service deliveries beginning in April 1941. The G4M1 was soon delivering raids deep into China, where lack of fighters meant that the Japanese bomber proved very successful. Initial combat operations in World War II were also successful: these included a major part in the sinking of the battleship *Prince of Wales* and the battle-cruiser *Repulse*, and the conquest of the Philippines. Operations against targets in New Guinea, however, were attended by heavy casualties, for here the Allies had deployed adequate fighter defences. In an effort to reduce these losses Mitsubishi developed the Model 12 (still given the company designation G4M1), with uprated engines, rudimentary fuel tank protection and fire extinguishers. Unfortunately range was reduced by some 200 miles (321 km).

Further modifications resulted in a redesignated model. This was the G4M2 or Model 22, which had 1,800-hp Kasei 21 engines with methanol-water injection, improved armament and aerodynamics, increased fuel capacity, and the provision of doors over the bomb-bay. The new model entered production in July 1943. The Models 22A and 22B featured revised and improved armaments. Although the type was by now growing obsolete, the failure of its replacements meant that further development had to be undertaken. This led to the G4M2a, or Model 24. Better engines, with a lower fuel consumption, were fitted, and various sub-marks were designated by their different armaments. Late production examples had air-sea search radar installed in the nose. A not very numerous, but nevertheless celebrated, variant of the Model 24 was the G4M2e Model 24J, which carried the Yokosuka MXY7 *Okha* kamikaze aircraft. Most Model 24J aircraft were conversions of Model 24B and Model 24C bombers. By October 1944 the G4M2 had replaced all G4M1 aircraft, which

were now relegated to lesser duties. Losses in combat, however, were very heavy for all types, and a new model was developed.

This was the G4M3, or Model 34, and featured a new wing with self-sealing rubber fuel tanks, armour protection for the crew, a revised tail turret, and dihedral on the tailplane. Small-scale production began in October 1944. Thus the G4M ended its wartime career. It had proved successful when there was little effective defence, but its losses had been enormous as Allied defences became more efficient. The G4M's last wartime duty was the transport of the Japanese surrender delegation to Ie Shima off Okinawa on 19 August 1945. In all, 2,146 G4M and G6M aircraft were built.

The development of the Yokosuka MXY7 suicide craft is indicative of the dire straits in which Japan found herself in the second half of 1944. The basic idea for the aircraft that was to emerge as the MXY7 was drafted by Mitsuo Ohta, and developed by Masao Yamana, Rokuro Hattori and Tadanao Mitsugi in a programme that was launched in August 1944.

The concept was of a rocket-powered aircraft with a large warhead that could be carried by a parent aircraft to within some 20 miles (32 km) of the target, where it could be released to dive down onto that target. Progress with the type was swift, and successful gliding trials were conducted in October 1944. Powered flights were made in November, and the type was ordered into production as the Navy Suicide Attacker Model 11 in September, 755 examples being built by March 1945. Only a few were used operationally, with very limited success, the laden G4M2e carriers proving very vulnerable.

A smaller version, designated Model 22, was designed for carriage by the Yokosuka P1Y1 *Ginga* bomber, but only a few were completed before the end of hostilities. Unbuilt projects included the jet-powered Model 33 to be carried by a Nakajima G8N1 *Renzan* bomber and the Models 43A and 43B, to be launched by catapult from surfaced submarines or caves on Japan's shore.

Above: An example of the first mark of the Navy Type 1 Attack Bomber, the Model 11, which was built under the manufacturer's designation G4M1. The type entered production in 1940

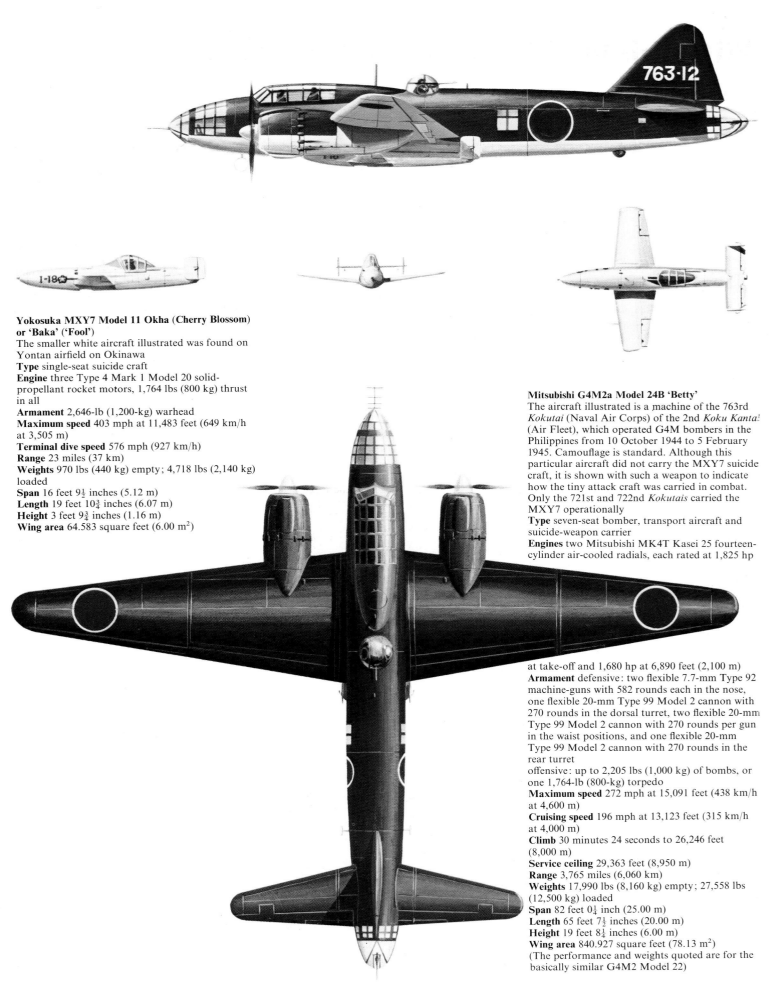

Yokosuka MXY7 Model 11 Okha (Cherry Blossom) or 'Baka' ('Fool')
The smaller white aircraft illustrated was found on Yontan airfield on Okinawa
Type single-seat suicide craft
Engine three Type 4 Mark 1 Model 20 solid-propellant rocket motors, 1,764 lbs (800 kg) thrust in all
Armament 2,646-lb (1,200-kg) warhead
Maximum speed 403 mph at 11,483 feet (649 km/h at 3,505 m)
Terminal dive speed 576 mph (927 km/h)
Range 23 miles (37 km)
Weights 970 lbs (440 kg) empty; 4,718 lbs (2,140 kg) loaded
Span 16 feet 9½ inches (5.12 m)
Length 19 feet 10¾ inches (6.07 m)
Height 3 feet 9¾ inches (1.16 m)
Wing area 64.583 square feet (6.00 m²)

Mitsubishi G4M2a Model 24B 'Betty'
The aircraft illustrated is a machine of the 763rd *Kokutai* (Naval Air Corps) of the 2nd *Koku Kantai* (Air Fleet), which operated G4M bombers in the Philippines from 10 October 1944 to 5 February 1945. Camouflage is standard. Although this particular aircraft did not carry the MXY7 suicide craft, it is shown with such a weapon to indicate how the tiny attack craft was carried in combat. Only the 721st and 722nd *Kokutais* carried the MXY7 operationally
Type seven-seat bomber, transport aircraft and suicide-weapon carrier
Engines two Mitsubishi MK4T Kasei 25 fourteen-cylinder air-cooled radials, each rated at 1,825 hp at take-off and 1,680 hp at 6,890 feet (2,100 m)
Armament defensive: two flexible 7.7-mm Type 92 machine-guns with 582 rounds each in the nose, one flexible 20-mm Type 99 Model 2 cannon with 270 rounds in the dorsal turret, two flexible 20-mm Type 99 Model 2 cannon with 270 rounds per gun in the waist positions, and one flexible 20-mm Type 99 Model 2 cannon with 270 rounds in the rear turret
offensive: up to 2,205 lbs (1,000 kg) of bombs, or one 1,764-lb (800-kg) torpedo
Maximum speed 272 mph at 15,091 feet (438 km/h at 4,600 m)
Cruising speed 196 mph at 13,123 feet (315 km/h at 4,000 m)
Climb 30 minutes 24 seconds to 26,246 feet (8,000 m)
Service ceiling 29,363 feet (8,950 m)
Range 3,765 miles (6,060 km)
Weights 17,990 lbs (8,160 kg) empty; 27,558 lbs (12,500 kg) loaded
Span 82 feet 0¼ inch (25.00 m)
Length 65 feet 7½ inches (20.00 m)
Height 19 feet 8¼ inches (6.00 m)
Wing area 840.927 square feet (78.13 m²)
(The performance and weights quoted are for the basically similar G4M2 Model 22)

47

Mitsubishi Ki-46 'Dinah'

The Mitsubishi Ki-46 was probably the finest reconnaissance aircraft of World War II, and certainly one of the most satisfying from both the aesthetic and aerodynamic aspects. The type also reflects the importance attached to long-range strategic reconnaissance by the Imperial Japanese Army's high command, which realized in the early 1930s that its forces would be operating at great distances from the centralized command, and hence would need the benefits of excellent reconnaissance. Thus whilst the Western powers were usually content to develop reconnaissance variants of bombers and fighters in service, the Japanese developed reconnaissance aircraft *ab initio*.

The standard Japanese reconnaissance machine 1937 was the Mitsubishi Ki-15, but in that year the army issued a requirement for an eventual replacement. The performance specified was very high, and the army wisely left it to the manufacturers to decide the exact layout of the aircraft to meet the requirements. Maximum speed was to be in the order of 375 mph (604 km/h), and range just under 1,500 miles (2,414 km).

The Mitsubishi team, led by Tomio Kubo, had some experience in the field of high-performance twin-engined monoplanes, and therefore opted to use this configuration. Mitsubishi was greatly aided by the co-operation of the Tokyo University Aeronautical Research Institute in the design of the undercarriage and the beautifully streamlined engine nacelles, but progress with the prototype was slow as a result of the need for considerable wind-tunnel testing.

The prototype, powered by two 900-hp Mitsubishi Ha-26 radials, flew in November 1939. Although performance was good in general, the maximum speed was still 40 mph (64 km/h) below that specified. As even this speed

was greater than those attained by the army's and the navy's latest fighters, the Nakajima Ki-43 and Mitsubishi A6M2, the army was nevertheless enthusiastic. The type was ordered into production as the Army Type 100 Command Reconnaissance Plane Model 1, with the company designation Ki-46-I.

Although the Model 1 was generally adequate, service units soon found that the undercarriage was weak, and therefore prone to break during a heavy landing, and that the ailerons and rudder were not as effective as they might be. In general, however, the Ki-46 was well received. But even while prototype testing was being carried out, Mitsubishi had received army approval to replace the Ha-26 engines with Mitsubishi Ha-102 radials, which were derived from the earlier engines and had the same dimensions, but were rated at 1,080 hp for take-off.

The first of the new machines, designated Ki-46-II, flew in March 1941, and proved to have a top speed of 375 mph (604 km/h). The new type entered production immediately, and quickly showed its worth in the campaigns in the Philippines, Malaya, the Dutch East Indies, and New Guinea. With the arrival of the latest Allied fighters in Australia and the Solomons, however, the Model 2 (Ki-46-II) began to suffer increasingly heavy losses. The Japanese had anticipated this, and in May 1942 ordered a version of the Ki-46 with two Ha-112-II radials of 1,500 hp each. The fuel consumption of the new engine was greater than that of the earlier Ha-102, so extra tankage was provided in the fuselage. At the same time the undercarriage was strengthened, and the whole nose redesigned into one smooth, extensively glazed canopy, without the step in front of the pilot.

The new model entered production in December 1942 as the Ki-46-III or Model 3. With a

top speed of over 390 mph (628 km/h) and fine high-altitude performance, the Model 3 was welcomed by service pilots. As the numbers of Model 3 aircraft reaching the front-line increased, the Model 2 was gradually relegated to training duties, sometimes with a stepped cockpit behind the pilot's position, as a three-seat radio navigation trainer. In this capacity the Model 2 became the Army Type 100 Operations Trainer, or Ki-46-II KAI.

Such was the performance of the Model 3 that the army evinced an interest in the basic machine as a high-altitude interceptor. The result was the not very successful Ki-46-III KAI or Army Type 100 Air Defence Fighter. This had a solid nose armed with a pair of 20-mm Ho-5 cannon, and the fuel tank between the pilot and the observer removed to make space for a 37-mm Ho-203 cannon firing obliquely forwards and upwards. The type entered service in November 1944, but proved disappointing as it did not have the rate of climb necessary for a fighter. A further development, the Ki-46-IIIc or Army Type 100 Assault Aircraft, was built only in very limited numbers.

The last reconnaissance variant was the Ki-46-IV or Model 4, which was powered by a pair of Ha-112-II Ru radials offering 1,100 hp at over 33,000 feet (10,058 m). Four prototypes were built, but problems with the exhaust-driven turbo-superchargers meant that neither the reconnaissance Ki-46-IVa (Model 4A) nor the equivalent Ki-46-IVb fighter entered service. 'Dinah' production totalled 1,742 aircraft.

Below: The definitive model of the 'Dinah', the Ki-46-III. Note the alteration of the nose contours compared with earlier models, helping to make the type aesthetically one of the most satisfying aircraft in the whole history of aviation

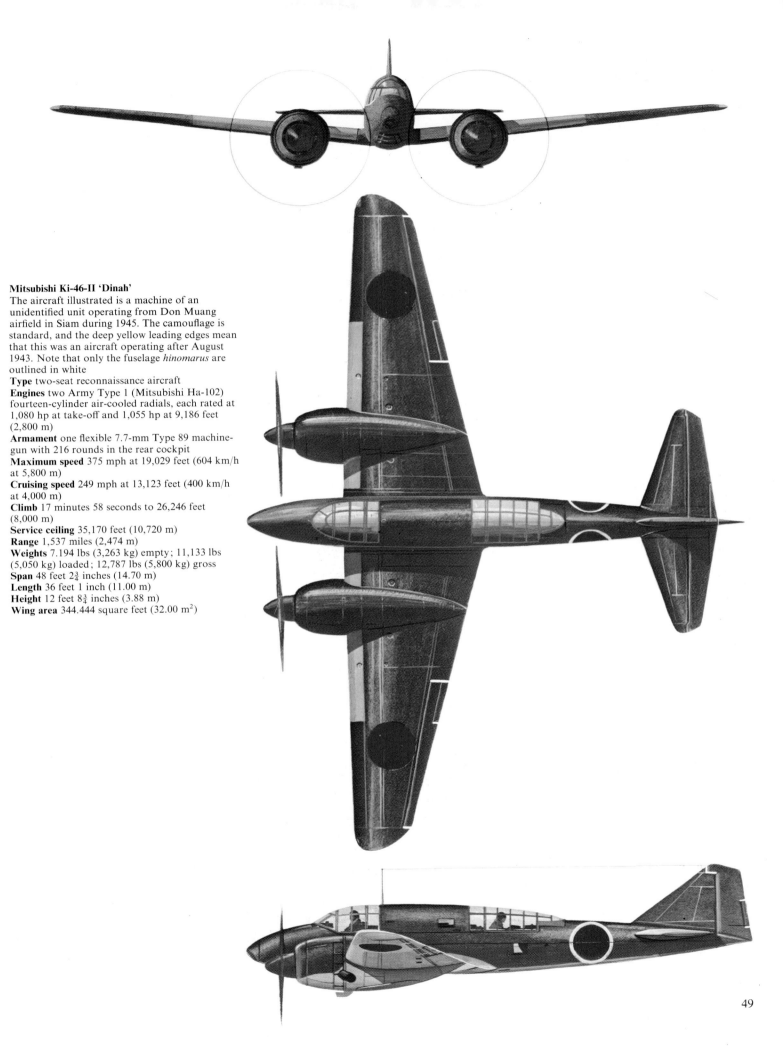

Mitsubishi Ki-46-II 'Dinah'
The aircraft illustrated is a machine of an
unidentified unit operating from Don Muang
airfield in Siam during 1945. The camouflage is
standard, and the deep yellow leading edges mean
that this was an aircraft operating after August
1943. Note that only the fuselage *hinomarus* are
outlined in white
Type two-seat reconnaissance aircraft
Engines two Army Type 1 (Mitsubishi Ha-102)
fourteen-cylinder air-cooled radials, each rated at
1,080 hp at take-off and 1,055 hp at 9,186 feet
(2,800 m)
Armament one flexible 7.7-mm Type 89 machine-
gun with 216 rounds in the rear cockpit
Maximum speed 375 mph at 19,029 feet (604 km/h
at 5,800 m)
Cruising speed 249 mph at 13,123 feet (400 km/h
at 4,000 m)
Climb 17 minutes 58 seconds to 26,246 feet
(8,000 m)
Service ceiling 35,170 feet (10,720 m)
Range 1,537 miles (2,474 m)
Weights 7.194 lbs (3,263 kg) empty; 11,133 lbs
(5,050 kg) loaded; 12,787 lbs (5,800 kg) gross
Span 48 feet 2¾ inches (14.70 m)
Length 36 feet 1 inch (11.00 m)
Height 12 feet 8¾ inches (3.88 m)
Wing area 344.444 square feet (32.00 m²)

Mitsubishi Ki-67 Hiryu

The Mitsubishi Ki-67 was the Imperial Japanese Army Air Force's equivalent of the Naval Air Force's G4M, and, although classified by the Japanese as a heavy bomber, by Western standards it was little more than a light to medium bomber. No matter what classification is put upon it, however, the Ki-67 was an excellent machine, and probably the best bomber operated by the Japanese army in World War II. As the Nakajima Ki-49 was entering service in the second half of 1940, the army started the process of producing a successor to the Nakajima bomber. Accordingly, a difficult set of requirements was issued to Mitsubishi, whose design team, led by Engineer Ozawa, had to produce a bomber powered by two 1,450-, 1,870- or 1,900-hp radials, with a bomb-load of 1,764 lbs (800 kg), a speed of 342 mph (550 km/h) and a range of 700 miles (1,127 km).

Ozawa chose to use the most powerful engines allowed, the 1,900-hp Mitsubishi Ha-104 radials, and designed a very clean monoplane with certain similarities to the same company's G4M naval bomber. Unusually for a Japanese aircraft, provision was made for protected self-sealing fuel tanks from the outset. The three prototypes ordered when the requirement was issued were completed late in 1942 and early in 1943. These aircraft were fitted with a defensive armament of two 12.7-mm and three 7.92-mm machine-guns. Flight trials began in December 1942, and although some problems with longitudinal stability and control sensitivity were experienced, performance was up to requirements except in the matter of speed. Subsequent prototype and pre-production aircraft had increased fuel tankage and armament amended to one 20-mm cannon, two 12.7-mm machine-guns, and two 7.92-mm machine-guns. All the early Ki-67 aircraft showed excellent handling characteristics, and without bombs on board the type could be looped.

Interest in the Ki-67 was also shown by the Imperial Japanese Naval Air Force, and early in 1943 Mitsubishi were ordered to install torpedo crutches in 100 production aircraft. So successful were trials that Mitsubishi was ordered to fit the crutches on all production aircraft after the 160th. The army agreed to allocate some of these for naval use. Paradoxical though it may seem, the success of the early Ki-67s was nearly the type's undoing. The reason is simple: the army wished to try so many permutations of equipment on this versatile aircraft that production could not be got under way on any particular model. After much remonstration, the army finally froze the design, and in December 1943 ordered Mitsubishi to commence production of the Army Type 4 Heavy Bomber Model 1, with the company designation Ki-67-I. This had the defensive armament further improved to one 20-mm cannon and four 12.7-mm machine-guns.

The new bomber went into action for the first time in October 1944, and thereafter played an important part in all army and navy operations to prevent the US forces closing in on Japan. In this capacity the Ki-67s were used mostly as torpedo-bombers, although many raids were made on the Marianas after their capture by

the Americans in an effort to destroy the heavy bombers and their bases being built up there for the assault on Japan.

In an attempt to rectify the shortages of the aircraft, caused by the failure to freeze the design for production sufficiently early, the Imperial Japanese Army Air Force tried not to ask for modifications to be implemented on the production lines. One exception to this, however, was that necessary for the provision of two 12.7-mm machine-guns in the tail turret in place of the earlier single gun. It was also planned to increase the bomb-load to 2,756 lbs (1,250 kg) in the 751st and subsequent aircraft. Production was severely curtailed by American bombing, however, and the earthquake of late 1944 also hampered production. Thus only 698 of this very efficient and versatile aircraft had been built by the end of the war.

Projected models, which did not enter production, included several very interesting projects: the Ki-67-II was to be powered by two Mitsu-

Top: A Mitsubishi Ki-67 on a Japanese airfield. Although it was classified by the Japanese as a heavy bomber, by Allied standards it was little more than a light bomber. Nevertheless it had a very respectable performance, and would have played a significant part in the war had the Japanese standardized the variant they wanted and put it into production more swiftly
Above: A Ki-67-Ib 'Peggy' in flight. Just visible under the fuselage are the shackles for carriage of a torpedo. With an extensively redesigned 'solid' nose fitted with a 75-mm Type 88 gun, the Ki-67 was developed into the Ki-109 heavy fighter

bishi Ha-204 radials of 2,400 hp each, giving the Ki-67 a spectacular performance; the Ki-67-I KAI suicide aircraft with a 6,393-lb (2,900-kg) explosive charge; and the Ki-109 heavy fighter. This last was a heavy two-seat interceptor fighter armed with a 75-mm cannon in the nose and a maximum speed of 342 mph (550 km/h). Only 32 had been built by the end of the war.

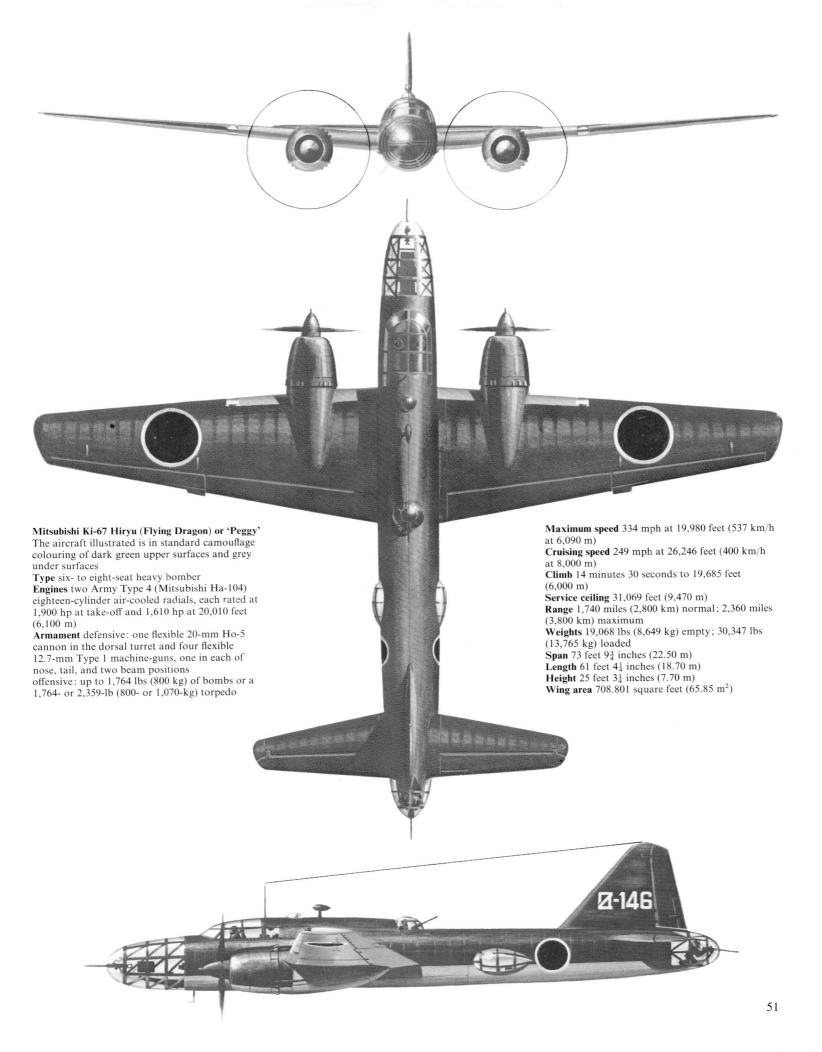

Mitsubishi Ki-67 Hiryu (Flying Dragon) or 'Peggy'
The aircraft illustrated is in standard camouflage
colouring of dark green upper surfaces and grey
under surfaces
Type six- to eight-seat heavy bomber
Engines two Army Type 4 (Mitsubishi Ha-104)
eighteen-cylinder air-cooled radials, each rated at
1,900 hp at take-off and 1,610 hp at 20,010 feet
(6,100 m)
Armament defensive: one flexible 20-mm Ho-5
cannon in the dorsal turret and four flexible
12.7-mm Type 1 machine-guns, one in each of
nose, tail, and two beam positions
offensive: up to 1,764 lbs (800 kg) of bombs or a
1,764- or 2,359-lb (800- or 1,070-kg) torpedo

Maximum speed 334 mph at 19,980 feet (537 km/h
at 6,090 m)
Cruising speed 249 mph at 26,246 feet (400 km/h
at 8,000 m)
Climb 14 minutes 30 seconds to 19,685 feet
(6,000 m)
Service ceiling 31,069 feet (9,470 m)
Range 1,740 miles (2,800 km) normal; 2,360 miles
(3,800 km) maximum
Weights 19,068 lbs (8,649 kg) empty; 30,347 lbs
(13,765 kg) loaded
Span 73 feet $9\frac{3}{4}$ inches (22.50 m)
Length 61 feet $4\frac{1}{4}$ inches (18.70 m)
Height 25 feet $3\frac{1}{4}$ inches (7.70 m)
Wing area 708.801 square feet (65.85 m²)

Nakajima B5N 'Kate'

Although it was produced only in relatively limited numbers, the Nakajima B5N had an enormous impact on the course of World War II, especially for its part in the surprise Japanese air strike on Pearl Harbor, the attack that finally brought the United States into the war. In other ways, too, the B5N was representative of the strengths and weaknesses of Japanese air power in World War II.

The origins of the B5N lay in a 1932 requirement for a high performance torpedo-bomber to replace the ageing Yokosuka B3Y. No suitable aircraft were forthcoming, and two years later the navy issued another specification. The Yokosuka B4Y was put into limited production to meet this, but the type was intended only as an interim torpedo-bomber.

In 1935 the navy again issued a requirement for an attack bomber, as torpedo-bombers were designated by the Imperial Japanese Navy, with a very high performance. Nakajima responded to the requirement with an advanced monoplane designed by a team led by Katsuji Nakamura. The prototype, designated B5N1, flew for the first time in January 1937, and soon proved to have excellent performance. The navy, however, was worried about certain advanced aspects of the design, which they feared might make maintenance too difficult, and Nakajima removed these. At the same time the Nakajima Hikari 2 radial was replaced by a Hikari 3, and with the new powerplant the B5N1 was judged superior to the rival Mitsubishi B5M1. The type was ordered into production as the Navy Type 97 Carrier Attack Bomber Model 1 in November 1937.

The type entered service in 1938, and was immediately issued to units on board Japanese aircraft-carriers and to units operating in support of the ground forces in China. In this latter capacity the B5N1 was used as a light, level bomber, and proved generally successful when escorted by fighters. During 1938 the designation of the Model 1 was changed to Model 11. The only modifications effected at this time were internal equipment changes to take advantage of the lessons learned in China. Combat experience in China led the Japanese navy to realize, however, that the B5N would have to be updated considerably to enable it to operate with any success in areas where strong fighter opposition might be met. Thus a new model appeared in 1939.

This was the B5N2 or Model 12, powered by a 1,000-hp Nakajima Sakae radial in place of the earlier 770-hp Hikari. The new engine was also more closely cowled than its predecessor, and a small spinner was provided over the propeller hub. Despite the increased power available, however, top speed was raised by only 6 mph (10 km/h). The navy nevertheless decided to place the latest model in production as the Sakae was a far more reliable engine than the Hikari. By the end of 1941 the B5N2 had replaced the B5N1 in all front-line units, the older model being relegated to training and liaison duties. The B5N2 was the most advanced carrier-borne torpedo-bomber in service anywhere in the world in 1941, as can be gauged from the success of the 144 such aircraft that took part in the raid on Pearl Harbor, and those that subsequently took part in the sinking of the three American aircraft-carriers *Lexington*, *Yorktown* and *Hornet* in 1942. B5N2 aircraft also operated as bombers in support of the Japanese amphibious assaults throughout the Pacific and South-east Asia during the early part of 1942.

By 1944 the B5N2 was obsolete, and the type suffered appalling casualties in the Philippines campaign. With the arrival of the Nakajima B6N1 *Tenzan* torpedo-bomber replacement that year, the B5N2 was relegated to second-line duties, the most important of which was the escort of Japanese convoys. In this capacity its long endurance and good visibility for the crew proved very useful in detecting Allied submarines. Visual sightings were quickly supplemented by radar ones when the type was equipped with air-sea search radar. This model could be distinguished by the antennae along the fuselage sides and wing leading-edges. Finally, the B5N2 replaced the B5N1-K, a modification of the standard B5N1, as a training, target-towing, and glider-tug aircraft. Total production was 1,149 aircraft.

Below: A Nakajima B5N accelerates down the flight-deck of a Japanese aircraft-carrier for an operational sortie. In the early months of the war the 'Kate' proved an excellent torpedo-bomber, capable of dropping its offensive load steadily and surely.

Nakajima B5N2 'Kate'
The aircraft illustrated is finished in the standard
natural metal finish of the Imperial Japanese Naval
Air Force in the first year of the war. Note the
matt black engine cowling and the dark green
patches applied to the wings of aircraft operated
from land bases
Type three-seat naval torpedo-bomber
Engine one Nakajima NK1B Sakae 11 fourteen-
cylinder air-cooled radial, 1,000 hp at take-off and
970 hp at 9,842 feet (3,000 m)
Armament defensive: one flexible 7.7-mm Type 92
machine-gun in the rear cockpit
offensive: up to 1,764 lbs (800 kg) of bombs or one
1,764-lb torpedo

Maximum speed 235 mph at 11,810 feet (378 km/h
at 3,600 m)
Cruising speed 161 mph at 9,842 feet (259 km/h
at 3,000 m)
Climb 7 minutes 40 seconds to 9,842 feet (3,000 m)
Service ceiling 27,099 feet (8,260 m)
Range 608 miles (979 km) normal; 1,237 miles
(1,990 km) maximum
Weights 5,024 lbs (2,279 kg) empty; 8,378 lbs
(3,800 kg) loaded; 9,030 lbs (4,100 kg) gross
Span 50 feet 11 inches (15.52 m)
Length 33 feet 9½ inches (10.30 m)
Height 12 feet 1¾ inches (3.70 m)
Wing area 405.798 square feet (37.70 m²)

Nakajima Ki-43 Hayabusa

The Nakajima 'Oscar' was the Imperial Japanese Army Air Force's standard fighter throughout World War II, and although it was available only in very limited numbers during the initial Japanese advances into Malaya, the Dutch East Indies, and Burma, its performance came as a very rude shock to the Allies. Convinced, despite several clear warnings, that the Japanese had only inferior types of aircraft, the Allies had deployed in the area only second-rate fighters, which proved wholly inadequate to deal with the Ki-43.

Design work on the Ki-43, led by Kideo Itokawa, started in December 1937 in response to an army requirement for a successor to the Nakajima Ki-27. Although the latter had an enclosed cockpit and a low-wing, all-metal construction, the undercarriage was a fixed, 'spatted' unit. The requirement for a successor, however, included some very stringent performance figures, and this meant that a retractable unit was almost inevitable. At the same time the requirement called for manoeuvrability equal to that of the Ki-27, which could best be obtained by the use of a lighter, fixed undercarriage.

The Nakajima team opted for the retractable unit, and the first prototype of the new fighter flew in January 1939. Powered by a Nakajima Ha-25 radial of 925 hp and armed with the specified two 7.7-mm machine-guns, the Ki-43 soon showed itself equal to the performance requirements. Manoeuvrability, however, was below that of the Ki-27 by a considerable margin, and for a time the fate of the Ki-43 hung in the balance. The army decided to let development work continue, however, and a series of trial aircraft was built with various engine and armament modifications, whilst a programme to improve the type's manoeuvrability resulted in a slimmer fuselage and the introduction of the so-called 'butterfly' combat flaps under the inboard wing panels. The latter led to a marked increase in the Ki-43's manoeuvrability, especially in the rate of turn, and the army authorities were now fully satisfied with its performance and agility.

The army ordered the Ki-43 into production with the Army Type 99 radial, the finalized version of the Ha-25, in April 1941, and deliveries started in October 1941. The first production variant was the Army Type 1 Fighter Model 1A, or Ki-43-Ia, but this was quickly followed by the Model 1B and Model 1C (Ki-43-Ib and Ki-43-Ic). The main differences between these three models lay in the armament, respectively two 7.7-mm machine-guns, one 12.7- and one 7.7-mm machine-gun, and two 12.7-mm machine-guns. The two-bladed propeller was also changed from a fixed-pitch wooden unit to a more efficient two-pitch metal unit.

In February 1942 the Ki-43-II appeared, powered by an Army Type 1 (Nakajima Ha-115) radial, the developed version of the Type 99, exerting 1,150 hp. The new type, which had a much enhanced performance, entered production in November 1942 as the Model 2A or Ki-43-IIa. This could be distinguished from the Model 1 by the re-location of the air intake for the supercharger in the upper portion of the cowling (previously it had been under the cowling), the reduction in wing span by almost two feet (59.7 cm) to increase speed, and provision of strongpoints under the wings for carrying bombs. Combat experience had also shown the need for protection, and so the fuel tanks were given a rudimentary form of self-sealing, and the pilot was given an armoured back to his seat. The Model 2B or Ki-43-IIb was basically similar but featured various equipment modifications, especially to the carburettor intake and oil cooler. These modifications were standardized in the next model to appear, the Ki-43-II KAI. This had the same three-bladed propeller as the earlier Ki-43-II models, but featured individual exhaust stacks to give greater speed with thrust augmentation.

In May 1944 the last Ki-43 variant appeared. This was the Ki-43-IIIa, powered by a 1,230-hp Ha-115-II radial. Production aircraft were designated Model 3A. Only two prototypes of the Ki-43-IIIb or Model 3B had been built by the end of the war. This last variant was intended as a high-altitude interceptor, and was powered by a 1,250-hp Mitsubishi (Ha-33) 42 (Ha-112) radial, with an armament of two 20-mm Ho-5 cannon.

By the end of 1944 the Ki-43 was obsolete, and was gradually replaced in front-line units by newer types. The Ki-43 ended its life as a training aircraft and as a *kamikaze* weapon. A total of 5,919 Ki-43 aircraft was built, more than any other fighter used by the Imperial Japanese Army Air Force. Although the type had achieved some notable success in the early stages of the war, this was as a result of its manoeuvrability and the poor quality of Allied fighter opposition. In fact the performance of the Ki-43 was never more than adequate, and its armament was always inferior.

Below: Two Nakajima Ki-43-Ia 'Oscar' fighters

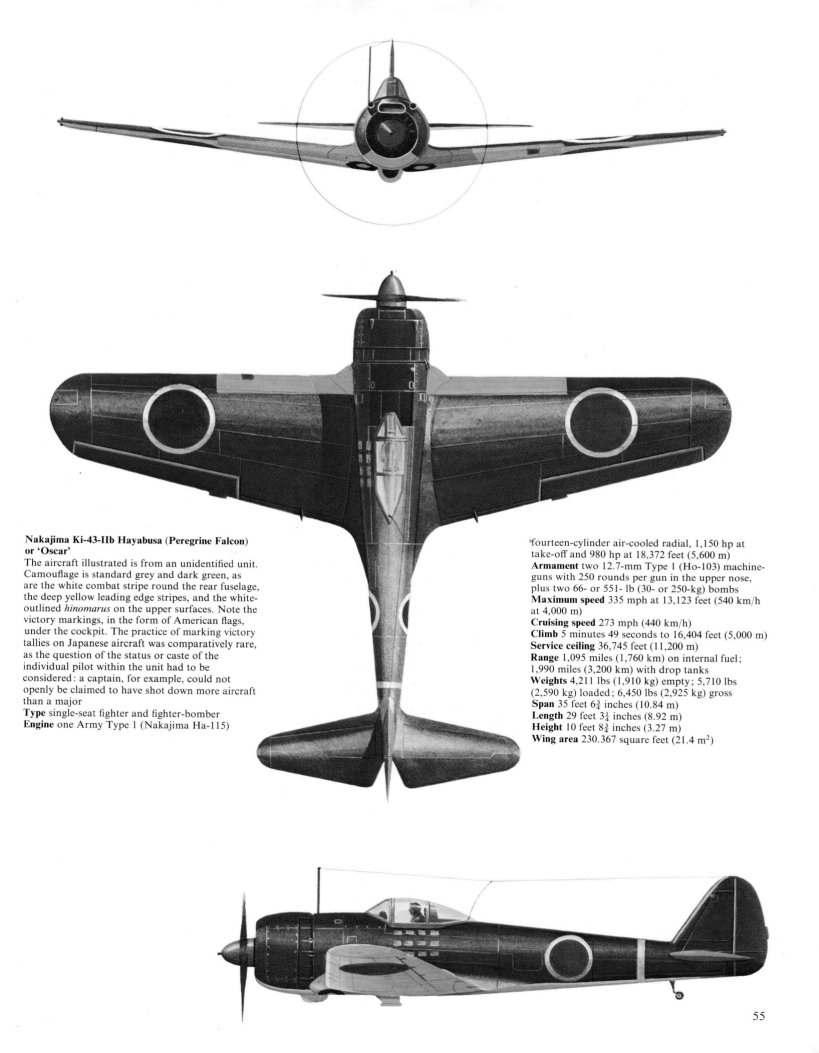

**Nakajima Ki-43-IIb Hayabusa (Peregrine Falcon)
or 'Oscar'**
The aircraft illustrated is from an unidentified unit.
Camouflage is standard grey and dark green, as
are the white combat stripe round the rear fuselage,
the deep yellow leading edge stripes, and the white-
outlined *hinomarus* on the upper surfaces. Note the
victory markings, in the form of American flags,
under the cockpit. The practice of marking victory
tallies on Japanese aircraft was comparatively rare,
as the question of the status or caste of the
individual pilot within the unit had to be
considered: a captain, for example, could not
openly be claimed to have shot down more aircraft
than a major
Type single-seat fighter and fighter-bomber
Engine one Army Type 1 (Nakajima Ha-115)

fourteen-cylinder air-cooled radial, 1,150 hp at
take-off and 980 hp at 18,372 feet (5,600 m)
Armament two 12.7-mm Type 1 (Ho-103) machine-
guns with 250 rounds per gun in the upper nose,
plus two 66- or 551- lb (30- or 250-kg) bombs
Maximum speed 335 mph at 13,123 feet (540 km/h
at 4,000 m)
Cruising speed 273 mph (440 km/h)
Climb 5 minutes 49 seconds to 16,404 feet (5,000 m)
Service ceiling 36,745 feet (11,200 m)
Range 1,095 miles (1,760 km) on internal fuel;
1,990 miles (3,200 km) with drop tanks
Weights 4,211 lbs (1,910 kg) empty; 5,710 lbs
(2,590 kg) loaded; 6,450 lbs (2,925 kg) gross
Span 35 feet 6¾ inches (10.84 m)
Length 29 feet 3¼ inches (8.92 m)
Height 10 feet 8¾ inches (3.27 m)
Wing area 230.367 square feet (21.4 m²)

GREAT BRITAIN

The story of the Royal Air Force in the years between the two world wars is, for the most part, one of sad decline. Great Britain had been the first power to create an independent air force, with the formation of the RAF on 1 April 1918, and at the end of World War I the RAF could muster 22,000 aircraft, of which 3,300 were first-line machines. Manpower was almost 300,000.

It was inevitable, however, that the size of the RAF should be reduced after the war. Peacetime conditions did not warrant so great a force, and the financial difficulties of the postwar world meant that high expenditure on armaments could not be tolerated. But instead of pruning the great tree of the RAF to a manageable size, which might therefore put forth new, healthy shoots where and when required, postwar planners truncated the RAF. Manpower was reduced from 300,000 to 31,500 and the number of operational squadrons from 188 to 12.

This truncation of the RAF affected not only its size, but also its nature: concerned with maintaining its existence, the RAF concentrated on well-proven ideas and tactical concepts, together with the aircraft to implement them, at the expense of progress in operational theories and technology. As a result of financial restrictions, the RAF had to limit its participation in technical developments to a few racing aircraft, such as the early Supermarine floatplanes.

Failure to keep up with developments in air fighting meant that the standard fighters used by the RAF up to the middle of the 1930s were mere developments of the biplane fighters of World War I. Agility was still considered to be more important than acceleration and rate of climb, and a high maximum speed was not considered to be worth an increase in landing speed. And while other countries were experimenting with cannon, larger numbers of machine-guns, and machine-guns of heavier calibres, British armament was still the two 0.303-inch (7.7-mm) Vickers machine-guns that had proved

adequate in World War I, with their breeches in reach of the pilot so that he could clear jams.

Adolf Hitler's accession to power in January 1933 at last brought home to the British that the 'war to end all wars' might not have done that. Front-line strength of the RAF at that time was some 850 aircraft, but by 1934 plans had been laid to raise this figure to 3,500 plus, with another 6,000 machines in reserve. Plans were also made to expand considerably the strength of the RAF in personnel and airfield capabilities, and production capacity was built up with the introduction of the 'shadow' factory system in 1936. This last scheme called for the duplication of aircraft and engine production capacity in specially built new factories, so that even if the parent factory was destroyed by bombing, the 'shadow' could continue production.

At the same time plans were put in hand for new aircraft types: fast, twin-engined medium bombers, which appeared as the Vickers Wellington, Bristol Blenheim and Handley Page Hampden; fast, single-engined fighters with retractable undercarriages and large batteries of machine-guns, which appeared as the Hawker Hurricane and Supermarine Spitfire; four-engined heavy bombers, which appeared as the Short Stirling and Handley Page Halifax, together with the Avro Lancaster four-engined derivative of the ill-starred Manchester; and other types such as the Short Sunderland maritime-reconnaissance flying-boat, the Westland Lysander army co-

operation aircraft, the Westland Whirlwind twin-engined long-range fighter, and the Fairey Battle single-engined light bomber.

Great strides had been made by the beginning of the war in September 1939, but the RAF was still low in strength compared with Germany. However, manpower recruitment and training had proceeded well and the quality of personnel at all levels was excellent. Somehow the RAF got through the desperate days of 1940, with the loss of Denmark, Norway, the Low Countries, and France, and the Battle of Britain. By 1941 offensive action against Germany had started, with fighters and medium bombers operating over occupied Europe, and the bomber offensive against Germany herself was tentatively getting under way. New aircraft, such as the de Havilland Mosquito, Bristol Beaufighter and Hawker Typhoon emerged, and with them new weapons such as cannon, and new equipment such as radar for night-fighting and navigation.

During 1942 RAF Bomber Command's night offensive against German industrial areas grew in strength, and in the second half of the year the US Army Air Forces joined in and tackled pinpoint targets by day. At the same time in the deserts of North Africa the RAF were developing another weapon into a potent instrument. This was the fighter-bomber, whose tactics were evolved in North Africa, polished in Italy during 1943, and brought to perfection in the campaign in north-west Europe during 1944 and

Supermarine Spitfire VB fighters of 81 Squadron, RAF Fighter Command, in flight. Perhaps the single type that epitomizes the RAF in World War II, the Spitfire was a magnificent aircraft, loved by all who flew it. The type had beauty of line, and also great development potential. By the end of the war the basic interceptor fighter had been adapted into a successful naval fighter, reconnaissance aircraft, fighter-bomber and training aircraft, and with its original machine-gun armament increased to cannon, bombs and rockets. Over 20,000 of the Spitfire were built, to make it the most numerous British aircraft ever built

1945. During these last two years the art of night bombing was also brought to a high pitch, with the aid of radar and pathfinder forces to mark targets, and completely devastated many German cities.

The threat of the German *V*-1 was successfully dealt with from the air during 1944, and as the war ended in 1945, Great Britain was just beginning to deploy her first jet fighter against Germany, and a new generation of fighting aircraft was about to enter service.

In 1939 the RAF had been a small but efficient force, with adequate fighter defences, a small medium bomber force, and grand ideas about strategic bombing. By 1945 the fighter defences had grown in size enormously, and had been transmogrified into a devastating tactical offensive weapon against enemy armour and strongpoints. The medium bomber force had grown into a powerful short-range strike weapon, paralysing the ability of the Germans to move their troops and *matériel* with speed and efficiency. And the heavy bombers had developed from a dream into a vast and powerful force capable of causing very considerable damage. It should be noted, however, that the strategic bomber offensive only began to achieve worthwhile results late in 1944, with the destruction of Germany's rail, road, and waterway networks, and the annihilation of synthetic fuel and rubber production plants.

Avro Lancaster

The Avro Lancaster was Great Britain's most successful bomber of World War II; indeed so effective was the initial version of the bomber that later marks and models differed from it significantly only in armament and equipment while the basic aircraft remained virtually unchanged. It was capable of lifting a heavier offensive load than any other comparable aircraft and hence bore the brunt of RAF Bomber Command's night offensive against Germany, from the middle of 1942 to the end of the war.

The origins of the Lancaster lay in the unsuccessful Avro Manchester. This latter had been designed, by a team led by Roy Chadwick, to a 1936 requirement for a twin-engined medium bomber powered by Rolls-Royce Vulture engines. The first prototype of the Manchester flew in July 1939, and performance soon proved to be good. The type was ordered into production and entered service in November 1940. But combat operations with the Manchester were unsuccessful: the engines had been rushed into service too quickly, and although powerful proved totally unreliable. Only 209 Manchesters were built, and the type was phased out of service in June 1942.

The problems with the Vulture engines led the Air Ministry in 1940 to consider a version with four lower-powered engines. These, coupled with the excellent Manchester airframe, promised to result in a good heavy bomber. The engine selected for the new model, which was to be known as the Manchester III, was the well-tried and reliable Rolls-Royce Merlin. The prototype of the new aircraft, fitted with a tall central fin and small fin and rudder units at the ends of the tailplane (inherited from the Manchester I), first flew in January 1941, and soon revealed an excellent performance. The original type of vertical tail surfaces was soon replaced by the larger endplate surfaces on a wider-span tailplane from the Manchester IA. The central fin was deleted. Exhaustive trials were conducted with the first two prototypes, and the type, now renamed Lancaster, was ordered into production.

The first production Lancaster I bombers, which differed from the prototypes in having dorsal and ventral machine-gun turrets and 1,280-hp Merlin XX engines in place of the earlier 1,145-hp Merlin X units, flew in October 1941, and squadrons began to receive their new aircraft early in 1942. The first combat operation was flown in March of that year, and from that time onwards the Lancaster quickly became the mainstay of RAF Bomber Command. A total of 3,425 Lancaster Is was built.

Early in the production life of the Lancaster there were fears that supplies of the Merlin would be insufficient to meet all the demands for the engine, hence the Lancaster B II. This differed from the initial version in being powered by four 1,650-hp Bristol Hercules VI radial engines. Performance with the Hercules engines differed little from that of the Merlin-engined B I, but as in the end there was no shortage of the latter engines, production of the B II amounted to only 301 machines.

From August 1943 there appeared the Lancaster B X. This was a version of the B I built by Victory Aircraft of Canada, and powered by Packard-built Merlin 28, 38 or 224 engines. A total of 430 of this mark was built. In Great Britain, meanwhile, production of the B I continued, later aircraft having 1,460-hp Merlin 20 and 22, or 1,640-hp Merlin 24 engines. The next British model of the Lancaster was the B III, which differed from the B I only in having Packard-built Merlin engines. Production of this model totalled 3,039 machines. To all intents and purposes the B III and B X were identical.

The B VI, which was built in very limited numbers in the summer of 1944 was the next model. This featured Merlin 87 engines with four-bladed propellers in place of the earlier marks' three-bladed units. The nose and dorsal turrents were also removed, the gaps thus left being faired over, and special equipment to jam German radar was installed. The last mark was the B VII with a new dorsal Martin turret fitted further forward up the fuselage than the earlier

Nash and Thompson turret; 180 were built. The last Lancaster was delivered to the RAF in February 1946, completing a grand total of 7,377 machines.

Two notable sub-marks of the B I were produced: the B I (Special) and the B I (FE). The first was designed to carry special loads such as the 'dam-buster' bomb, the 12,000-lb (5,443-kg) 'Tallboy' deep penetration bomb, and the 22,000-lb (9,979-kg) 'Grand Slam' earthquake bomb (the largest bomb used in the war); the second had the dorsal turret removed and a large saddle tank, extending from just behind the wing trailing edge to the cockpit, added to the top of the fuselage. This held 1,200 gallons (5,455 l) of fuel to allow the Lancaster to bomb Japan over long ranges; however, the B I (FE) was too late to see service in the war. (FE stood for Far East.) Final development of the Lancaster from the so-called B IV and B V led to the RAF's last piston-engined heavy bomber, the Avro Lincoln.

During the course of the war the Lancaster was fitted with a variety of radar aids to help bombing in cloud and fog conditions, and the record of the aircraft speaks for itself: more than 150,000 missions during which over 600,000 tons of bombs were dropped. Losses were also comparatively light: in 1943 one aircraft for each 132 tons of bombs dropped, compared with 56 tons for each Handley Page Halifax and 41 tons for each Short Stirling.

Growth potential had been built into the basic design; bombs of the 4,000-lb (1,814-kg) type were catered for in the first model but ever increased bomb-loads could be carried internally and only the 'Tallboy', 'Grand Slam' and 'dam-buster' bombs had to be carried externally. The aircraft itself was manoeuvrable for its size, and the one major fault which it shared with other British bombers was its lack of heavy-calibre defensive armament, especially after the ventral turret had been abandoned.

Below: Avro Lancaster heavy bombers at their dispersal points on a Bomber Command airfield

Avro Lancaster B I

The aircraft illustrated is machine G of No 15 Squadron (code-letters LS), serial number LM110, which was flown by Flight-Lieutenant M Johnston, Royal Australian Air Force. The aircraft was lost on 13 September 1944 after it had flown 244 hours. Camouflage is standard, with matt black under-surfaces, extending three-quarters of the way up the fuselage, and dark green and dark earth upper surfaces.

Type seven-seat heavy bomber

Engines four Rolls-Royce Merlin 22 twelve-cylinder liquid-cooled inlines, each rated at 1,460 hp at take-off

Armament defensive: two flexible 0.303-inch (7.7-mm) Browning machine-guns in the nose turret, two flexible 0.303-inch Browning machine-guns in the dorsal turret, and four flexible 0.303-inch Browning machine-guns in the rear turret (some aircraft also had one or two flexible 0.303-inch Browning machine-guns in a ventral turret)

offensive: up to 18,000 lbs (8,165 kg) of bombs (22,000 lbs (9,979 kg) on BI Specials)

Maximum speeds 275 mph at 15,000 feet (443 km/h at 4,572 m) at maximum take-off weight; 245 mph (394 km/h) at sea level at maximum take-off weight; 287 mph (462 km/h) maximum

Cruising speed 200 mph at 15,000 feet (322 km/h at 4,572 m)

Initial climb rate 250 fpm (76 m/minute)

Climb 41 minutes 36 seconds to 20,000 feet (6,096 m)

Service ceiling 22,000 feet (6,706 m)

Range 2,530 miles (4,072 km) with 7,000-lb (3,175 kg) bomb-load; 1,730 miles (2,784 km) with 12,000-lb (5,443 kg) bomb-load

Weights 36,900 lbs (16,738 kg) empty; 68,000 lbs (30,845 kg) loaded; 72,000 lbs (32,659 kg) gross

Span 102 feet (31.09 m)

Length 69 feet 6 inches (21.18 m)

Height 20 feet 6 inches (6.25 m)

Wing area 1,297 square feet (120.45 m²)

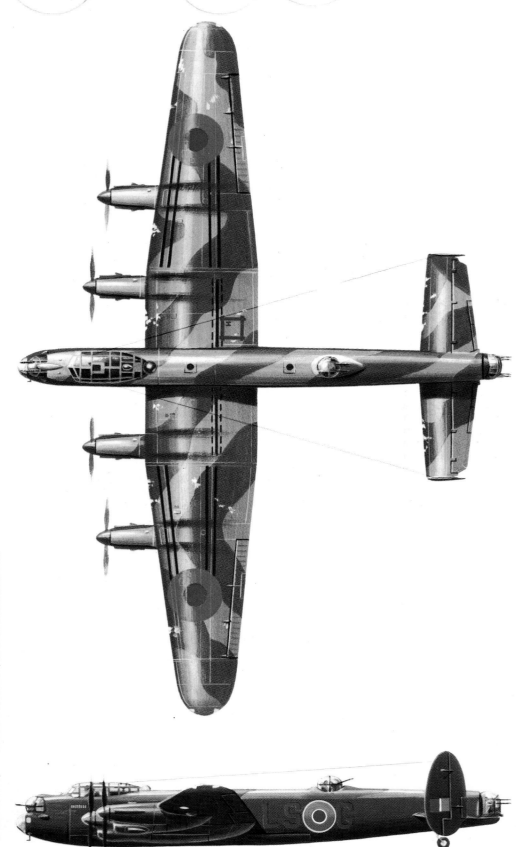

Bristol Beaufighter

At a first glance the Bristol Beaufighter appears to be an ungainly and unattractive aircraft. Closer examination, however, reveals this great aircraft's better points: large wings for heavy load carrying, massive engines for high speed and performance, a sturdy fuselage to contain equipment and absorb battle damage, and a cockpit right at the front of the fuselage to afford the pilot an excellent field of vision forwards. In fact, despite its superficial ugliness, the Beaufighter looked right, and following the old airmen's adage that what looks right is right, it was a superlative aircraft.

The Beaufighter was designed in 1938 as a private-venture fighter aircraft, using as much of the unsuccessful Bristol Beaufort torpedo-bomber as possible including the wings, rear fuselage, empennage and many of the components. A new front fuselage and more powerful engines were fitted. Just before the first prototype flew in July 1939 the Air Ministry expressed an interest in the new type by ordering 300 'off the drawing board'. Initial flight trials were very successful, few modifications were found to be necessary and aircraft began to roll off the production lines in July 1940, reaching RAF squadrons in September.

These first aircraft were to the Mark IF standard, with four 20-mm cannon and six 0.303-inch (7.7-mm) machine-guns, which became the ordinary forward-firing armament for Beaufighter fighters. The new type's performance was good, with a top speed of 323 mph (520 km/h), and the new Air Interception Mark IV radar was fitted, the marriage of the two producing the world's first really effective night-fighter – the Blenheim had been an interim model without the performance to make it properly effective in this role. The AI Mark IV radar was distinguishable by its aerials: a double arrow-head on the nose and vertical aerials on the outer wing panels.

In the spring of 1941 the Beaufighter entered service with units in North Africa as a long-range day fighter. To provide the necessary range, extra fuel tanks were located in the fuselage; these were later moved to the outer wing bays, which necessitated the removal of the six Browning machine-guns previously located there. At about the same time, March 1941, a new model entered service with RAF Coastal Command as a long-range fighter. This was the Beaufighter IC, which featured extra radio and navigation equipment for long flights over water.

Fears that production of the Bristol Hercules radial engine would not be able to keep pace with Beaufighter deliveries led to the next model, the Beaufighter IIF. This had two 1,280-hp Rolls-Royce Merlin XX inlines in place of the Mark I's 1,425-hp Hercules III radials. The Merlin engines produced less drag, and performance was thereby improved slightly, but the loss of forward keel area made the Beaufighter's directional stability less than adequate. The answer, found after a series of exhaustive experiments, was to give the tailplane pronounced dihedral, and the modification was incorporated on this and subsequent models. Only 450 Beaufighter IIFs were built as production of the Hercules radial engine proved sufficient to meet all aircraft production demands.

Among experiments carried out on the Beaufighter were the testing of a new centimetric radar with its aerial in a 'thimble' nose, an armament of two 40-mm cannon, and special air brakes. None of these reached production status early in the Beaufighter's development life and only the radar was widely used. In an effort to improve the type's firepower for night-fighting the Mark V was developed with a four-gun turret in a dorsal position over the wing. But the modification was not successful, and only two Beaufighter V aircraft were built. The next type to attain widespread service use was the Mark VI, built as the VIF and VIC for Fighter Command and Coastal Command respectively. Power for the Mark VI was provided by a pair of 1,650-hp Hercules VI or XVI radials. For the first time rearward defence was provided in the form of a single 0.303-inch (7.7-mm) Vickers K machine-gun in the observer's cockpit. The Mark VIC was also given vastly enhanced offensive power by the provision of gear enabling it to carry either rockets or a torpedo. The Mark VI entered service in summer 1942; in all 1,833 were built.

The Beaufighter III (to be powered by Hercules VI radials) and Beaufighter IV (to be powered by Rolls-Royce Griffon inlines) had not been built, and neither had the Beaufighter VII (to be powered by Hercules VIII radials) and Beaufighters VIII and IX (reserved for aircraft built in Australia). The Mark XIC, of which 163 were built, was an interim version of the VIC without torpedo-dropping gear.

The next major version was the Torpedo-Fighter X or TF X; 2,206 examples were built. The TF X appeared in 1943, and used two Hercules XVIII radials with cropped impeller blades for the low-altitude superchargers. The TF X was the best anti-shipping strike fighter of the war, able to deliver a formidable quantity of rockets, bombs, torpedoes and cannon fire over very long ranges and at high speed. The chief external distinguishing marks of the TF X were the thimble nose, housing the centrimetric air-surface vessel search radar, and the dorsal fillet, extending the fin up the fuselage to improve directional stability. A total of 364 Beaufighters similar to the TF X was built in Australia as the Beaufighter 21. Production of the Beaufighter ceased in Great Britain in September 1945 after 5,562 machines had been built.

Although it had been the world's first truly effective night-fighter until supplanted by the de Havilland Mosquito, the Beaufighter found it real *métier* as a long-range strike fighter. In this role it was unsurpassed, and performed invaluable service in every theatre in which the RAF was involved.

Below: A Bristol Beaufighter TF X, aircraft T of 236 Squadron, RAF Coastal Command, in the air. Note the forward pair of shackles for the carriage of a torpedo under the pilot's cockpit, eight rockets carried on launchers under the outer wing panels (necessitating the deletion of the six 0.303-inch machine-guns normally carried in the wings), provision of defensive armament for the second crew member, and a pronounced dihedral angle on the tailplane. Later aircraft had a dorsal fillet extending the fin up the rear fuselage to increase directional stability. The excellent position of the pilot, right in the nose of the great fuselage where he enjoyed an unparalleled field of vision, is also apparent. Also noteworthy are the prominent 'invasion stripes' of all aircraft of the Allied Expeditionary Air Forces in the second half of 1944. The upper surface parts of these were often painted over

Bristol Beaufighter TF X

The aircraft illustrated is machine M of 404
Squadron (code-letters EE). Camouflage is a
variation on the standard Temperate Sea Scheme,
with Dark Slate Grey (appearing almost as green)
and Medium Sea Grey (instead of the specified
Extra Dark Sea Grey). The under surfaces are in
Sky Grey. National markings are the usual ones.
Note the black and white 'invasion' stripes, applied
to all combat aircraft of the Allied Expeditionary
Forces in June 1944

Type two-seat anti-shipping strike fighter

Engines two Bristol Hercules XVII fourteen-
cylinder air-cooled radials, each rated at 1,770 hp
at take-off

Armament four 20-mm Hispano cannon with 283
rounds per gun in the lower nose, plus one 1,650-
or 2,127-lb (748- or 965-kg) torpedo, or eight
90-lb (41-kg) rockets and two 250-lb (113-kg)
bombs

Maximum speed 303 mph at 1,300 feet (488 km/h
at 396 m)

Cruising speed 249 mph at 5,000 feet (401 km/h
at 1,524 m)

Climb 3 minutes 30 seconds to 5,000 feet (1,524 m)

Service ceiling 15,000 feet (4,572 m)

Range 1,470 miles at 205 mph at 5,000 feet
(2,366 km at 330 km/h at 1,524 m)

Weights 15,600 lbs (7,076 kg) empty; unknown
loaded; 25,200 lbs (11,431 kg) gross

Span 57 feet 10 inches (17.63 m)

Length 41 feet 8 inches (12.70 m)

Height 15 feet 10 inches (4.83 m)

Wing area 503 square feet (46.73 m^2)

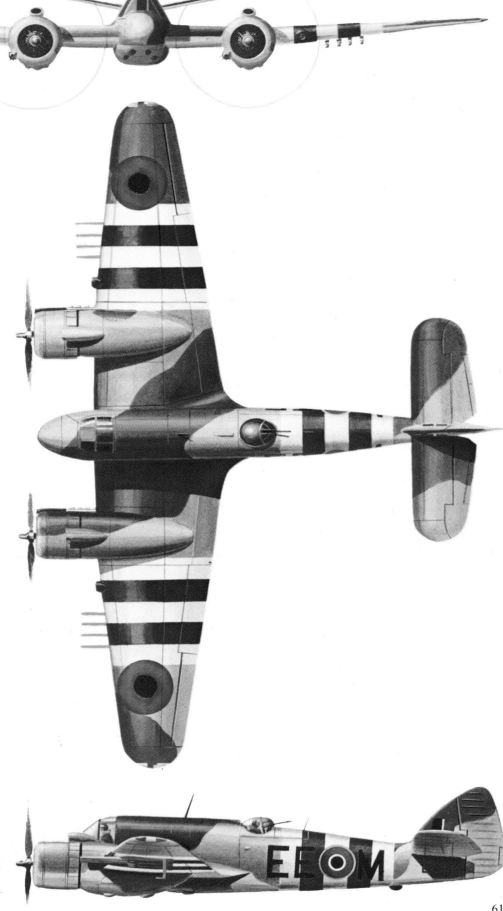

Bristol Blenheim

At the time of introduction to service in 1937, the Bristol Blenheim was one of the Royal Air Force's great hopes: its speed was superior to that of any of the biplane fighters then in service with the RAF, and little inferior to the latest monoplanes in service with the *Luftwaffe*. But despite these early hopes the Blenheim was destined to play a relatively minor and little publicized part in the British effort during World War II.

The origins of the Blenheim lay in the Bristol Type 142 high-speed civil transport of 1935, which had been presented to the RAF by the newspaper magnate Lord Rothermere. From this there emerged a 1935 requirement for a light bomber. The first prototype flew in June 1936: it had an extensively glazed nose extending a little further forward than the propellers. By August 1936 150 of the new bombers, designated Blenheim I, had been ordered, the first appearing in November 1936. It entered service in March 1937, and 1,134 of this model were built during the next 18 months before production of the Blenheim IV took over.

Late in 1938 the RAF realized the need for a specialized night-fighter, for which role the high performance of the Blenheim I seemed very useful. The Blenheim IF night fighter entered service with the RAF in December 1938 – the night-fighter conversion consisting of a ventral gun-pack containing four 0.303-inch (7.7-mm) Browning machine-guns and their ammunition.

Some 200 conversion kits were produced to enable service units to turn their Blenheim I bombers into Blenheim IF night fighters. Radar was also pioneered on the Blenheim IF in June 1940, thus producing the world's first true night fighter.

Early service use had revealed that the Blenheim I's chief failings lay in its lack of adequate defensive armament – only two 0.303-inch (7.7-mm) machine-guns – and insufficient room for the navigator. These failings were rectified in the Blenheim IV, which appeared late in 1938 and entered service use in March 1939. This had an extended nose with more room for the navigator, increased fuel tankage for greater range, and more powerful engines to boost performance and permit a heavier bomb-load to be carried. The increased fuel tankage was incorporated only after the first 80 Blenheim IVs had been built, the improved model being designated Blenheim IVL. A total of 3,297 Blenheim IVs was built. Wartime improvements included the provision of defensive armour, the doubling of the dorsal turret's firepower to two machine-guns, and the addition of a twin-gun blister under the nose. A fighter version, the Blenheim IVF, was also produced with a four-gun ventral pack similar to that of the Blenheim IF. Although the Blenheim was phased out of front-line service in Europe in August 1942, the type continued in such service in North Africa and the Far East after this date.

The Blenheim was an excellent aircraft technically, and an adequate aircraft so far as performance was concerned, but its lack of sturdiness and load-carrying capacity – which stemmed from its civil aircraft origins – was always a disadvantage. Nevertheless, the Blenheim performed useful service before it was replaced by the de Havilland Mosquito and Douglas Boston. Perhaps the Blenheim's greatest contribution to the Allied war effort was the fact that from it was developed the unsuccessful Bristol Beaufort torpedo-bomber which was the basis of the superlative Bristol Beaufighter night fighter and anti-shipping strike fighter. Also developed from the Blenheim was the Bristol Blenheim V, originally known as the Bristol Bisley. This entered service as a light bomber in November 1942, but was unsuccessful and was withdrawn in the autumn of 1943.

Below: An example of the last of the Blenheim family, a Blenheim V. The type resulted from an attempt to increase the Blenheim's basic performance by fitting more powerful engines, and increasing the type's operational effectiveness by increasing the armour protection. The Blenheim V appeared in service in North Africa in November 1942, and the last was delivered to the RAF in June 1943. Note the flame-damper fitted to the port exhaust of the port Mercury 30 engine. The turret was also a marked improvement to that fitted to the Blenheim IV

Bristol Blenheim IV

The aircraft illustrated is a standard Mark IV
bomber with the exception of the Vokes air filters
under the engine nacelles and the additional air
intakes on the starboard side of each upper engine
cowling. The markings are standard, with Azure
under surfaces.

Type three-seat light bomber
Engines two Bristol Mercury XV nine-cylinder air-
cooled radials, each rated at 905 hp at take-off and
995 hp at 9,250 feet (2,819 m)
Armament defensive: one fixed 0.303-inch (7.7-mm)
Browning machine-gun in the port wing, two
flexible 0.303-inch Browning machine-guns in the
blister under the nose, and two flexible 0.303-inch
Browning machine-guns in the dorsal turret
offensive: up to 1,320 lbs (599 kg) of bombs
Maximum speed 266 mph at 11,800 feet (428 km/h
at 3,597 m)
Cruising speed 220 mph at 15,000 feet (354 km/h
at 4,572 m)
Initial climb rate 1,500 fpm (457 m/minute)
Climb 15 minutes to 15,000 feet (4,572 m)
Service ceiling 22,000 feet (6,706 m)
Range 1,460 miles (2,350 km) at maximum take-off
weight
Weights 9,823 lbs (4,211 kg) empty; 14,500 lbs
(6,577 kg) loaded; 15,000 lbs (6,804 kg) gross
Span 56 feet 4 inches (17.17 m)
Length 42 feet 7 inches (12.98 m)
Height 9 feet 10 inches (3.00 m)
Wing area 469 square feet (43.57 m²)

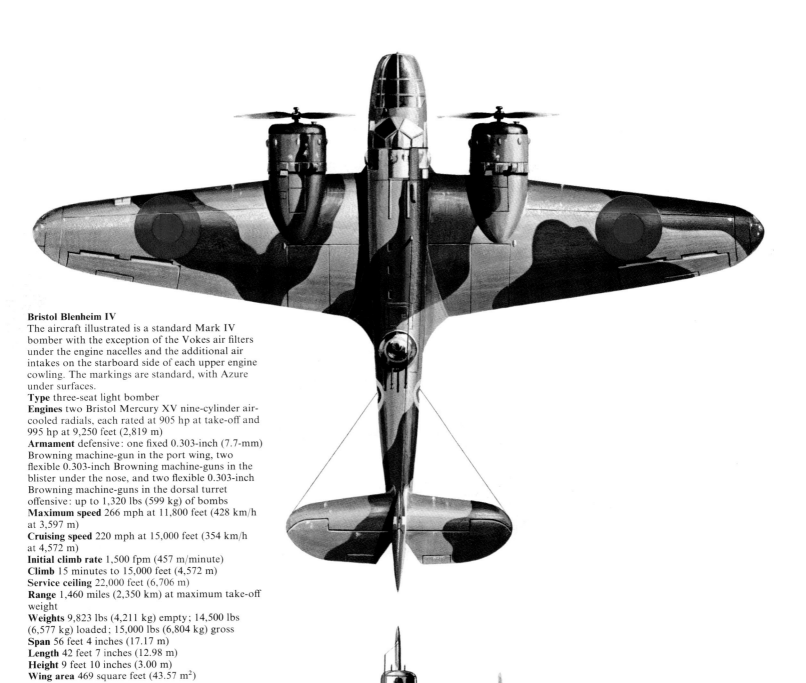

63

de Havilland Mosquito

Its versatility and basically wooden construction would be enough to ensure the immortality of the de Havilland Mosquito. And it deserves to be remembered, too, as an absolutely delightful aircraft – beautiful to look at and superb to fly. Although the Mosquito was originally designed as an unarmed high-speed bomber, relying on its pace to evade enemy fighters, the roles in which the aircraft eventually operated included those of bomber, fighter, fighter-bomber, night fighter, photographic-reconnaissance aircraft, minelayer, strike fighter, pathfinder, transport and trainer.

The de Havilland concern began design work on the aircraft that was to emerge as the Mosquito in October 1938 as a private venture high-speed bomber with two Rolls-Royce Merlin inline engines. Wooden construction was chosen as it was light and strong, because de Havilland had experience with it, and also because work of this type could be sub-contracted to other firms without disrupting an aircraft industry already fully extended. The Air Ministry began to display an interest in the de Havilland design in December 1939, and in the following March an order for 50 Mosquitoes was placed.

The exigencies of the Battle of Britain period of 1940 meant that Mosquito prototype construction enjoyed only a low priority; however, the first prototype flew in November 1940. It was a very clean, attractive aeroplane, and quickly showed itself to be possessed of exceptional performance and handling characteristics. Service trials were swiftly instituted, and so successful were these that the type was already mentioned being subdivided into 10 PR Mark 1, 10 B Mark IV and 30 NF Mark II aircraft. As the majority of Mosquitoes fall into one of these three categories (photographic-reconnaissance, bomber, and fighter), it is convenient to discuss the Mosquito according to type rather than in a strictly chronological order of marks.

The first Mosquitoes to enter service, in September 1941, were examples of the photographic-reconnaissance PR I mark. These aircraft were unarmed, but in deep-penetration missions over German-occupied Europe quickly showed themselves able to outpace even the latest German fighters. To improve the Mosquito's high-altitude performance the PR VIII was developed, powered by Merlin 61 engines with two-stage superchargers; but only five were built. In May 1943 the PR IX appeared, developed from the B IX high-altitude bomber mark and 90 examples were delivered. Late in 1943 the first pressurized version of the Mosquito for PR work appeared, the PR XVI; some 432 were produced making it the most numerous PR mark of the Mosquito. The last wartime version, the PR 34, was intended for very long-range missions with two drop-tanks under the wings and further fuel tanks in the bulged belly.

The second type of Mosquito to enter service was a bomber variant, the B IV, in November 1941. This carried 2,000 lbs (907 kg) of bombs, and was powered by a pair of 1,250-hp Merlin XXI engines. B IV aircraft were built in two series, the Series 2 differing from the Series 1 in having engine nacelles that extended aft of the trailing edge. Like the early PR aircraft, the unarmed B IV proved to be too fast for German fighters to catch, and its losses were therefore very light. Mosquitoes soon acquired an enviable reputation for their ability to deliver their bomb-loads with pinpoint accuracy over long ranges. In mid 1943 the B IX was introduced, with increased bomb capacity and an 'Oboe' radar aid for 'pathfinding'. The last major wartime variant, the B XVI, had a pressurized cockpit, enabling it to operate at altitudes of up to 40,000 feet (12,192 m) and a top speed of 415 mph (668 km/h), compared with the B IV's 380 mph (612 km/h). Some 1,200 of this mark were built, mostly for use in independent solo raids to disrupt German nights.

So spectacular was the performance of the Mosquito that very early in its career thought was given to producing a fighter version of the basic aircraft. The designers had catered for this, leaving the fuselage nose empty to enable cannon and machine-gun armament to be located there. The first fighter Mosquito, the NF II, entered service in January 1942. It had an armament of four 20-mm cannon and four 0.303-inch (7.7-mm) machine-guns in the nose, and was fitted with AI Mark IV (later Mark V) radar. The type proved an immediate success over northern Europe and in the Mediterranean theatre. The 97 NF XII fighters which followed were all conversions from NF II standard, with centimetric AI Mark VIII radar but no machine-gun armament – a feature of all night-fighter Mosquitoes with radar. The NF XII was succeeded by 270 NF XIIIs with underwing drop-tanks. The next model was the NF XVII – a redesignation of the 100 NF II aircraft re-equipped with the American AI Mark X radar. Similar radar was fitted to the NF XIII, but in this case 220 new aircraft were built as the NF XIX. The last wartime variant of the night-fighting Mosquito was the NF 30. This was essentially similar to the NF XIX except for the power units.

The success of the first armed Mosquito, the NF II, led to the development of a fighter-bomber variant, the FB VI, early in 1943. This entered service in May 1943, and became the most numerous of all Mosquito marks. Series 1 aircraft, of which 300 were built, were powered by 1,460-hp Merlin 21 or 23 engines, and carried a bomb-load of four 250-lb (113-kg) bombs in addition to a fixed armament of four 20-mm cannon and four 0.303-inch (7.7-mm) machine-guns. Series 2 aircraft, of which some 2,200 were built, had 1,635-hp Merlin 25 engines, and carried 500-lb (227-kg) bombs.

A total of 7,781 of this magnificent British aircraft was built before production ceased in November 1950.

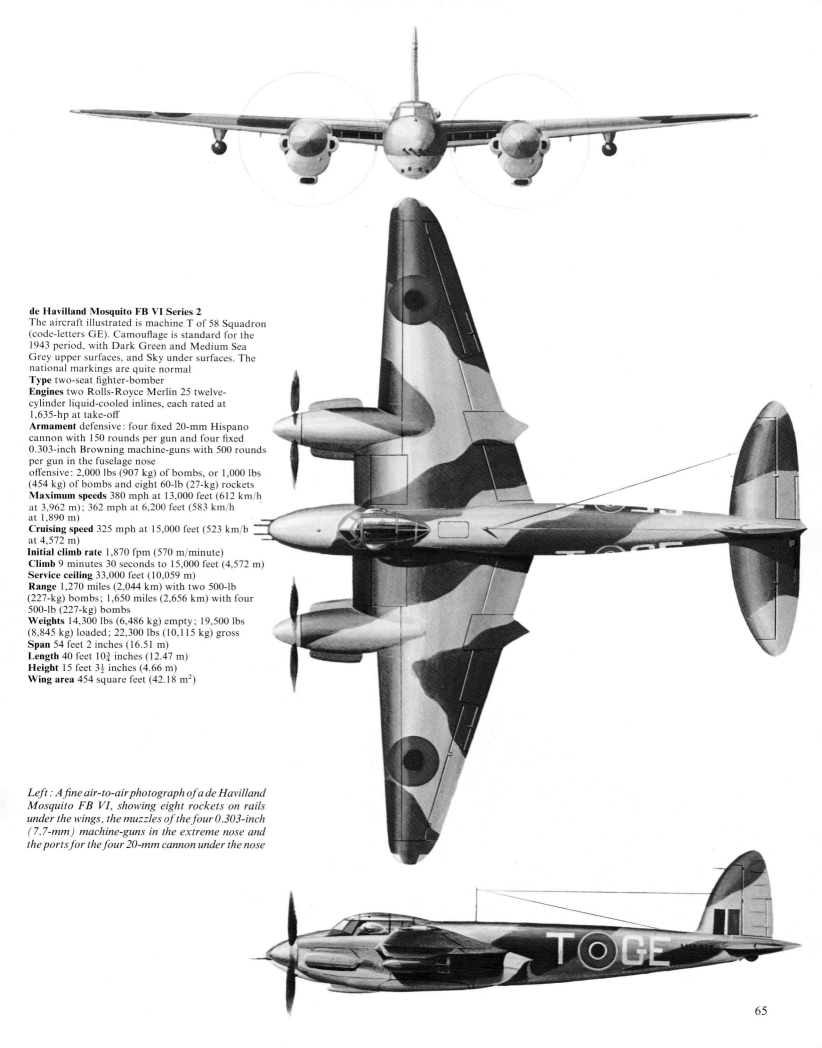

de Havilland Mosquito FB VI Series 2
The aircraft illustrated is machine T of 58 Squadron (code-letters GE). Camouflage is standard for the 1943 period, with Dark Green and Medium Sea Grey upper surfaces, and Sky under surfaces. The national markings are quite normal
Type two-seat fighter-bomber
Engines two Rolls-Royce Merlin 25 twelve-cylinder liquid-cooled inlines, each rated at 1,635-hp at take-off
Armament defensive: four fixed 20-mm Hispano cannon with 150 rounds per gun and four fixed 0.303-inch Browning machine-guns with 500 rounds per gun in the fuselage nose
offensive: 2,000 lbs (907 kg) of bombs, or 1,000 lbs (454 kg) of bombs and eight 60-lb (27-kg) rockets
Maximum speeds 380 mph at 13,000 feet (612 km/h at 3,962 m); 362 mph at 6,200 feet (583 km/h at 1,890 m)
Cruising speed 325 mph at 15,000 feet (523 km/h at 4,572 m)
Initial climb rate 1,870 fpm (570 m/minute)
Climb 9 minutes 30 seconds to 15,000 feet (4,572 m)
Service ceiling 33,000 feet (10,059 m)
Range 1,270 miles (2,044 km) with two 500-lb (227-kg) bombs; 1,650 miles (2,656 km) with four 500-lb (227-kg) bombs
Weights 14,300 lbs (6,486 kg) empty; 19,500 lbs (8,845 kg) loaded; 22,300 lbs (10,115 kg) gross
Span 54 feet 2 inches (16.51 m)
Length 40 feet $10\frac{3}{4}$ inches (12.47 m)
Height 15 feet $3\frac{1}{2}$ inches (4.66 m)
Wing area 454 square feet (42.18 m²)

Left: A fine air-to-air photograph of a de Havilland Mosquito FB VI, showing eight rockets on rails under the wings, the muzzles of the four 0.303-inch (7.7-mm) machine-guns in the extreme nose and the ports for the four 20-mm cannon under the nose

Fairey Swordfish

Although it was obsolescent by the beginning of World War II, the Fairey Swordfish remained in production until late in 1944; it performed both gallantly and usefully up to the end of hostilities in front-line service, and was in fact the last biplane combat aircraft to be used by the British armed forces. Nicknamed the 'Stringbag' by its crews, the Swordfish earned affection as an excellent torpedo-launching platform and as a remarkably sturdy and reliable aircraft which would get its crew home with damage that would have downed most other aircraft. The Swordfish was undeniably slow by World War II standards, but it was manoeuvrable for its size, very steady, and an ideal aircraft for operations from the small escort-carriers that came into service later in the war.

Derived from Fairey's Torpedo-Spotter-Reconnaissance I private-venture aircraft of 1933, the prototype Swordfish flew for the first time in April 1934. It was originally designated TSR II, and was developed to meet an Air Ministry request for a carrier-borne torpedo-bomber also capable of undertaking reconnaissance missions too. Trials with the new aircraft proved immediately successful with both wheel and float undercarriages, and it was ordered into production.

The Swordfish entered service with the Fleet Air Arm in July 1936, the main external difference between service and prototype aircraft being the three-bladed propeller of the former, in place of the two-bladed unit of the latter. By the beginning of World War II there were 13 squadrons equipped with the Swordfish, and during the war a further 13 were formed, the last in June 1943.

The Swordfish I, as the first production type was named, continued to be built up to 1943, when two improved marks appeared. The first of these, the Swordfish II, had metal skinning on the under surfaces of the lower wings, in place of the Mark I's cloth. This gave the lower wings enough strength to take eight 60-lb (27-kg) rockets, which proved very useful in anti-shipping strikes and attacks on U-boats. The 690-hp Pegasus IIIM 3 radial was retained on the first Mark IIs, but the improved 750-hp Pegasus 30 was installed on later aircraft of the Mark II series and all subsequent aircraft.

The second new mark to appear in 1943 was the Swordfish III. This featured the addition of Air-Surface Vessel Mark X radar, mounted in a large and clumsy radome under the fuselage between the undercarriage legs. This radar greatly improved the Swordfish's efficiency in the anti-shipping strike role. The last version of the Swordfish to appear was the Mark IV. This had an enclosed cockpit, and was intended for use in Canada. Total production of the Swordfish amounted to 2,392 aircraft, the last being delivered in August 1944.

In the war the Swordfish proved remarkably effective, its low speed and steadiness making it an excellent launching platform for torpedoes. Swordfish made the first torpedo strike of the war in April 1940, and continued to devastate German and Italian shipping with torpedoes and later rockets up to the end of hostilities.

Operating from escort-carriers in the mid-Atlantic, which land-based aircraft could not reach until the end of the war, the Swordfish proved an invaluable weapon in the final defeat of the U-boat menace in 1943. It was very effective against Axis surface vessels too: evidence for this need be sought no further than the crippling of the Italian battle fleet in Taranto in November 1940 and the damage inflicted on the German battleship *Bismarck* in May 1940, allowing elements of the British navy to close her and then sink her with gunfire and torpedoes. Perhaps the most courageous action fought by Swordfish aircraft was the vain attempt by six aircraft of 825 Squadron to disable the German battle-cruisers *Scharnhorst* and *Gneisenau*, and the heavy cruiser *Prinz Eugen* during their 'Channel dash' in February 1942. All six Swordfish torpedo-bombers were destroyed by AA gunfire and the massive German fighter screen. In conclusion, perhaps there can be no finer tribute to the qualities of the Swordfish than the fact that it outlived its supposed successor, the Fairey Albacore, as a front-line aircraft.

Above right: A Swordfish III, showing the large radome for the ASV X radar between the undercarriage legs
Below: This overhead photograph of a Swordfish reveals the type's angular flying surfaces, and the open nature of the triple cockpit. This last made long flights in poor weather very uncomfortable for the crew. The Swordfish IV, with an enclosed cockpit, was used in Canada

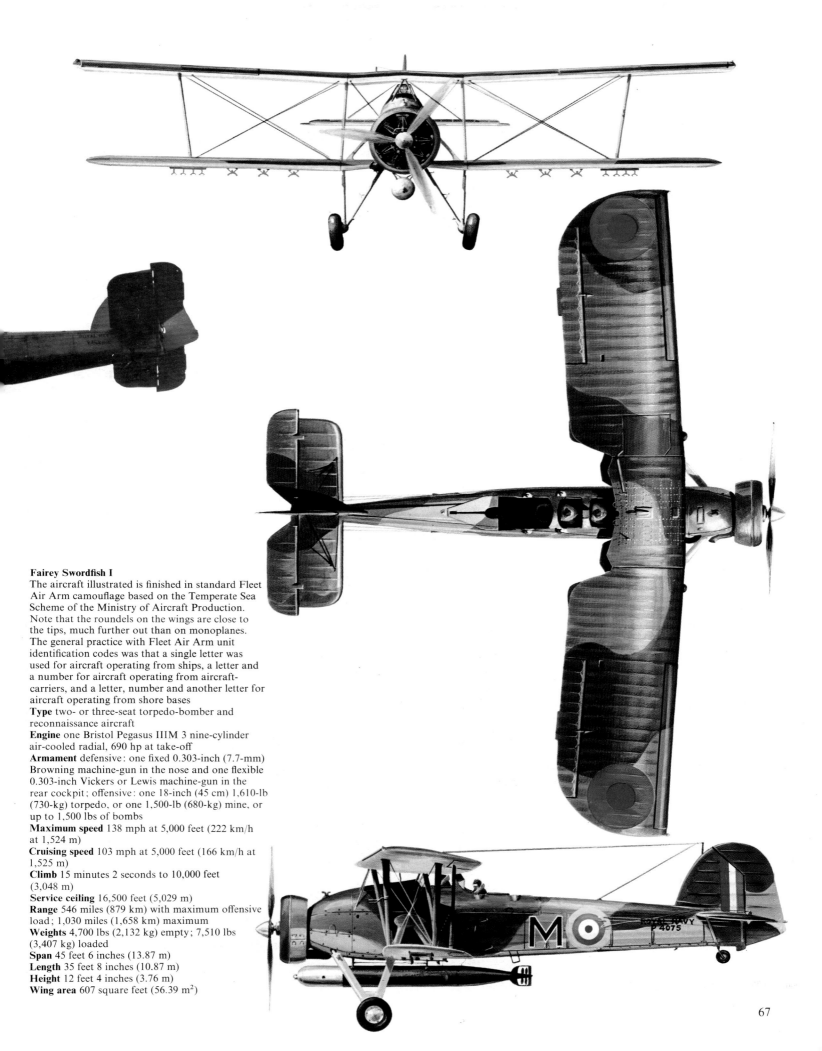

Fairey Swordfish I
The aircraft illustrated is finished in standard Fleet
Air Arm camouflage based on the Temperate Sea
Scheme of the Ministry of Aircraft Production.
Note that the roundels on the wings are close to
the tips, much further out than on monoplanes.
The general practice with Fleet Air Arm unit
identification codes was that a single letter was
used for aircraft operating from ships, a letter and
a number for aircraft operating from aircraft-
carriers, and a letter, number and another letter for
aircraft operating from shore bases
Type two- or three-seat torpedo-bomber and
reconnaissance aircraft
Engine one Bristol Pegasus IIIM 3 nine-cylinder
air-cooled radial, 690 hp at take-off
Armament defensive: one fixed 0.303-inch (7.7-mm)
Browning machine-gun in the nose and one flexible
0.303-inch Vickers or Lewis machine-gun in the
rear cockpit; offensive: one 18-inch (45 cm) 1,610-lb
(730-kg) torpedo, or one 1,500-lb (680-kg) mine, or
up to 1,500 lbs of bombs
Maximum speed 138 mph at 5,000 feet (222 km/h
at 1,524 m)
Cruising speed 103 mph at 5,000 feet (166 km/h at
1,525 m)
Climb 15 minutes 2 seconds to 10,000 feet
(3,048 m)
Service ceiling 16,500 feet (5,029 m)
Range 546 miles (879 km) with maximum offensive
load; 1,030 miles (1,658 km) maximum
Weights 4,700 lbs (2,132 kg) empty; 7,510 lbs
(3,407 kg) loaded
Span 45 feet 6 inches (13.87 m)
Length 35 feet 8 inches (10.87 m)
Height 12 feet 4 inches (3.76 m)
Wing area 607 square feet (56.39 m²)

Gloster Gladiator

The Gloster Gladiator was the last biplane fighter to serve with the Royal Air Force, and as such was the ultimate expression of the fighter philosophy that had dominated RAF thinking from 1916 to 1935. Apart from such refinements as an enclosed cockpit, a simplified undercarriage, and four machine-guns, the Gladiator conformed to this philosophy which called for a relatively lightly armed aircraft that was manoeuvrable and possessed a high rate of climb. Yet despite its obsolescence by the outbreak of World War II, the Gladiator enjoyed a remarkably successful operational career up to 1942.

The Gladiator was in essence an aerodynamically refined version of the Gloster Gauntlet fighter, with the improvements mentioned above and single-bay instead of double-bay wings. The design team which produced this very clean and attractive little biplane was led by H P Folland, and the prototype first flew in September 1934. Although the new fighter was a private venture, it conformed basically to a 1930 fighter requirement. The Air Ministry thus developed an interest in the machine, and a specification was written around it in 1935 when, after exhaustive trials, the Gladiator was ordered for the RAF.

The first 70 production aircraft, like the prototype, had drum-fed Lewis or Vickers guns under the wings, but all subsequent machines had belt-fed Browning guns. Production aircraft, unlike the prototype, also had an enclosed

cockpit and the engine was changed – an 830-hp Mercury IXS in place of a 645-hp Mercury VIS. Deliveries started in July 1936, and the Gladiator entered service with front-line squadrons in January 1937. Some 231 Gladiator I fighters were built.

The next model was the Gladiator II. This was very similar to the Mark I, but had a Mercury VIIIA or Mercury VIIIAS engine, a Vokes air filter, and a three-bladed propeller in place of the Mark I's two-bladed unit. The Gladiator II was intended for use by RAF squadrons in the Middle East and North Africa, and entered service in that area in February 1938. Basically similar to the Gladiator was the Sea Gladiator. This naval version of the fighter had an arrester hook, catapult points, and a faired bulge under the fuselage for a dinghy. Production of the Gladiator II amounted to 252 aircraft, and that of the Sea Gladiator to 98 machines. The first 38 Sea Gladiators were converted from Mark II standard. The final Gladiator, a Mark II, was delivered in April 1940.

Considerable enthusiasm for the Gladiator was also displayed by other nations: Mark I aircraft were ordered by Latvia, Lithuania, Norway, Sweden, Belgium, China, Ireland, Greece and Iraq; and Mark II aircraft by Sweden, Portugal, Norway, Finland, Greece, Egypt and Iraq. In all, 216 Gladiators were exported.

The Gladiator was Britain's main front-line

fighter during the period of the Munich crisis in 1938, but by the outbreak of war in 1939 the main strength of RAF Fighter Command lay with the Hawker Hurricane and Supermarine Spitfire. Nevertheless, there were 114 Gladiators serving as front-line aircraft in September 1939 compared with 102 at the time of Munich the year before. The Gladiator flew with distinction during the Norwegian campaign of 1940, operating from a frozen lake, but it was definitely outclassed by German aircraft. In the Mediterranean theatre, however, the boot was on the other foot. In combat against Italian biplanes and first generation monoplanes, the agility of the Gladiator enabled it to destroy a large number of enemy aircraft. The most celebrated episode in the Gladiator's career must be the 18-day defence of Malta by three Sea Gladiators in June 1940. But the Gladiator also served with distinction in North Africa and during the German invasion of Greece in April 1941.

Below: A Gloster Gladiator II of 25 Squadron RAF Fighter Command. Note the gun under each lower wing, and that the sliding portion of the cockpit canopy has been pushed back. This latter reflects the unpopularity of such canopies in the late 1930s with service pilots

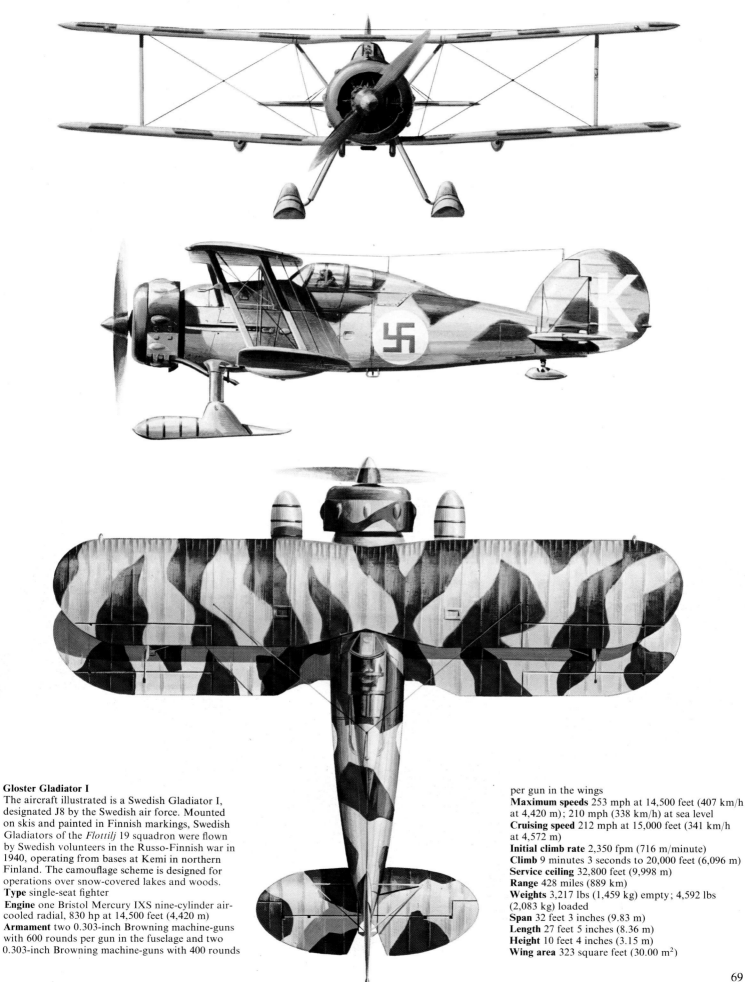

Gloster Gladiator I

The aircraft illustrated is a Swedish Gladiator I, designated J8 by the Swedish air force. Mounted on skis and painted in Finnish markings, Swedish Gladiators of the *Flottilj* 19 squadron were flown by Swedish volunteers in the Russo-Finnish war in 1940, operating from bases at Kemi in northern Finland. The camouflage scheme is designed for operations over snow-covered lakes and woods.

Type single-seat fighter

Engine one Bristol Mercury IXS nine-cylinder air-cooled radial, 830 hp at 14,500 feet (4,420 m)

Armament two 0.303-inch Browning machine-guns with 600 rounds per gun in the fuselage and two 0.303-inch Browning machine-guns with 400 rounds per gun in the wings

Maximum speeds 253 mph at 14,500 feet (407 km/h at 4,420 m); 210 mph (338 km/h) at sea level

Cruising speed 212 mph at 15,000 feet (341 km/h at 4,572 m)

Initial climb rate 2,350 fpm (716 m/minute)

Climb 9 minutes 3 seconds to 20,000 feet (6,096 m)

Service ceiling 32,800 feet (9,998 m)

Range 428 miles (889 km)

Weights 3,217 lbs (1,459 kg) empty; 4,592 lbs (2,083 kg) loaded

Span 32 feet 3 inches (9.83 m)

Length 27 feet 5 inches (8.36 m)

Height 10 feet 4 inches (3.15 m)

Wing area 323 square feet (30.00 m²)

69

Gloster Meteor

The Gloster Meteor was the first British turbojet-powered aircraft to enter service, and the only Allied aircraft with such powerplants to be flown operationally in World War II. Although the Meteor was thus a milestone in aviation history, it is worth noting that it was preceded into service by the Messerschmitt Me 262, and that despite the fact that the Me 262 was the earlier aircraft, it was the progenitor of today's jet aircraft, not the Meteor. The reason for this is quite simple: the Meteor, with its unswept wings, was in concept a 'piston-engined' aircraft with jet engines, whereas the Me 262, with its swept wings, took advantage of the latest developments in aerodynamics, such as the means for delaying the onset of compressibility problems.

By 1940, interest in jet engines at the Air Ministry was sufficient for that body to issue a specification for a fighter powered by the new type of engine. The Gloster firm, which was building the first British jet aircraft, the Gloster-Whittle E 28/39, entered the lists with a machine designed by a team led by W G Carter. As the jet engines under construction had only a relatively small thrust, the Gloster aircraft was designed to use two small jets mounted in the wings. The first prototype was ready for ground tests with derated Whittle 2B engines built by Rover in July 1942, and after the completion of successful taxiing trials, the first Meteor was returned to its manufacturer to await the delivery of flight-cleared Whittle 2/500 jets built by Power Jets. As severe difficulties were being experienced with these motors, the Meteor prototype first

flew in July 1943 with Rover B 23 engines. Further prototypes followed, with engines such as the Halford H 1, Metrovick F 3, and Rolls-Royce W 2B (Rolls-Royce having taken over development work on the Whittle-designed series of engines previously handled by Rover).

The first production order for the new fighter, at first called Thunderbolt and then changed to Meteor to avoid confusion with the Republic P-47 Thunderbolt fighter, was placed in September 1941. The engine chosen for production Meteors was the 1,700-lb (771-kg) static thrust Rolls-Royce W 2B/23 Welland I. The Meteor I entered squadron service in July 1944, just in time to join the latest Allied piston-engined fighters in combatting the menace posed by the German V-1 flying bomb. For this task the top speed of the Meteor I (385 mph or 620 km/h at sea level) was only just sufficient. Only 20 examples of the Meteor I were built, the first being given to the United States in exchange for a Bell YP-59A jet fighter.

The next model planned, the Meteor II, which was to have used the 2,700-lb (1,225-kg) static thrust de Havilland Goblin I jet, was not proceeded with and the next model to enter service was the Meteor III. The first 16 of the new mark differed from the Mark I only in having additional fuel tankage, a sliding instead of a hinging canopy over the cockpit, and minor structural refinements. However, from the 17th Mark III onwards Meteor III aircraft were fitted with Rolls-Royce W 2B/37 Derwent I engines of 2,000-lb (907-kg) static thrust each. These boosted performance considerably, top speed

being raised from 410 mph to 493 mph at 30,000 feet (660 km/h to 793 km/h at 9,144 m).

After working up in Great Britain, the units equipped with the new fighter moved to north-west Europe in the spring of 1945 with every expectation of meeting the Me 262 in combat. The deteriorating state of the *Luftwaffe*, however, meant that this clash never occurred, the few Meteor aircraft available being used mostly for ground-attack missions. In all, some 280 Meteor III aircraft were built before the type was succeeded in production by the Meteor IV in 1945. This latter had the more powerful Derwent V engines with improved engine nacelles, and pointed the way towards the fighter development of the late 1940s.

The Meteor deserves its place in history, but any objective analysis must conclude that it was inferior to the Me 262 for two basic reasons: its engines, of the centrifugal compressor type, were bulkier and less powerful than the axial flow units used in the German aircraft, and its aerodynamics were far less sophisticated, paying no heed to the problems of compressibility.

Below: Three Gloster Meteor F 4 fighters of 124 Squadron. This model of the Meteor was basically similar to the wartime F 3 except for the provision of uprated Derwent engines with a slightly enlarged tailpipe. A comparison between the Me 262's sleek lines and the comparatively unsophisticated shape of the Meteor provides an interesting contrast between the design philosophies of the two countries in the closing stages of the war. Nevertheless, the Meteor was a useful aircraft

Gloster Meteor III

The aircraft illustrated is machine Q of 616 Squadron (code-letters YQ), the first squadron to operate both the Meteor I and the Meteor III. 616 Squadron operated Meteor III fighters with the 2nd Tactical Air Force from its base at Nijmegen from April 1945 onwards. Camouflage is standard for the later stages of the war, with the Ministry of Aircraft Production Pattern No 1, in the Temperate Land Scheme of colours, being used. This produced Dark Green and Ocean Grey upper surfaces and Sky Type 'S' under surfaces. National insignia are the normal ones except for the flash on the fin, made necessary by the shape of the fin and the positioning of the tailplane half way up it. Other distinguishing features worthy of note are the yellow leading edges, introduced from September 1941 for all fighters, and the 18-inch wide blue band round the fuselage just in front of the fin, introduced on all day fighters from December 1940. This was supposedly painted in Sky Type 'S', the same colour as that used for the under surfaces, but such was the discrepancy in the interpretation of the colour intended by Sky Type 'S' that it was variously described as duck-egg green, duck-egg blue, and grey-green with a yellowish aspect

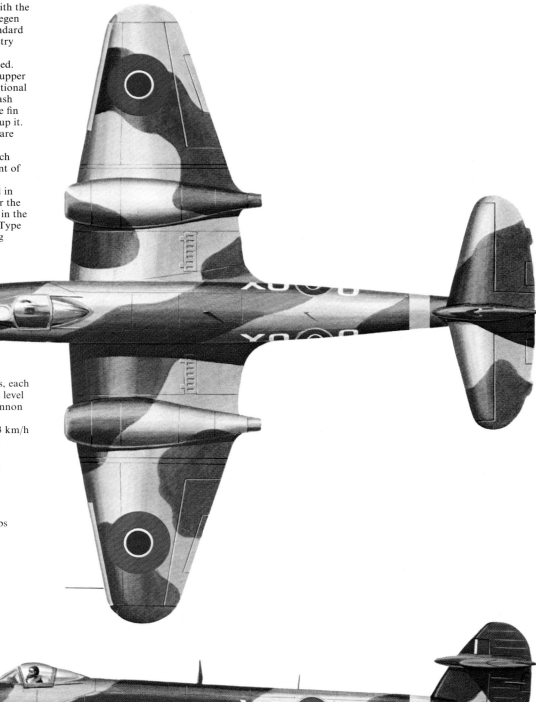

Type single-seat fighter
Engines two Rolls-Royce Derwent I turbojets, each rated at 2,000 lbs (907 kg) static thrust at sea level
Armament four 20-mm Hispano Mark III cannon with 195 rounds per gun
Maximum speeds 493 mph at 30,000 feet (793 km/h at 9,144 m); 458 mph (737 km/h) at sea level
Cruising speed unknown
Initial climb rate 3,980 fpm (1,213 m/minute)
Climb 15 minutes to 30,000 feet (9,144 m)
Service ceiling 44,000 feet (13,411 m)
Range 1,340 miles at 350 mph at 30,000 feet (2,157 km at 563 km/h at 9,144 m)
Weights 8,810 lbs (3,996 kg) empty; 13,300 lbs (6,033 kg) loaded
Span 43 feet (13.11 m)
Length 41 feet 3 inches (12.57 m)
Height 13 feet (3.96 m)
Wing area 374 square feet (34.75 m²)

Handley Page Halifax

Although it was not as successful a heavy bomber as the Avro Lancaster, the Handley Page Halifax nevertheless deserves more praise than it is usually given. The Halifax was the second of Great Britain's heavy bombers, becoming operational only a month after the unsuccessful Short Stirling, and was used for a variety of other tasks including transport, maritime reconnaissance and as a glider tug. It stayed in production after the end of the war.

The genesis of the Halifax was from the same 1936 requirement for a medium-heavy bomber powered by two Rolls-Royce Vulture engines that led to the ill-starred Avro Manchester. In 1937, however, the Air Ministry instructed Handley Page to redesign their contender to use four Rolls-Royce Merlins, as it was expected that Vulture production would not be able to match demand. Although Handley Page complied, the firm was unhappy about the decision. But the Air Ministry's directive was finally vindicated by the failure of the Vulture and the demise of the Manchester.

The prototype flew in October 1939, and the first production Halifax almost a year later. Service introduction followed in November, and the first operation mission was flown in March 1941. Naturally enough, these first production Halifaxes were built to Mark I standard, but in three groups, Series I, II and III. Top speed, with four 1,280-hp Merlin X engines, was 265 mph (426 km/h), and the three series differed from each other as follows: the Series I was stressed for take-off weights of 55,000 lbs (24,948 kg); the Series II for take-off weights of 60,000 lbs (27,216 kg); and the Series III had increased fuel tankage.

The lessons learned on operations were applied to the next Halifax model, the Mark II. This again was produced in three series. The Halifax II Series I (of which the prototype flew in July 1941 and the first production machine in September 1941) were powered by four 1,390-hp Merlin XX engines and had increased fuel tankage. A more radical departure from the Mark I standard, however, was the elimination of the two hand-held machine-guns in the waist position for beam defence, and their replacement by a Boulton Paul twin-gun turret in the dorsal position. Combat experience with this series led to the Series I (Special). The muffs which had previously been fitted to cut down exhaust flames were now removed as they reduced performance by an unacceptable margin; the little-used twin-gun nose turrent was removed, the gap thus left being faired over; and the dorsal turret was once again removed as its drag had affected performance adversely.

Further improvement was attained in the Halifax II Series IA. This series was powered by 1,460-hp Merlin 22 engines in improved cowlings; had a redesigned nose of perspex (mounting a single gun for forward defence), which lengthened the aircraft by 18 inches (45.7 cm) but produced far less drag than the old nose; and once again brought in a dorsal turret, this time a four-gun model which developed relatively little drag. These improvements raised the speed by 20 mph (32 km/h) compared with the

Mark I. Late production Series IA aircraft also introduced the rectangular vertical tail surfaces that became a hallmark of all later Halifaxes. The new surfaces eliminated the Halifax's tendency to yaw when the bomb-doors were open which reduced bombing accuracy. With these improvements the Halifax, now being built in large numbers, was one of the most useful types available to RAF Bomber Command. The efficiency of the Halifax was also improved by the introduction of the H2S radar blind-bombing and navigation device, which was pioneered in service by Halifax aircraft.

By the end of 1942 Halifax II Series IA aircraft were also serving with Coastal Command, under the designation Halifax GR II; all were armed with a 0.5-inch (12.7-mm) machine-gun in the nose, in place of Bomber Command aircraft's 0.303-inch (7.7-mm) weapons. The next Halifax model was the Mark V. This had a Dowty undercarriage in place of the earlier marks' Messier one – a change occasioned not by operational requirements but by a shortage of Messier units – but was otherwise identical with the Mark II. The Halifax V was built in two series, the Series I (Special) and Series IA, which corresponded to series of the same designation in the Mark II model. The type also served with Coastal Command as the Halifax GR V, with a 0.5-inch (12.7-mm) machine-gun in a ventral position when H2S was not carried.

The next model substituted a Bristol Hercules radial in place of the Rolls-Royce Merlin inline as the basic powerplant. The first example of the Mark III, which flew in July 1943, had four 1,615-hp Hercules XVI engines. The tailwheel was also made retractable for the first time, and

H2S or a ventral gun was made standard. On late production examples extended wingtips were introduced, raising the span to 104 feet 2 inches (31.76 m). This new wing was used on all subsequent Halifaxes. Despite all the early modifications and improvements the Halifax was now beginning to show its age as a combat aircraft, and it was increasingly relegated to attacks on less heavily defended targets from September 1943. The widespread introduction of the Halifax III, however, meant that the type was put back into full front-line service from February 1944. In October 1944 the Halifax VI appeared. This was intended for eventual operations against Japan, and was powered by 1,800-hp Hercules 100 engines. The last Halifax bomber model was the Mark VII, which was basically the same as the Mark VI except for its Hercules XVI engines.

It is worth noting that unlike the Lancaster the Halifax was also called upon to tow gliders (it was the only aircraft capable of towing the mighty General Aircraft Hamilcar glider), and to undertake the dropping of paratroopers and agents. Finally, amongst the other roles played by the Halifax, mention must be made of the vital job it did as a radio- and radar-countermeasures aircraft. In all, 6,176 Halifaxes were built.

Below: A Halifax II Series IA bomber with the rectangular vertical tail surfaces introduced in late production models
Bottom: A fine study of a Halifax II Series IA with the original vertical tail surfaces. Note the four-gun dorsal turret and the bulge for H2S radar under the fuselage

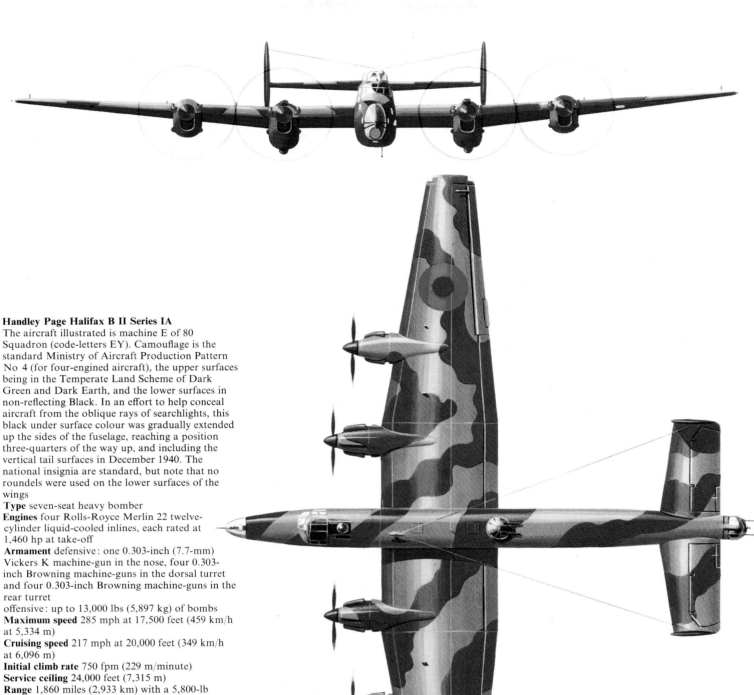

Handley Page Halifax B II Series IA
The aircraft illustrated is machine E of 80
Squadron (code-letters EY). Camouflage is the
standard Ministry of Aircraft Production Pattern
No 4 (for four-engined aircraft), the upper surfaces
being in the Temperate Land Scheme of Dark
Green and Dark Earth, and the lower surfaces in
non-reflecting Black. In an effort to help conceal
aircraft from the oblique rays of searchlights, this
black under surface colour was gradually extended
up the sides of the fuselage, reaching a position
three-quarters of the way up, and including the
vertical tail surfaces in December 1940. The
national insignia are standard, but note that no
roundels were used on the lower surfaces of the
wings
Type seven-seat heavy bomber
Engines four Rolls-Royce Merlin 22 twelve-
cylinder liquid-cooled inlines, each rated at
1,460 hp at take-off
Armament defensive: one 0.303-inch (7.7-mm)
Vickers K machine-gun in the nose, four 0.303-
inch Browning machine-guns in the dorsal turret
and four 0.303-inch Browning machine-guns in the
rear turret
offensive: up to 13,000 lbs (5,897 kg) of bombs
Maximum speed 285 mph at 17,500 feet (459 km/h
at 5,334 m)
Cruising speed 217 mph at 20,000 feet (349 km/h
at 6,096 m)
Initial climb rate 750 fpm (229 m/minute)
Service ceiling 24,000 feet (7,315 m)
Range 1,860 miles (2,933 km) with a 5,800-lb
(2,631-kg) bomb-load
Weights 38,250 lbs (17,350 kg) empty; 54,400 lbs
(24,676 kg) loaded; 60,000 lbs (27,216 kg) gross
Span 98 feet 10 inches (30.43 m)
Length 70 feet 1 inch (21.36 m)
Height 20 feet 9 inches (6.32 m)
Wing area 1,250 square feet (116.13 m²)

Hawker Hurricane

Although it is not as famous as the Supermarine Spitfire, the Hawker Hurricane should have as great, if not greater, claim to our remembrance: during the momentous days of the Battle of Britain, Hurricane fighters of RAF Fighter Command destroyed more enemy aircraft than all the other aircraft and ground defences involved. Apart from this, the Hurricane was the first eight-gun fighter to enter service with the RAF, and that force's first aircraft to be capable of a speed in excess of 300 mph (483 km/h) in level flight. The Hurricane was, moreover, an extremely sturdy machine, with viceless handling characteristics and excellent manoeuvrability at medium altitudes.

The origins of the Hurricane can be traced back to Sydney Camm's project for a 'Fury Monoplane', powered by a Rolls-Royce Goshawk engine, in October 1933. This project was shelved at the beginning of 1934 in favour of a revised version powered by a Rolls-Royce PV 12 (later the Merlin), renamed 'Interceptor Monoplane'. The Air Ministry soon became interested in the new type, and a prototype was ordered to two 1934 specifications early in 1935.

This flew for the first time in November 1935, and immediately displayed excellent performance and handling characteristics. An order for 600 of the new fighter was placed in June 1936 and raised to 1,000 in November 1938. The Hurricane was originally to be armed with four machine-guns, but this was altered to eight guns in July 1935. Experiments and assessments by the armaments branch of the Air Ministry had shown that the concentrated firepower of such an armament would be required to destroy the latest aircraft which, with their high speed, would only be in the fighter's gun-sights for a very short time.

Deliveries of production Hurricane I fighters started in October 1937, entering squadron service in December of the same year. These first machines had Merlin II engines, improved cockpit and exhausts, and modified undercarriage leg fairings. A small strake was subsequently fitted to the underneath of the rear fuselage to aid recovery from spins. As with the later Spitfire, the original fixed-pitch two-bladed wooden propeller was replaced first with a two-pitch three-bladed metal propeller and finally with a constant-speed three-bladed unit as they became available. The later propellers greatly aided the aircraft's rate of climb.

In comparison with other monoplane fighters of the World War II period, which were all-metal with a stressed-skin covering, the structure of the Hurricane was somewhat antiquated. A basic metal tube construction covered with fabric was used as the makers were very experienced in it, and thus the Hurricane could be brought into service more quickly and in greater numbers than would have otherwise been possible up to the early stages of the war. It is interesting to note that by the outbreak of war 497 Hurricanes had been delivered, compared with 310 Spitfires. By August 1940 deliveries were 2,309 and 1,400 respectively. The fabric-covered fuselage stayed with the Hurricane all its life, but later production examples had metal-skinned wings, which allowed a heavier armament to be carried, and higher diving speeds to be attained.

Much valuable combat experience was gained with the Hurricane during the 'Phoney War' period, and the type was the mainstay of the RAF fighter units in France after the invasion by Germany in May 1940, while the Spitfire was kept in Great Britain for metropolitan defence. During the Battle of Britain, the primary role of the Hurricane squadrons was the destruction of German bombers, while the Spitfires engaged the German fighters; the Hurricane was extremely successful, inflicting very heavy losses at a rate favourable to themselves.

Meanwhile the next model of the Hurricane, the Mark II, was under development. This had the 1,280-hp Merlin XX engine in place of the Mark I's 1,030-hp Merlin II or III, and also had a two-stage supercharger, giving a better performance at all altitudes. The armament, too, was revised. The first production Hurricane IIs, delivered in September 1940, retained the eight-gun armament of the Mark I, and were designated Hurricane IIA. But from April 1941 there appeared the Hurricane IIB, which had 12 0.303-inch (7.7-mm) machine-guns in the wings. In June 1941 there followed the Hurricane IIC, armed with four 20-mm cannon in place of the machine-guns. Other modifications of the period included provision of tropical equipment for use in the Middle Eastern and Mediterranean theatres, drop-tanks, and the ability to carry 250- or 500-lb (113- or 227-kg) bombs under the wings. Armed with bombs, the Hurricane became the 'Hurribomber', and as such soon proved itself an admirable fighter-bomber. It first went into service in Malta in September 1941, in Great Britain in October, and in North Africa in November. The Hurricane's armament was further improved in 1942, firstly by the addition of eight 60-lb (27-kg) rockets on underwing rails, and then by the fitting of 40-mm cannon. Rocket-armed Hurricanes entered service in the autumn of 1943, being preceded by the 'tank-busting' Hurricane IID. This mark was armed with a pair of 40-mm cannon, and entered service in North Africa during June 1942.

No Hurricane IIIs, intended to use Packard-built Merlins, were built, and thus the next model was the Mark IV. This had a Universal wing, which could carry 40-mm cannon, bombs, drop-tanks or rockets. It was at first designated Hurricane IIE. The final version of the Hurricane was the Mark V, of which only two were built. The Hurricane was also used at sea, the first being 'Hooked Hurricanes', converted from Mark II standard to carry an arrester hook. Full navalization led to the Sea Hurricane II, and later the Sea Hurricane XIIA, a carrier version of the Canadian Hurricane XIIA. Some 1,451 Hurricanes were built by the Canadian Car and Foundry Company, to a basic Mark II standard, as the Hurricanes X, XI, XII, and XIIA. British production of the Hurricane ended in September 1944, after a grand total of 14,223 had been built.

Below: An example of the Hurricane IV's predecessor, the Hurricane IIE (the designation was changed after 270 had been built). The IIE was the first model to have Universal wings, capable of taking 40-mm cannon, bombs, drop-tanks or rockets

Hawker Hurricane I

The aircraft illustrated is machine H of 32 Squadron (code-letters GZ), flown by Squadron-Leader J Worrall, DFC, from Biggin Hill during the opening stages of the Battle of Britain in July 1940. Standard upper surface camouflage of Dark Green and Dark Earth (Temperate Land Scheme), in Ministry of Aircraft Production Pattern No 1 for single-engined monoplanes, is carried. The under surfaces are finished in a washed-out Sky Blue. National insignia are the normal ones. Note the red fabric patches doped over the gun ports in the wing leading edge. These were applied before take-off to reduce drag and thus improve the climb to combat altitudes, and were shot through on entering combat

Type single-seat fighter

Engine one Rolls-Royce Merlin III twelve-cylinder liquid-cooled inline, 1,029 hp at 16,250 feet (4,953 m)

Armament eight 0.303-inch (7.7-mm) Browning machine-guns with 334 rounds per gun

Maximum speeds 328 mph at 20,000 feet (528 km/h at 6,096 m); 280 mph (451 km/h) at sea level

Cruising speed unknown

Initial climb rate 2,300 fpm (701 m/minute)

Climb 8 minutes 30 seconds to 20,000 feet (6,096 m)

Service ceiling 34,200 feet (10,424 m)

Range 425 miles (684 km) on internal fuel; 900 miles (1,448 km) with drop-tanks

Weights 4,670 lbs (2,118 kg) empty; 6,600 lbs (2,994 kg) loaded

Span 40 feet (12.19 m)

Length 31 feet 4 inches (9.55 m)

Height 13 feet 1½ inches (4.00 m)

Wing area 258 square feet (23.97 m²)

Left: A fine study of a Hurricane IV, armed with a pair of 40-mm cannon, in a tight bank to port Inset left: A Hurricane IIC, armed with four 20-mm cannon, and fitted with a 44-gallon (200 l) fixed long-range fuel tank under each wing

Hawker Hurricane IID
The aircraft illustrated is machine Z of 6 Squadron (code-letters JV). Camouflage is standard Middle East Scheme of Dark Earth and Middle Stone on the upper surfaces, with Sky Blue under surfaces
Type single-seat fighter-bomber and tank-busting aircraft
Engine one Rolls-Royce Merlin XX twelve-cylinder liquid-cooled inline, 1,280 hp at take-off and 1,160 hp at 20,750 feet (6,325 m)
Armament two 40-mm Rolls-Royce BF cannon with 12 rounds per gun or Vickers Type S cannon

with 15 rounds per gun under the wings and two 0.303-inch (7.7-mm) Browning machine-guns with 334 rounds per gun in the wings
Maximum speed 322 mph at 20,750 feet (518 km/h at 6,235 m)
Cruising speed unknown
Initial climb rate 2,750 fpm (832 m/minute)
Climb 12 minutes 24 seconds to 20,000 feet (6,096 m)
Service ceiling 32,100 feet (9,784 m)
Range 420 miles (676 km) on internal fuel; 900 miles (1,448 km) with drop-tanks
Weights 5,550 lbs (2,517 kg) empty; 7,850 lbs (3,561 kg) loaded; 8,100 lbs (3,674 kg) gross
Span 40 feet (12.19 m)
Length 32 feet (9.75 m)
Height 13 feet 1½ inches (4.00 m)
Wing area 258 square feet (23.97 m²)

Hawker Tempest

The Hawker Tempest was the result of an attempt to improve on the failings that manifested themselves early in the development career of the Typhoon. These failings in performance, especially at altitude, were largely attributable to the problems of compressibility, exaggerated by the thick, bluff wing-section of the aircraft. Hawker therefore proposed a Typhoon II, which would have an elliptical wing of laminar-flow section. This would delay the onset of compressibility problems and, coupled with the use of the latest Napier Sabre engine driving a four-bladed propeller, would guarantee a much higher performance at the altitudes at which interceptor fighters worked.

The idea was submitted to the Air Ministry in August 1941. It was approved and even expanded upon, but meanwhile the third Tornado, which had been modified to use a Bristol Centaurus radial engine, had been tested, with very encouraging results. With the cancellation of the Tornado programme, development of the Centaurus-powered derivative continued under the designation Typhoon II with a revised fuselage. The Air Ministry wished to explore the possibility of several powerplants for the elliptical wing Typhoon II, and to avoid confusion a new name was selected. This was Tempest, and the following prototypes were ordered: Tempest I with a Napier Sabre IV engine, Tempest II with a Bristol Centaurus engine, Tempest III and IV with Rolls-Royce Griffon engines, and Tempest V with a Napier Sabre II engine. Hawker elected to concentrate on the Tempest I, II and V, for which prototypes flew in February 1943, June 1943, and September

1942 respectively. The Tempest V preceded the others into the air as its engine was more readily available. The new thin-section laminar-flow wing of the Tempest could not accommodate the fuel tanks which had been placed there in the Typhoon, so extra fuel tankage had to be provided in a lengthened fuselage. A larger fin, provided by extending the Typhoon-type fin with a dorsal fillet, was required to compensate for the extra keel area.

The Tempest I, which had its radiators placed in the wings instead of the large chin radiator of the Typhoon and Tempest V, had an excellent performance and was ordered into large-scale production. Delays with the Sabre IV engines, however, led to the transference of Tempest I orders to the Tempest V. The first production Tempest V flew in June 1943, and the type entered squadron service in April 1944, proving to be an excellent low- and medium-altitude interceptor and fighter-bomber. As with the Typhoon, however, problems with the Sabre II had first to be eliminated.

Some 805 Tempest V fighters were built, the first 100 as Series 1 and the rest as Series 2 aircraft. Series 1 machines had a non-detachable rear fuselage and cannon that projected slightly in front of the wings, whereas Series 2 machines had a detachable rear fuselage, cannon that did not project ahead of the wing leading edge, smaller wheels, and spring tabs on the rudder and one aileron to increase manoeuvrability. Engine horsepower available eventually reached 2,260 with the Sabre IIC. Production ceased in August 1945. The Tempest VI was a development of the Mark V, with a 2,340-hp Sabre V engine and the

air intakes moved from the radiator to the wings. This was intended for tropical operations, and 142 were delivered between July 1945 and June 1947. None saw service during World War II.

The other major version of the Tempest to see service was the radial-engined Mark II. This was derived from the Bristol Centaurus-powered Tornado prototype, and eventually became the most powerful single piston-engined fighter to serve with the RAF. The engine used was the 2,520-hp Centaurus V or VI. A combination of vibration problems associated with the Centaurus installation and the production priority enjoyed by the Tempest V delayed production deliveries until October 1944. The Tempest II was intended primarily for operations in the Far East, but the first squadron to re-equip with the type did not do so until November 1945, after the end of the war; with a speed of 440 mph (708 km/h) and a range of 1,700 miles (2,736 km), it would have proved extremely useful had hostilities against Japan continued into 1946. The final expression of the Typhoon/Tempest design philosophy was reached in the postwar Hawker Fury and Sea Fury fighters, which were essentially lightened versions of the Tempest II aircraft.

Below: Three Hawker Tempest V Series 2 fighter-bombers. Series 2 aircraft were distinguishable by the fitting of Hispano Mark V short-barrelled 20-mm cannon, whose muzzles did not protrude in front of the wing leading-edge. Note the thin wings compared with the Typhoon's much thicker-section surfaces

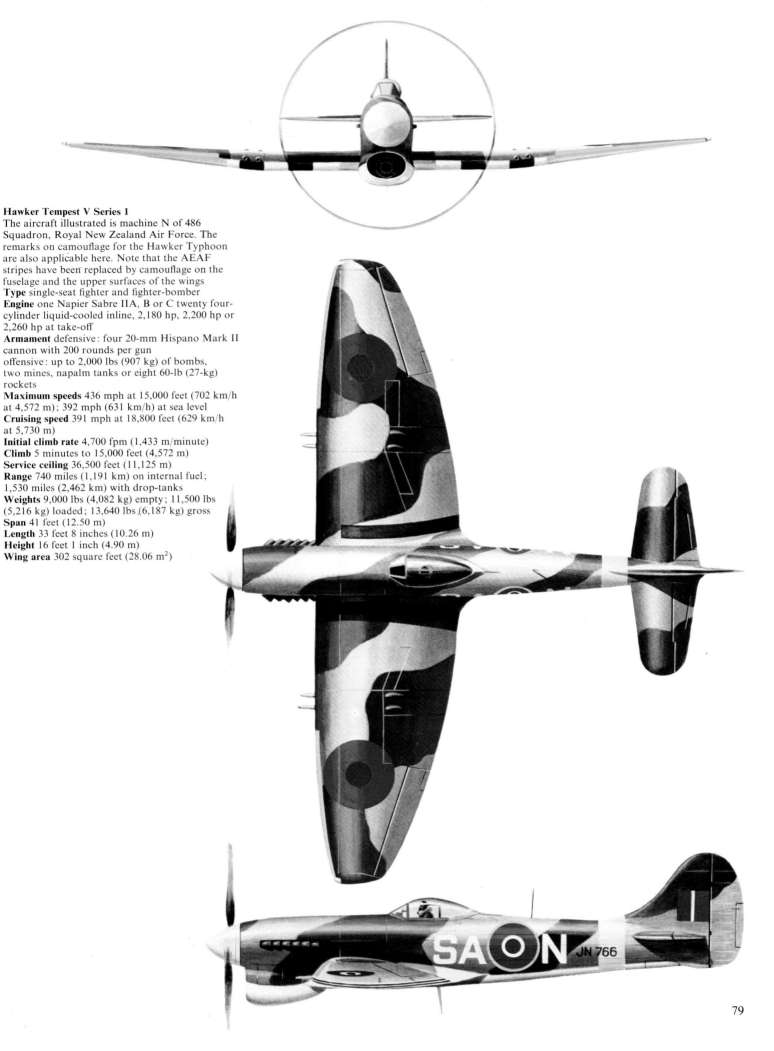

Hawker Tempest V Series 1
The aircraft illustrated is machine N of 486
Squadron, Royal New Zealand Air Force. The
remarks on camouflage for the Hawker Typhoon
are also applicable here. Note that the AEAF
stripes have been replaced by camouflage on the
fuselage and the upper surfaces of the wings
Type single-seat fighter and fighter-bomber
Engine one Napier Sabre IIA, B or C twenty four-
cylinder liquid-cooled inline, 2,180 hp, 2,200 hp or
2,260 hp at take-off
Armament defensive: four 20-mm Hispano Mark II
cannon with 200 rounds per gun
offensive: up to 2,000 lbs (907 kg) of bombs,
two mines, napalm tanks or eight 60-lb (27-kg)
rockets
Maximum speeds 436 mph at 15,000 feet (702 km/h
at 4,572 m); 392 mph (631 km/h) at sea level
Cruising speed 391 mph at 18,800 feet (629 km/h
at 5,730 m)
Initial climb rate 4,700 fpm (1,433 m/minute)
Climb 5 minutes to 15,000 feet (4,572 m)
Service ceiling 36,500 feet (11,125 m)
Range 740 miles (1,191 km) on internal fuel;
1,530 miles (2,462 km) with drop-tanks
Weights 9,000 lbs (4,082 kg) empty; 11,500 lbs
(5,216 kg) loaded; 13,640 lbs (6,187 kg) gross
Span 41 feet (12.50 m)
Length 33 feet 8 inches (10.26 m)
Height 16 feet 1 inch (4.90 m)
Wing area 302 square feet (28.06 m²)

Hawker Typhoon

The Typhoon, like the Hurricane, was designed by Sydney Camm, Hawker's chief designer. Intended as an interceptor fighter to replace the Hurricane, the Hawker Typhoon was not successful in this role, and found its real *métier* as a ground-attack aircraft. In this latter role it was arguably the best ground-attack fighter of World War II.

Design work on the Typhoon began in 1937, the intention being to produce a stressed-skin all-metal fighter, powered by the new Napier Sabre engine of 2,000 hp. The Air Ministry was also looking into the possibility of a Hurricane replacement to be powered by either the Sabre or the Rolls-Royce Vulture, which was also intended to develop more than 2,000 hp. Thus when Hawker approached the Air Ministry with their project, the ministry instructed the firm to build four prototypes, two to be powered by each of the new engines. The Vulture-engined type, which appeared as the Tornado, was bedevilled by engine problems, and the type was abandoned after three examples had been built.

The Sabre-engined type, which became the Typhoon, first flew in February 1940. Although it had been hoped to have the new fighter in service by the middle of that year, production aircraft began to be delivered only in May 1941, entering service in September of the same year. These first aircraft were Typhoon IA fighters, armed with 12 0.303-inch (7.7-mm) Browning machine-guns in the wings.

But although the Typhoon was a welcome addition to Fighter Command's inventory, as the RAF's first fighter capable of a speed greater than 400 mph (644 km/h), its initial service career was far from smooth. This was to a great extent the result of the type's too swift entry into service, before all the teething problems with the engine and the airframe had been eliminated. The two chief problems were the unreliability of the Sabre engine, which was especially dangerous at take-off, and a structural weakness in the rear fuselage, which resulted in a disastrous tendency for the empennage to shake itself off. The engine problems were finally solved after further testing and the structural ones by the addition of a band of strengthening fishplates right round the fuselage, but not before the withdrawal of the Typhoon had been seriously mooted. Fighter Command was disappointed with the Typhoon's low rate of climb and lack of performance at high altitude, and only the type's outstanding capabilities at low altitudes saved it. At this time, the end of 1941 and the beginning of 1942, the Focke-Wulf 190 had entered service with the *Luftwaffe*, and was engaged in making low-level hit-and-run raids on targets in the south of England. Only the Typhoon was able to catch the intruders, the latest mark of Spitfire, the Mark V, being too slow.

The Typhoon IA was soon replaced on production lines by the Mark IB, which had four 20-mm cannon instead of machine-guns as its chief armament. The new model went into action for the first time in August 1942. At the end of the same year models equipped to carry two 250-lb (113-kg) bombs under the wings also began to reach squadrons. During 1943 this bomb-load was increased from 500 to 2,000 lbs (227 to 907 kg), and rockets were added to the type's armament. With these weapons, the Typhoon quickly added to its laurels as a fast and very hard-hitting low-level attack aircraft, devastating German transport all over northern Europe. With the Allied invasion of Europe in June 1944, the Typhoon really came into its own. Enough aircraft were now in service to allow 'cab-rank' patrols to be mounted. These could be called in by the ground forces at a moment's notice to blast any and every German tank, emplacement, gun position or other impediment to progress encountered.

The first production Typhoons had featured a framed cockpit canopy and a sideways-opening door for entry into the cockpit, but this cumbersome arrangement was replaced on later production aircraft by a sliding 'bubble' canopy, which greatly increased the pilot's all-round vision. Other modifications were the replacement of the earlier aerial mast behind the cockpit with a whip aerial and the provision of a four-bladed instead of a three-bladed propeller. Production of the Typhoon ceased in November 1945 with the delivery of the 3,330th and last machine. The importance of the Typhoon in the campaign in north-west Europe during 1944 and 1945 was very considerable. Its thick wings enabled it to carry a heavy offensive load in addition to its cannon armament, and its powerful engine bestowed an excellent low-altitude performance. The Typhoon was the scourge not only of German front-line units, but also of their corps and army headquarters, which it could attack with pinpoint accuracy.

Below: RAF groundcrew at work on a Hawker Typhoon IB. Note the barrels of the four cannon and the launching rails for eight 60-lb (27-kg) rockets. The drum-shaped object in the foreground is the radiator for the huge, but at times unreliable, Napier Sabre inline engine

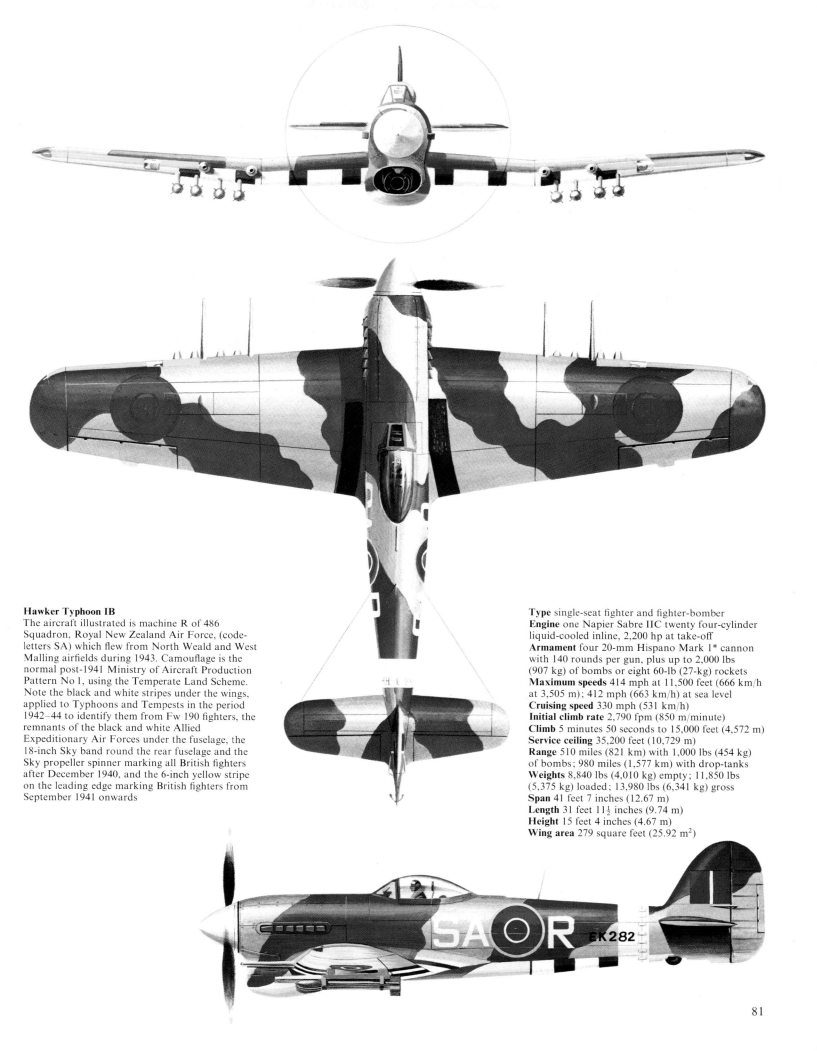

Hawker Typhoon IB
The aircraft illustrated is machine R of 486 Squadron, Royal New Zealand Air Force, (code-letters SA) which flew from North Weald and West Malling airfields during 1943. Camouflage is the normal post-1941 Ministry of Aircraft Production Pattern No 1, using the Temperate Land Scheme. Note the black and white stripes under the wings, applied to Typhoons and Tempests in the period 1942–44 to identify them from Fw 190 fighters, the remnants of the black and white Allied Expeditionary Air Forces under the fuselage, the 18-inch Sky band round the rear fuselage and the Sky propeller spinner marking all British fighters after December 1940, and the 6-inch yellow stripe on the leading edge marking British fighters from September 1941 onwards

Type single-seat fighter and fighter-bomber
Engine one Napier Sabre IIC twenty four-cylinder liquid-cooled inline, 2,200 hp at take-off
Armament four 20-mm Hispano Mark 1* cannon with 140 rounds per gun, plus up to 2,000 lbs (907 kg) of bombs or eight 60-lb (27-kg) rockets
Maximum speeds 414 mph at 11,500 feet (666 km/h at 3,505 m); 412 mph (663 km/h) at sea level
Cruising speed 330 mph (531 km/h)
Initial climb rate 2,790 fpm (850 m/minute)
Climb 5 minutes 50 seconds to 15,000 feet (4,572 m)
Service ceiling 35,200 feet (10,729 m)
Range 510 miles (821 km) with 1,000 lbs (454 kg) of bombs; 980 miles (1,577 km) with drop-tanks
Weights 8,840 lbs (4,010 kg) empty; 11,850 lbs (5,375 kg) loaded; 13,980 lbs (6,341 kg) gross
Span 41 feet 7 inches (12.67 m)
Length 31 feet $11\frac{1}{2}$ inches (9.74 m)
Height 15 feet 4 inches (4.67 m)
Wing area 279 square feet (25.92 m²)

Short Sunderland

Although it was built in relatively limited numbers compared with other major RAF combat aircraft, the Short Sunderland holds an enviably high place in the annals of World War II air history. Its only contenders for the title of the best flying-boat of the war are the Japanese Kawanishi H8K 'Emily' and the American Consolidated PBY Catalina series. The Sunderland played a greater part than the Catalina in the defeat of Germany's U-boats in the Atlantic, and therefore played a more important role in the eventual Allied victory.

The Sunderland was a military derivation of the famous Short C class civilian flying-boats of the early 1930s, and was designed to a specification for a monoplane replacement for the Royal Air Force's elderly fleet of biplane maritime-reconnaissance flying-boats. The specification had been issued in 1933, and the first prototype flew in October 1937. Before this, however, the Air Ministry had placed orders for the new aircraft to a revised 1936 specification. The Sunderland entered service in the middle of 1938; by the outbreak of war three squadrons were flying the new machine and others followed as soon as production allowed.

The Sunderland I soon proved itself to be a useful anti-submarine aircraft and a formidable opponent in the air. With its two power-operated machine-gun turrets, the first to be fitted to a British flying-boat, a Sunderland often managed to shoot down or drive off several German fighters. The type's most vulnerable spot was the planing bottom of its hull, and to protect this the pilot normally flew as close to the water as possible when being attacked. Although its normal work was patrolling over the sealanes, the Sunderland was also called upon at times to serve as a rescue and transport aircraft. In the former capacity it picked up the crews of torpedoed ships, and in the latter capacity it helped in the evacuation of Norway and Crete. It was even used to evacuate the wounded and sick from the second Chindit operation in Burma during 1944, flying off lakes far from the sea.

Production of the Sunderland I reached 90 before the next mark, the Sunderland II, began to appear in August 1941. The new model, which was powered by 1,065-hp Pegasus XVIII radials and had a power-operated twin-gun dorsal turret in place of the two hand-held beam guns, entered service at the end of 1941. After 43 examples had been built, the Mark II was replaced by the Mark III. The first production Sunderland III flew in December 1941. It differed from the Mark II in having a revised bottom to the hull, the forward step of the planing surface being reduced in depth. A total of 456 Sunderland III boats was built, making it the most numerous mark of the basic type.

The next version, the Sunderland IV, first flew in August 1944. This had 1,700-hp Bristol Hercules radial engines, and it was soon found that a larger fin and rudder and tailplane were needed. As it was realized that it would take some time to get this new model into full production, it was scheduled for use in the Pacific. Defensive armament was to include two 20-mm cannon and eight 0.5-inch (12.7-mm) machine-guns. Performance was disappointing, however, and only eight Seafords, as the Sunderland IV with all its modifications had been renamed, were built for military use.

The last Sunderland model was the Mark V. To obtain adequate performance with the Mark III it had been necessary to fly with the engines running flat out much of the time, and this wore out the Pegasus engines very quickly. Service pilots therefore suggested that 1,200-hp Pratt & Whitney Twin Wasp radials replace the Pegasus engines. The first of the new Mark V aircraft flew in March 1944, and the type entered squadron service in February 1945. In all, 150 Sunderland V flying-boats were built before production ceased in June 1946, making a grand total of 739.

To improve the type as a reconnaissance aircraft, Sunderlands from the Mark II onwards had been fitted with air-surface vessel search radar. In the Mark II this had been ASV Mark II equipment, which was readily identifiable by its four masts rising vertically from the top of the hull, and the 16 transmitting loops in four rows of four, two on each side of the hull. On late production Mark III aircraft this radar was replaced by ASV Mark VIC, and this equipment was made standard on the Mark V. This later radar could be distinguished by the bulges underneath the wings outboard of the outer float bracing wires. Each of these two bulges housed a scanner. It is worth noting that the Sunderland's offensive armament was carried on racks in the hull. These had to be winched out under the wings before the bombs could be dropped.

The last Sunderlands were retired from RAF service in May 1959, after a career of 17 years. They had proved to be magnificent aircraft, acquiring for themselves a special niche in aviation history. Perhaps the Sunderland can best be described by the epithet bestowed upon it by German aircrew operating against it, *fliegende Stachelschwein* – Flying Porcupine – due to its formidable armament.

Below: A Short Sunderland Mark V long-range maritime-reconnaissance flying-boat in the air. This last production model of the Sunderland was distinguishable by the scanners for its air-to-surface vessel search radar, mounted in a small radome under each outer wing panel, and Pratt & Whitney Twin Wasp radials in place of earlier marks' Bristol Pegasus engines, with which the aircraft was slightly underpowered

Short Sunderland I

The aircraft illustrated is the 12th production Sunderland, machine B of 204 Squadron, Coastal Command (code-letters KG). Camouflage is standard for the period 1941-mid 1942, with a Temperate Sea Scheme of Dark Slate Grey and Extra Dark Sea Grey on the upper surfaces, with Sky Type 'S' on the under surfaces. National insignia are the normal ones except for the fin stripes, which at this time should have been three equal stripes of red, white and blue in a block 24 inches wide and 27 inches high

Type ten-seat maritime patrol and reconnaissance flying boat

Engines four Bristol Pegasus XXII nine-cylinder air-cooled radials, each rated at 1,010 hp at take-off

Armament defensive: two flexible 0.303-inch (7.7-mm) Browning machine-guns in the nose turret, four flexible 0.303-inch Browning machine-guns in the tail turret and two flexible 0.303-inch Vickers K machine-guns, one in each of two beam positions

offensive: up to 2,000 lbs (907 kg) of bombs

Maximum speed 210 mph at 6,500 feet (338 km/h at 1,981 m)

Cruising speed 178 mph at 5,750 feet (286 km/h at 1,753 m)

Initial climb rate 830 fpm (253 m/minute)

Service ceiling 17,000 feet (5,182 m)

Range 2,900 miles (4,667 km)

Weights 28,290 lbs (12,832 kg) empty; 44,600 lbs (20,230 kg) loaded; 50,100 lbs (22,725 kg) gross

Span 112 feet 9 inches (34.37 m)

Length 85 feet 8 inches (26.11 m)

Height 32 feet 10½ inches (10.02 m)

Wing area 1,487 square feet (138.15 m²)

Supermarine Spitfire

The Supermarine Spitfire is certainly the most famous aircraft ever used by the Royal Air Force, and probably the most celebrated aircraft of World War II. It was a superlative fighter, a match for any of its opponents at the beginning of World War II, and still a match for any fighter powered by a piston engine at the end of that conflict. It had enormous development potential, and its successor, the Supermarine Spiteful, was the ultimate expression of the piston-engined fighter concept. Finally, the Spitfire's capabilities as a warplane were matched by its aesthetic qualities.

The designer of the Spitfire, R J Mitchell, who died just after it went into production, had been concerned with high-speed flight with monoplanes since the middle of the 1920s, when he had been responsible for the design of the Supermarine S 4 racing floatplane. Subsequently he had designed the S 5, S 6 and S 6B floatplanes which had won the Schneider Trophy for Great Britain. He had designed a single-seat monoplane fighter to a 1930 Air Ministry requirement, and was working on a more advanced design, to be powered by a Rolls-Royce Goshawk engine, with an enclosed cockpit and a retractable undercarriage, when two factors made him start afresh. These two factors were a 1934 Air Ministry requirement for a monoplane fighter armed with eight machine-guns, and the introduction of the 1,000-hp Rolls-Royce PV 12 engine, later the Merlin. Mitchell completely

redesigned his interim design to incorporate the new factors, and the result first flew in March 1936.

This was the prototype Spitfire, and its performance, combined with its handling characteristics, led to a first production order for 310 machines in June 1936. By October 1939 production orders totalled 4,000 machines. Production of the Spitfire I began in 1937, deliveries beginning in June 1938, the first squadron to re-equip with the new fighter doing so in July of the same year. These early Mark Is were fitted with a Merlin II engine with a fixed-pitch two-bladed wooden propeller, but improvements in these latter matched those already described for the Hurricane. The first few aircraft, designated Spitfire I, had only four machine-guns and an unbulged cockpit like the prototype's. Later machines had a domed cockpit canopy, and the Spitfire IA introduced an eight-gun armament. The Spitfire IB, of which 30 were delivered in August 1940, had two 20-mm cannon and four machine-guns. Spitfire I production totalled 1,583 aircraft before production was changed to the next model.

This was the Spitfire II, which was powered by a Merlin XII of 1,175-hp. It entered service in August 1940, and two major versions were built: 750 Mark IIAs with eight machine-guns, and 170 Mark IIBs with two 20-mm cannon and four 0.303-inch (7.7-mm) Browning machine-guns. The designation Spitfire IIC was used for

the Mark II variant in service with air/sea rescue squadrons. Apart from being used as a fighter, the Spitfire was also employed as a photographic-reconnaissance aircraft under the designations A, B, C, D, E, F, and G. The first definitive PR Spitfire was the PR IV, with a 1,100-hp Merlin 46; 229 were built.

The Spitfire III proved a useful development aircraft, but did not enter production. It was strengthened to take a 1,480-hp Merlin XX, and had clipped wings of 30 feet 6 inches (9.3 m) span. The Spitfire IV tested a Rolls-Royce Griffon IIB installation. With the introduction of the PR IV, the Griffon-engined Mark IV became the Mark XX. The Mark IV/XX prototype also had the mock-up of a six-cannon wing armament.

The Spitfire V, the next major production model, entered service in February 1941. This was powered by a 1,440-hp Merlin 45 series engine, and was the first model to be fitted with tropical equipment for service in the Mediterranean and Middle Eastern theatres, and the first to be used as a fighter-bomber, with one 500- or two 250-lb (227- or 113-kg) bombs. Production of the Spitfire V totalled 6,479 aircraft, in three major versions: the VA with eight machine-guns, the VB with two cannon and four machine-guns, and the VC with the Universal wing, capable of accepting either A or B armament, or four cannon. With the decline of Axis air strength, the Spitfire V was used increasingly for

Left: RAF groundcrew at work on three Spitfire VC fighter-bombers of 253 Squadron in the Middle East theatre. Note the details of the engine installation, made visible by the removal of the Merlin, and the belt of 20-mm cannon shells ready for loading into the ammunition tank in the starboard wing. Visible under the nose of the middle aircraft is the Vokes air-filter so essential for operations in dusty climates to prevent the engines from wearing out too soon

Supermarine Spitfire IA
The aircraft illustrated is machine D of 603 'City of Edinburgh' Squadron, Royal Auxiliary Air Force. The squadron was based at Dyce, Hornchurch and Montrose during the Battle of Britain. Camouflage is the standard Ministry of Aircraft Production Pattern No 1, in the Temperate Land Scheme of 1940, with Dark Green and Dark Earth upper surfaces and an unusual under surface finish of white. National insignia are normal
Type single-seat fighter
Engine one Rolls-Royce Merlin III twelve-cylinder liquid-cooled inline, 1,030 hp at take-off
Armament eight 0.303-inch (7.7-mm) Browning machine-guns with 300 rounds per gun
Maximum speed 362 mph at 19,000 feet (583 km/h at 5,791 m)
Cruising speed 315 mph at 20,000 feet (507 km/h at 6,096 m)
Initial climb rate 2,530 fpm (771 m/minute)
Climb 9 minutes 24 seconds to 20,000 feet (6,096 m)
Service ceiling 31,900 feet (9,723 m)
Range 395 miles (636 km) normal; 575 miles at 210 mph (925 km at 338 km/h)
Weights 4,810 lbs (2,182 kg) empty; 5,784 lbs (2,624 kg) loaded
Span 36 feet 10 inches (11.23 m)
Length 29 feet 11 inches (9.12 m)
Height 8 feet 10 inches (2.69 m)
Wing area 242 square feet (22.48 m²)

low-level attacks. In this capacity it was fitted with Merlin 45M, 50M, or 55M engines and clipped wings of 32 feet 2 inches (9.80 m). Other Spitfire variants of this time were the production versions of the F and G PR models as the PR VI and PR VII. An increasingly difficult problem for the RAF from 1941 onwards was that of intercepting high-altitude German raiders and reconnaissance aircraft. To meet this threat the Spitfire VI was developed with a Merlin 47 engine of 1,415 hp at 14,000 feet (4,267 m) and a pressurized cockpit. Production of the Spitfire VI, which could reach 40,000 feet (12,192 m), totalled 100 aircraft. The wingtips were extended, to give a span of 40 feet 2 inches (12.24 m).

The Spitfire VI was essentially an interim model, the Spitfire VII being intended as the definitive high-altitude interceptor. The first of the 140 built flew in April 1942. The Mark VII used the 1,700-hp Merlin 60 series of engines, with a two-stage supercharger. The new engine needed a revised cooling system and the two underwing radiators were made symmetrical. The area of the fin and rudder also had to be increased to compensate for the increased area forward of the centre of gravity, resulting in a wider and slightly more pointed fin and rudder. The FR VII fighter-reconnaissance model was derived from the PR IV and was powered by a Merlin 45 or 46, with an armament of eight machine-guns. Some 16 of these FR VII aircraft were later converted to low-level PR XIIIs, with 1,645-hp Merlin 32 engines.

The modifications incorporated in the Mark VII, with the exception of the pressurized cockpit, were also incorporated in the Spitfire VIII. This was basically similar to the Mark VII in function, but intended for operations at lower altitudes. The type was introduced into service in August 1943, and 1,658 were built in three major versions: the F VIII with standard wings and a Merlin 61 or 63 engine, the HF VIII with extended wings and a Merlin 70 engine, and the LF VIII with clipped wings and a Merlin 66.

With the introduction of the Focke-Wulf in 1941 the Spitfire V was definitely outclassed, and Supermarine gave thought to a radically improved version of the Spitfire. Pending deliveries of the Mark VII and VIII, an interim model based on the Spitfire VC, using the Merlin 60 series of engines, was developed. This became the Mark IX, and despite the fact that it was intended only as a stopgap, 5,665 were built, making it the most numerous Spitfire mark. It was built in F, LF, and HF versions, with only the engines distinguishing the three sub-marks. The Mark IX was an improvement on the Mark V, but was still not quite a match for the Fw 190. Later in the Mark IX's production, the C wing was replaced by the E wing, with the cannon

moved outboard and the four 0.303-inch (7.7-mm) machine-guns replaced by a pair of 0.5-inch (12.7-mm) guns. The PR X and PR XI – the former with, and the latter without, a pressurized cockpit – were developed from the Mark IX.

The final version of the Spitfire to be powered by a Merlin engine was the LF XVI. This had a Packard-built Merlin 266, enlarged vertical tail surfaces, and a bubble canopy for the cockpit, together with a cut-down rear fuselage. This last greatly improved the pilot's field of vision. A total of 1,054 Mark XVIs was built with C or E wings.

It had been intended to number Griffon-engined Spitfires from XX onwards, but in the event the first Griffon version was the Spitfire XII. This was based on the Mark V, and 100 were built. The type was powered by a Griffon III or IV engine rated for low-altitude work, and was intended as a counter to Fw 190 sneak-raiders over southern England. The Spitfire XII was put into service from the spring of 1943. Tests with a Griffon-engined Mark VIII had proved so encouraging that another interim model, the Spitfire XIV powered by a Griffon 65, was produced, entering service in January 1944. This had the vertical tail surfaces widened still further, and had either a C or an E wing. Mark XIV production totalled 957. A further development of the Mark XIV idea led to the Mark XVIII, with fuselage and undercarriage strengthened to allow more fuel to be carried. By the end of the war 100 F XVIII and 200 FR XVIII models had been built. The Griffon-engined PR XIX was based on the Spitfire XIV with a Mark VC type of wing.

With the Mark 21 the Spitfire underwent a radical change, losing its elliptical wing plan-form for an aerodynamically superior wing allowing higher diving speeds. The Mark 22 was basically similar, but had a cut-down rear fuselage and a bubble canopy. The Mark 21 appeared in February 1944 and entered service just before the end of hostilities. The Mark 22 appeared in March 1945, and 278 were built. The last version, the Mark 24, appeared after the war, 54 being built. Total Spitfire production reached 20,334 before it ceased in October 1947.

Naval versions of the Spitfire were also built, but the outward retracting undercarriage, with its inherently narrow track, always proved a weakness. The Seafire IB was derived from the Spitfire VB, the Seafire IIC from the Spitfire VC, the Seafire III was the first model with folding wings, the Seafire XV had a Griffon engine but was otherwise similar to the Seafire III, and the final wartime Seafire was the Mark XVII, basically a Seafire XV with a cut-down rear fuselage and bubble canopy.

Supermarine LF VB
The aircraft illustrated is finished in standard Ministry of Aircraft Production Pattern No 1 in the Middle East Scheme of Dark Earth and Middle Stone upper surfaces and Sky Blue under surfaces. The 18-inch Sky Type 'S' fighter band round the rear fuselage was not used in the Middle East. National insignia are standard
Type single-seat fighter and fighter-bomber
Engine one Rolls-Royce Merlin 50M twelve-cylinder liquid-cooled inline, 1,585 hp at 2,750 feet (838 m)
Armament defensive: two 20-mm Hispano cannon with 60 or 120 rounds per gun and four 0.303-inch Browning machine-guns with 350 rounds per gun offensive: up to 500 lbs (227 kg) of bombs
Maximum speeds 357 mph at 6,000 feet (575 km/h at 1,829 m); 332 mph (534 km/h) at sea level
Cruising speed 272 mph at 5,000 feet (438 km/h at 1,524 m)
Initial climb rate 4,750 fpm (1,448 m/minute)
Climb 7 minutes to 20,000 feet (6,096 m)
Service ceiling 35,500 feet (10,821 m)
Range 470 miles (756 km) on internal fuel; 1,135 miles (1,827 km) with drop-tank
Weights 5,050 lbs (2,291 kg) empty; 6,650 lbs (3,016 kg) loaded; 6,710 lbs (3,044 kg) gross
Span 32 feet 2 inches (9.80 m)
Length 29 feet 11 inches (9.12 m)
Height 9 feet 11 inches (3.02 m)
Wing area 231 square feet (21.46 m²)

Supermarine Seafire III
The aircraft illustrated is finished in the Temperate Sea Scheme of Dark Slate Grey and Extra Dark Sea Grey upper surfaces with white under surfaces. The national insignia are those used by the British Pacific Fleet, with the markings placed as on American aircraft. Note that the roundels contain no red, to avoid confusion with the Japanese *hinomaru* marking
Type single-seat naval fighter and fighter-bomber
Engine one Rolls-Royce Merlin 55 twelve-cylinder liquid-cooled inline, 1,470 hp at take-off
Armament defensive: two 20-mm Hispano cannon with 120 rounds per gun in the wings and four 0.303-inch (7.7-mm) Browning machine-guns with 350 rounds per gun in the wings offensive: up to 500 lbs (227 kg) of bombs
Maximum speed 352 mph at 12,250 feet (567 km/h at 3,734 m)
Cruising speed 218 mph at 20,000 feet (351 km/h at 6,096 m)

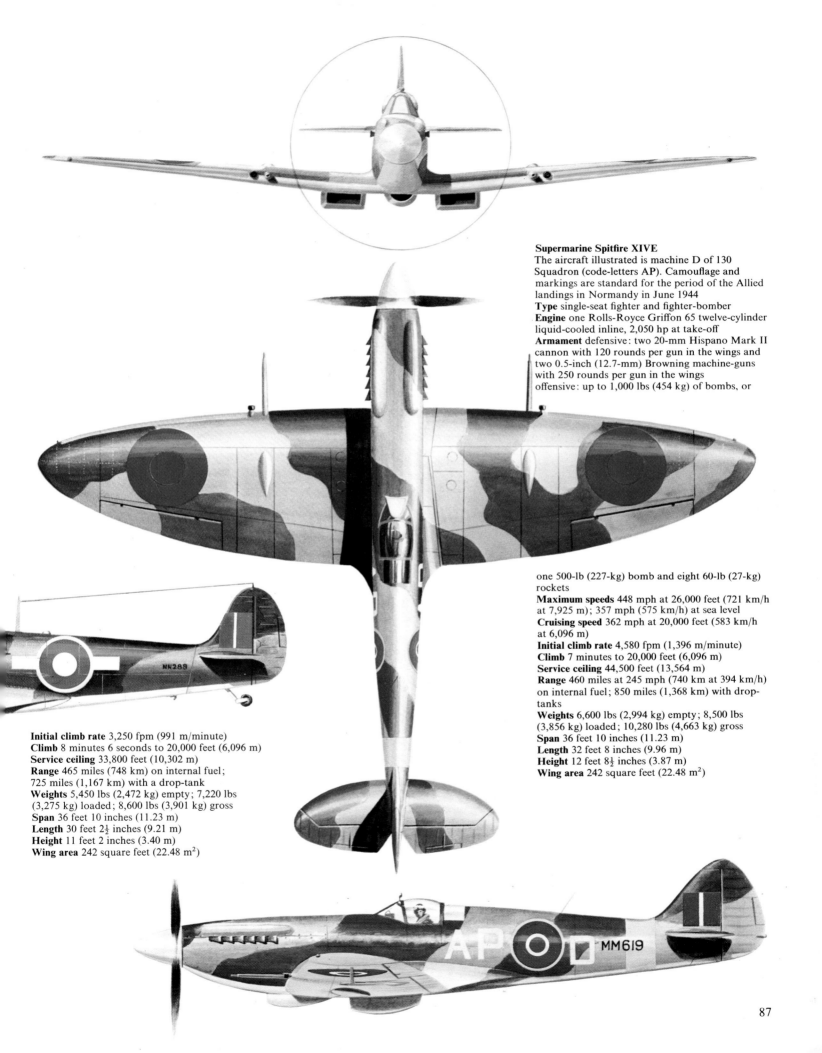

Supermarine Spitfire XIVE
The aircraft illustrated is machine D of 130
Squadron (code-letters AP). Camouflage and
markings are standard for the period of the Allied
landings in Normandy in June 1944
Type single-seat fighter and fighter-bomber
Engine one Rolls-Royce Griffon 65 twelve-cylinder
liquid-cooled inline, 2,050 hp at take-off
Armament defensive: two 20-mm Hispano Mark II
cannon with 120 rounds per gun in the wings and
two 0.5-inch (12.7-mm) Browning machine-guns
with 250 rounds per gun in the wings
offensive: up to 1,000 lbs (454 kg) of bombs, or
one 500-lb (227-kg) bomb and eight 60-lb (27-kg)
rockets
Maximum speeds 448 mph at 26,000 feet (721 km/h
at 7,925 m); 357 mph (575 km/h) at sea level
Cruising speed 362 mph at 20,000 feet (583 km/h
at 6,096 m)
Initial climb rate 4,580 fpm (1,396 m/minute)
Climb 7 minutes to 20,000 feet (6,096 m)
Service ceiling 44,500 feet (13,564 m)
Range 460 miles at 245 mph (740 km at 394 km/h)
on internal fuel; 850 miles (1,368 km) with drop-
tanks
Weights 6,600 lbs (2,994 kg) empty; 8,500 lbs
(3,856 kg) loaded; 10,280 lbs (4,663 kg) gross
Span 36 feet 10 inches (11.23 m)
Length 32 feet 8 inches (9.96 m)
Height 12 feet 8½ inches (3.87 m)
Wing area 242 square feet (22.48 m²)

Initial climb rate 3,250 fpm (991 m/minute)
Climb 8 minutes 6 seconds to 20,000 feet (6,096 m)
Service ceiling 33,800 feet (10,302 m)
Range 465 miles (748 km) on internal fuel;
725 miles (1,167 km) with a drop-tank
Weights 5,450 lbs (2,472 kg) empty; 7,220 lbs
(3,275 kg) loaded; 8,600 lbs (3,901 kg) gross
Span 36 feet 10 inches (11.23 m)
Length 30 feet 2½ inches (9.21 m)
Height 11 feet 2 inches (3.40 m)
Wing area 242 square feet (22.48 m²)

FRANCE

A Potez 631 three-seat fighter of the Armée de l'Air patrols over the English Channel in the early months of the war. This aircraft, the fighter version of the basic Potez 63 series, was one of France's more successful aircraft

The history of the French Air Force, or *Armée de l'Air*, in the 20 years between the two world wars is a strange one, marked by the improbable combination of fear for renewed German militarism and of complacency about France's ability to cope with such a problem. The fear was best exemplified by the construction of the 'impregnable' Maginot Line to shield France from direct invasion from Germany, and the complacency by the trusting belief that Germany would not once again outflank the French defences by moving through one or more of the neutral states along France's northern frontiers. The complacency, coupled with the usual reluctance of civilian governments to 'lavish' money on their armed forces, also meant that the quality of personnel and *matériel* slowly declined in the 1920s and early 1930s.

The French air force suffered the same decline as the air forces of the other victorious Allies in the aftermath of World War I – there was neither the money nor the inclination to support what had been the world's second largest air force.

Aircraft types which had been in service or under development at the end of World War I soldiered on into the late 1920s, whilst advanced new types were built in limited numbers as record-breaking and racing aircraft. But by the early 1930s the French had begun to lose touch with progress in military aircraft; and the bombers of the small-scale re-equipment programme of this time have the distinction of being amongst the ugliest flying machines ever built and barely mediocre in performance. The Amiot 143, for example, was an extraordinarily unattractive, slab-sided twin-engined machine and intended to serve in the triple role of bomber, fighter and reconnaissance aircraft. Equally improbable as a combat type was the Farman F221 and with it the modified Farman F222. Completing a trio of ugly French bombers in the early 1930s was the Potez 540.

Fighter developments of the same period were slightly better. The aircraft of the Dewoitine D37 series were parasol-winged monoplanes with maximum speeds in the order of 239 mph

(385 km/h); the Dewoitine D500 series all had a low-wing monoplane configuration with a fixed undercarriage of extremely wide track, and could reach speeds of 224 to 250 mph (360 to 400 km/h); the Loire 46 had a gull monoplane wing, and was capable of 255 mph (410 km/h); and the Morane-Saulnier MS 225 was another parasol-wing monoplane, with a top speed of 199 mph (320 km/h).

These aircraft formed the backbone of the French air force at the time that most other European powers were beginning to develop more sophisticated bombers, using the latest structural techniques and a fair measure of streamlining. In the field of fighter aircraft other powers were revealing the prototypes of fast cantilever monoplanes with retractable undercarriages and enclosed cockpits. The one advantage that French fighters of the period enjoyed was cannon armament, a legacy of French interest in such weapons as armament for both fighters and bombers in World War I.

The French realized how far behind the rest

of the world they had slipped during 1935 and 1936, when some 80 per cent of the French aircraft industry was nationalized. A crash programme to develop new types was immediately put in hand, and this produced some advanced and extremely attractive types before World War II. Unfortunately, however, the effort to revitalize France's defence potential with new *matériel* was seriously hampered by lack of strict control at the top. Instead of ordering, for each type of aircraft needed, a small number of prototypes, which could then be tested and evaluated quickly and rigorously, the French called for multitudes of prototypes, the testing and evaluation of which were pursued slowly and lethargically. Thus in the time during which Great Britain and Germany tested and got into production a new type, the French were still insisting on numerous small changes in the several prototypes under evaluation. Naturally enough this meant that although the air force finally received excellent aircraft, quantity production had started too late to enable the

aircraft industry to deliver worthwhile numbers of the new types before the crushing of France in May and June 1940. This was one of the reasons why France had to go to the United States with a considerable number of orders for American combat aircraft. Few of these could be delivered in time, however, and the majority were then diverted to Great Britain.

As noted above, France's final rearmament led to some first rate types. Of the bombers the best were the Bloch 175 twin-engined light bomber, the superlative Lioré et Olivier 451 twin-engined medium bomber with a top speed of 311 mph at 18,044 feet (500 km/h at 5,486 m), and the sturdy Potez 631 twin-engined light-bomber, fighter and tactical reconnaissance machine. Of the fighters the best were the Bloch 150 series low-wing monoplanes (principally the 151, 152, 155, and finally the Bloch 157, which was built only in prototype form, but had a performance years in advance of most other contemporary fighters), the Dewoitine D 520, the Morane-Saulnier MS 406, and several other

aircraft types that attained only prototype status.

Few of these types attained widespread service use except the Morane-Saulnier MS 406 and the Potez 631, for the reasons mentioned above. Thus although French pilots and crews fought valiantly against the Germans, they had little or no chance of halting the Germans, who by 1940 had the benefits of a centralized aircraft industry, and aircrew experienced in the combat over Spain, Poland, Denmark and Norway. Quite apart from their numerical and *matériel* inferiority compared with the Germans, the French also suffered from the grave difficulties posed by constant retreat, lack of adequately trained replacements, and the inevitable shortage of spares for aircraft and engines, the last a result of slow production and too many types of combat aircraft in front-line service. This last situation was partially remedied by the Vichy French air force, which continued to operate in the unoccupied zone of France from June 1940 onwards, and in the French colonies overseas controlled by the Vichy government.

Dewoitine 520

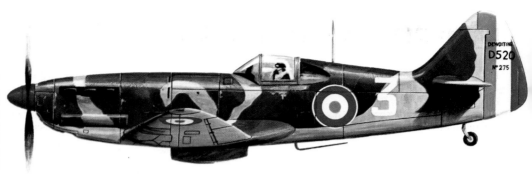

Although it was slightly slower than the Messer-schmitt Bf 109E and the Supermarine Spitfire I, the Dewoitine D 520 fighter had a slight edge over the German fighter in manoeuvrability while the British aircraft was itself slightly less agile than the Bf 109E. Despite this agility and an adequate armament, the Dewoitine 520 was destined to play a relatively minor role in World War II. The reason for this is simple: the development of new types of aircraft in France started so late that few production models had reached the French air force by the time of France's capitulation in June 1940.

Design work on the D 520 began in 1936 under a team led by Emile Dewoitine. Although the initial design failed to win the approval of the French Air Ministry, it was reworked in 1937 to suit a fighter requirement issued in January of that year. Three prototypes were ordered, the first flying in October 1938. This had an 890-hp 12Y21 engine driving a two-bladed wooden propeller and radiators in the wings. During the course of the trials, the wing radiators were replaced by a ventral one, and the two-bladed propeller by a three-bladed one which improved speed considerably. The vertical tail surfaces were also enlarged for greater longitudinal stability. The type was ordered into production in March 1939.

It had been planned to use the 1,100-hp 12Y51 engine on production aircraft, but the non-availability of this engine meant that the 910-hp 12Y45 had to be used. The first production aircraft, which flew in November 1939, was atypical in having a 12Y31 engine, a one-piece curved windscreen, a tailskid and an armament of only two drum-fed machine-guns in the wings. The second production machine was finished to full service standards. By the time of the German invasion of the West in May 1940 the production rate of D 520 fighters had reached 100 aircraft per month, but only one unit, *Groupe de Chasse*

I/3, was operational with it. Other units were re-equipped with the D 520 during the campaign, but it was not enough to sway the outcome of the battle of France. Despite their hurried entry into combat, the D 520s of the French air force did well. They were credited with a total of 108 confirmed kills and 39 probables against the loss in combat of 54 of their own number.

By the time of the French surrender in June 1940, some 437 D 520 fighters had been built, and production of the D 521 had been scheduled to start. The D 520 was also fitted with a 1,030-hp Merlin III engine, with which it attained 354 mph (570 km/h) at 16,240 feet (4,950 m), but the project was cancelled in November 1939. Other D 520 derivatives were: the 12Z89*ter*-engined D 524 of June 1940, which attained 382 mph (615 km/h); the 12Y51-engined D 523 of May–June 1940; the D 520 Z of September–December 1941, with ejector exhaust stubs, an improved undercarriage, and a heat exchanger instead of the oil cooler; the 1,600-hp 12Z-engined SE 520Z of February 1943, which never flew; the 12Ycrs-engined D 550 racer of June 1939–February 1940, which reached 435 mph (700 km/h); and the D 551 of 1940–1941, a military version of the D 550.

The D 520 continued to serve with the Vichy French air force both in France and overseas, where it was met by Allied types in subsequent campaigns. Production resumed for Vichy in August 1941, and an additional 349 D 520s were built before production ceased in December 1943.

Dewoitine D 520

The aircraft illustrated is the 275th production aircraft, as indicated by the markings in black over the rudder stripes. The camouflage is a mottling of dark green and dark brown over a grey basic finish. The national insignia are standard, and it is worth noting that roundels were only applied to the fuselage sides of French aircraft from the spring of 1940, after British requests. The hook-shaped object under the fuselage below the cockpit is a semi-retractable radio aerial

Type single-seat fighter
Engine one Hispano-Suiza 12Y45 twelve-cylinder liquid-cooled inline, 930 hp at take-off and 850 hp at sea level
Armament one-20-mm Hispano-Suiza HS 404 cannon with 60 rounds firing through the propeller shaft and four 7.5-mm MAC 1934 M1939 machine-guns with 500 rounds per gun in the wings
Maximum speeds 332 mph at 18,040 feet (535 km/h at 5,500 m); 264 mph (425 km/h) at sea level
Cruising speed 310 mph at 13,123 feet (485 km/h at 4,000 m)
Initial climb rate 2,362 fpm (720 m/minute)
Climb 8 minutes 59 seconds to 19,685 feet (6,000 m)
Service ceiling 33,628 feet (10,250 m)
Range 553 miles at 230 mph at 16,732 feet (890 km at 370 km/h at 5,100 m) normal; 956 miles at 230 mph at 16,730 feet (1,540 km at 370 km/h at 5,100 m) maximum
Weights 4,679 lbs (2,122 kg) empty; 5,900 lbs (2,676 kg) loaded; 6,144 lbs (2,787 kg) gross
Span 33 feet 5½ inches (10.12 m)
Length 28 feet 8½ inches (8.75 m)
Height 8 feet 5 inches (2.57 m)
Wing area 171.886 square feet (15.97 m²)

Morane-Saulnier 406

In terms of numbers, the Morane-Saulnier MS 406 was the most important fighter operated by the *Armée de l'Air*, or French air force, during World War II. But although it was a relatively advanced aircraft at the time of its introduction, the design was beginning to show its age when it entered combat with German fighters.

In 1934 the French air ministry issued a requirement for a single-engined monoplane fighter to replace the three fighters then in service. The Morane-Saulnier offering was the MS 405, which was powered by a Hispano-Suiza 12Ygrs engine and first flew in August 1935. Trials against the other contenders were carried out in the spring of 1936, and the MS 405 performed well, attaining a speed of 298 mph (480 km/h). Later in the year the MS 405 was fitted with the improved 12Ycrs engine, and this model was finally selected for large-scale production in July 1937. In August 1936, however, Morane-Saulnier had been instructed to deliver a pre-production batch of 15 MS 405 fighters and these were produced between February and December 1939. A number of engine, equipment and structural alterations were tested in this batch. The semi-retractable radiator of the other models was dispensed with on the 12th and 13th models, and this type, redesignated MS 408, was built under licence in Switzerland.

The definitive model, redesignated MS 406, was finally evolved, and this was ordered into production in March 1938. The first example flew in June 1938. Production was slow to gather momentum, because of the nationalization of the French aircraft industry in 1936, and the limited production capacity of the Morane-Saulnier factory at Puteaux, which meant that major components had to be subcontracted and then delivered to a government factory at Bouguenais or the parent factory at Puteaux for final assembly. With the arrival of further new types, the Bouguenais facility was turned over to other designs at the end of 1939, and production slowed down still further. Nevertheless, by the end of the French campaign, 1,098 MS 406 fighters had been delivered to the *Armée de l'Air*. The only other French type to pass the 1,000 mark in production during this period was the Potez 63.

The MS 406 enjoyed mixed fortunes between September 1939 and June 1940. Its major failing in combat was its lack of speed, which enabled many German bombers to outrun it. Manoeuvrability was good, however, as numerous German pilots who tried to dogfight with experienced MS 406 pilots discovered to their cost. In all, of the fighters operating with the *Armée de l'Air* during the battle of France (MS 406, Dewoitine D 520, Bloch MB 152, and Curtiss H 75), the MS 406 was the least successful. About 150 MS 406s were lost in combat, while the type's victory tally included 191 confirmed and 89 probable kills – a poor ratio of losses to kills for a first-line fighter. Moreover, the high ratio of probables to confirmed indicates that the armament of the MS 406 was inadequate. The type continued in service with the Vichy French air force after the armistice, but it was relegated to training duties after November 1942.

It is worth noting that the best and most successful MS 406s were not French ones, but those delivered to Finland. Some 30 had been delivered by France in January 1940, and a further 57 captured aircraft were delivered by Germany from August 1940. Re-engined with the Russian 1,100-hp Klimov M-105P inline in a neat cowling, these 'Super-Moranes', as they were dubbed, were 28 mph (45 km/h) faster than the French model, and possessed outstanding climb rate and ceiling (4,921 feet per minute and 39,370 feet or 1,500 m/minute and 12,000 m). MS 406 fighters were also exported by France to Switzerland and Turkey. Planned deliveries to Poland, Lithuania, Yugoslavia and China were not made.

The final development of the MS 406 was the MS 410, 75 of which were produced as conversions from the MS 406. The later type had four belt-fed machine-guns in the wings instead of two drum-fed guns. All but one were converted after the fall of France, and several were supplied to Croatia.

Never more than a sound design, the MS 406 was a mediocre fighter. It lacked the aerodynamic refinements of contemporary fighters, was underpowered, and lacked a sufficiently heavy armament. Only as the Finnish 'Super-Morane' did the type really become a useful warplane.

Morane-Saulnier MS 406
The aircraft illustrated is the 192nd production MS 406 Cl, as indicated by the markings over the rudder stripes. 'Cl' shows that the type was a single-seat fighter (*avion de chasse*). The markings at the bottom of the rudder show the aircraft's weights and the octane of the fuel to be used. Camouflage is standard for all MS 406 aircraft except the first 100 built: dark brown and dark green on the upper surfaces, and a light grey-blue on the under surfaces. The national insignia are standard. The fuselage roundel was added in January 1940. After the armistice, a white outline was painted round the fuselage roundel, together with a white line along each side of the fuselage. Later the aircraft of the Vichy French air force were painted with horizontal stripes of yellow and red round the nose and tail, together with an oblique tricolour on the wings
Type single-seat fighter
Engine one Hispano-Suiza 12Y31 twelve-cylinder liquid-cooled inline, 860 hp at take-off and at 13,123 feet (4,000 m)
Armament one 20-mm Hispano-Suiza HS 59 or 404 cannon with 60 rounds firing through the propeller shaft and two 7.5-mm MAC 1934 machine-guns with 300 rounds per gun in the wings
Maximum speeds 304 mph at 14,700 feet (490 km/h at 4,480 m); 248 mph (400 km/h) at sea level
Cruising speed 248 mph at 16,404 feet (400 km/h at 5,000 m)
Initial climb rate 3,543 fpm (1,080 m/minute)
Climb 9 minutes 3 seconds to 19,685 feet (6,000 m)
Service ceiling 32,808 feet (10,000 m)
Range 497 miles (800 km) on internal fuel; 932 miles (1,500 km) with external fuel
Weights 4,177 lbs (1,895 kg) empty; 5,610 lbs (2,545 kg) loaded; 6,000 lbs (2,722 kg) gross
Span 34 feet 9¾ inches (10.61 m)
Length 26 feet 9¼ inches (8.08 m)
Height 9 feet 3¾ inches (2.84 m)
Wing area 172.223 square feet (16.00 m²)

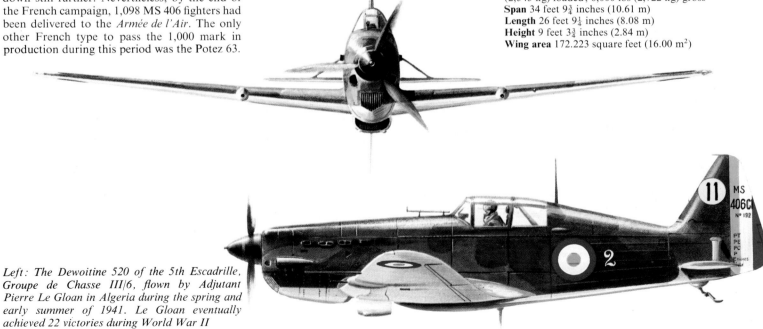

Left: The Dewoitine 520 of the 5th Escadrille, Groupe de Chasse III/6, flown by Adjutant Pierre Le Gloan in Algeria during the spring and early summer of 1941. Le Gloan eventually achieved 22 victories during World War II

THE SOVIET UNION

As with all things Russian, the nature of the Russian air forces in World War II, or the 'Great Patriotic War' as it is known to the communist world, was strongly affected by the revolution of November 1917. Had it not been for this revolution, and the rise to absolute power of the Communist Party, the Russian air force might well have stagnated into the mediocre force most Westerners thought it was.

The Imperial Russian Flying Corps was the basis upon which the Reds built. The Imperial force had flown a mixed bag of Russian and foreign types, in about equal proportions, and this policy was adhered to in the years immediately after the successful conclusion of the wars against the 'White' Russians and 'Interventionist' armies. The policy meant that the Russians kept abreast of technological advances in the West, while building up their own design and production capacities. Engines were imported from Great Britain, France and the

United States, and were placed in widespread licence production with modifications to suit them to Russian manufacturing techniques and climatic conditions. This programme led to the developed of a series of cheap, light and very reliable radial and inline aircraft engines, most of them slightly more powerful than equivalent Western engines.

In the late 1920s and early 1930s the Russians, in common with Great Britain, France, Italy and the United States, placed great store in record-breaking aircraft as a means of experimenting with the latest technological advances without the cost of large-scale production of fighting aircraft that might have been rendered obsolete quickly in an era of rapid advances in aerodynamics and structures. In particular the Russians concentrated on long-distance and high-altitude machines, with their emphasis on engine reliability and performance. At the same time heavy bomber development – culminating

in the vast Tupolev ANT-20 of 1930 – led the world in the practical application of strategic bombing theories that had become voguish since World War I. But with the decision to concentrate on a tactical air force in the late 1930s, development of heavy bombers was dropped, with the exception of the Petlyakov Pe-8 during World War II.

It is worth noting how adventurous the Russians were in experimenting with novel tactical ideas. For example, schemes for heavy bombers to carry their own defending fighters with them on long-range missions were tested in the early 1930s with the ANT-6. This aircraft could carry up to five fighters, two on top and three below the wings, but the idea was dropped after successful tests as only superb fighter pilots could land back on their parent aircraft.

At the same time as she was experimenting with the idea of a heavy bomber fleet, Russia was also leading the world in the introduction

of the single-seat, low-wing monoplane fighter, which was to become the standard during World War II. Polikarpov led the way with the I-16, which the incredulous West immediately assumed was derived from the latest American design, the P-26. The American design, which entered service as the Russian fighter was being tested, was a far inferior machine, having a fixed undercarriage and a lower performance. The I-17 derivative of the I-16, with a neatly cowled inline engine, also led the world in the development of its type. Despite their advanced designs, however, these Russian fighters received little but derision at the Western aeronautical *salons* at which they were exhibited. Western experts scorned the poor workmanship of their construction but failed to see the laudable advances in their concepts, and totally ignored the fact that their simple, robust structures were ideally suited to swift production by semi-skilled workers and for operations from poor airfields in appal-

ling climatic conditions. Indeed the Germans were to regret the sophistication of their aircraft with the onset of Russian winters.

Unlike most countries, Russia saw a place for both monoplane and biplane fighters in her inventory, realizing that the agile biplane might prove very useful in short-range battlefield defence. The validity of the two-fighter concept was proved in the Spanish Civil War, in which several Russian types, including the I-16 and the I-15 series of biplanes, received a useful blooding. By the time of Russia's forced entry into World War II, however, the biplane was being phased out of front-line service.

Reassessment of the relationship between the Red Army and the Red Air Force in the 1930s led to the conclusion that what was needed of the latter was quick, powerful tactical support for the former. Fighters should be capable of acting as light bombers with rockets and cannon, whilst being able to hold their own against enemy

machines at medium and low altitudes, and a new generation of medium bombers and attack aircraft should be developed. The Russians found the right fighters in the Lavochkin and Yakovlev series of machines, the bombers in the Ilyushin DB-3, the Tupolev SB-2 and the Petlyakov Pe-2, and the ground-attack aircraft in the Ilyushin Il-2.

Once operations against the exceptionally able German *Luftwaffe* had disposed of its obsolete and obsolescent aircraft, and once combat had started to improve the performance of Russian pilots, the Red Air Force rapidly became probably the best, and certainly the largest, tactical air force yet produced. And whilst in absolute terms Russian aircraft might have been inferior to their Western counterparts, they were ideally suited for the tasks for which the Russians intended them, and therefore as useful in combat as the 'better' and more expensive Western aircraft.

Ilyushin Il-2 Shturmovik

The Ilyshin Il-2 *Shturmovik* was the most celebrated, and perhaps the best, aircraft used by the Red Air Force during World War II. So successful was the type that the designation *Shturmovik*, meaning ground-attack aircraft, was applied only to the Il-2, in much the same way as the epithet *Stuka*, meaning dive-bomber, was applied only to the Junkers 87.

Design work on ground-attack aircraft began in Russia during 1930, but so stringent were the provisions of the requirement that no suitable aircraft was forthcoming. The main reason for this was that while the demands for protection and firepower could be met, those for high speed and manoeuvrability could not with the fairly low-powered engines then available. The first aircraft to approach the performance required was Sergei V Ilyushin's *TsKB*-55 of 1938 (*TsKB* stands for *Tsentralnoye Konstruktorskoye Byuro* or Central Design Bureau.) From this the design team evolved the *TsKB*-57 late in 1939. This can be considered the true progenitor of the Il-2. Initial flight trials, however, proved disappointing as the 1,370-hp Mikulin AM 35 was too low-powered for so massive an aircraft. A far more satisfactory performance was achieved with the 1,680-hp AM 38 engine in October 1940.

The most interesting feature of the *TsKB*-57 was its excellent armour protection. This in fact formed the basis of the structure of the forward fuselage, and consisted of an armour-plate 'bath', between 5 and 12 mm thick, forming the bottom and sides of the fuselage between the rear of the cockpit and the front of the engine. Armament consisted of two 20-mm cannon, two 7.62-mm machine-guns, eight 82-mm rockets, and up to 882 lbs (400 kg) of bombs. The *TsKB*-57 was ordered into production as the Il-2 in March 1941. Only 249 had been delivered by the time of the German invasion in June 1941, but these proved very useful in hampering the progress of the German armoured columns. But it proved

impossible to halt the German advance before the winter of 1941–1942, and in the evacuation of Russian industry from western Russia to the Ural mountains area, production of the Il-2 ceased for two months.

By the early summer of 1942 certain complaints were being voiced about the Il-2. The two most important of these were the lack of rear defence at a time of almost total German air superiority, and the increasing inadequacy of the 20-mm cannon against the latest German armoured vehicles. The first complaint was dealt with by the addition of a second crew member, a rear gunner, armed with a single 12.7-mm BS or UBT machine-gun. The gunner was located behind the pilot, and to protect him the armoured bath was extended to the rear. The second complaint was remedied by the replacement (already tested on the Il-2 Modified) of the 20-mm cannon with 23-mm VJa cannon, which had a considerably higher muzzle velocity, and therefore penetrative power. As the weight of the aircraft was increased, the power of the engine was boosted to 1,750 hp by increasing the compression ratio.

With these modifications the new type entered service in August 1942 as the definitive Il-2m3. (The 'm3' stood for model 3.) As the addition of the gunner's cockpit improved the aerodynamic lines of the fuselage, top speed rose to 252 mph (405 km/h) despite the increase in loaded weight. In parallel with the Il-2m3 was produced the Il-2U trainer, with duplicated controls in the rear cockpit.

The main armament needed revision again in 1943 to deal with improved German armour. The VJa cannon were therefore replaced by a pair of 37-mm N-37 or P-37 cannon with good armour-piercing capabilities; a container for 200 small 5½-lb (2.5-kg) hollow-charge anti-tank bombs was installed, as was a grenade-launcher which fired grenades on small parachutes in

front of pursuing aircraft. These modifications were incorporated in the Il-2m3 (Modified), which entered service just in time to wreak terrible devastation on the latest German *PzKpfw* V and VI tanks in the Battle of Kursk in July 1943.

At the same time structural modifications were effected to the basic airframe. The original type, which had featured a wooden rear fuselage, was now designated the Basic type. A new structure of metal, introduced in the spring of 1944, was used on the Il-2m3 (Modified). This also had a rear bulkhead for the armoured bath in place of the gunner's previous front and back plates. During 1944 provision was also made for the carriage of 132-mm instead of 82-mm rockets for use against strongpoints, and an increased bomb-load of 1,323 lbs (600 kg) in the wing bays. The Il-2 was also used by the Red Naval Air Force as the Il-2T. This carried a 21.7-inch (55-cm) torpedo beneath the fuselage. The final development of the Il-2 occurred after the end of the war.

In combat the Il-2 *Shturmovik* proved a devastating weapon. It usually operated at extremely low altitudes, so that its hail of cannon shells and rockets hit the target horizontally, taking the Axis forces completely by surprise. The most favoured tactic for Il-2 units was the 'circle of death'. In this the unit would cross the lines and attack the target from the rear, flying past it towards the lines and then circling back to attack it again until it was destroyed or all the ammunition expended. In this tactic the target could be kept under continued fire for up to 30 minutes. To the Russians the Il-2 was the *Ilyusha*, the Flying Tank, the Flying Infantryman, or the Hunchback. To the Germans the Il-2 was, with very great justification, the *schwarz Tod* or Black Death.

Below: Line-up of the Red Air Force's superlative Il-2m3 on a Russian airfield

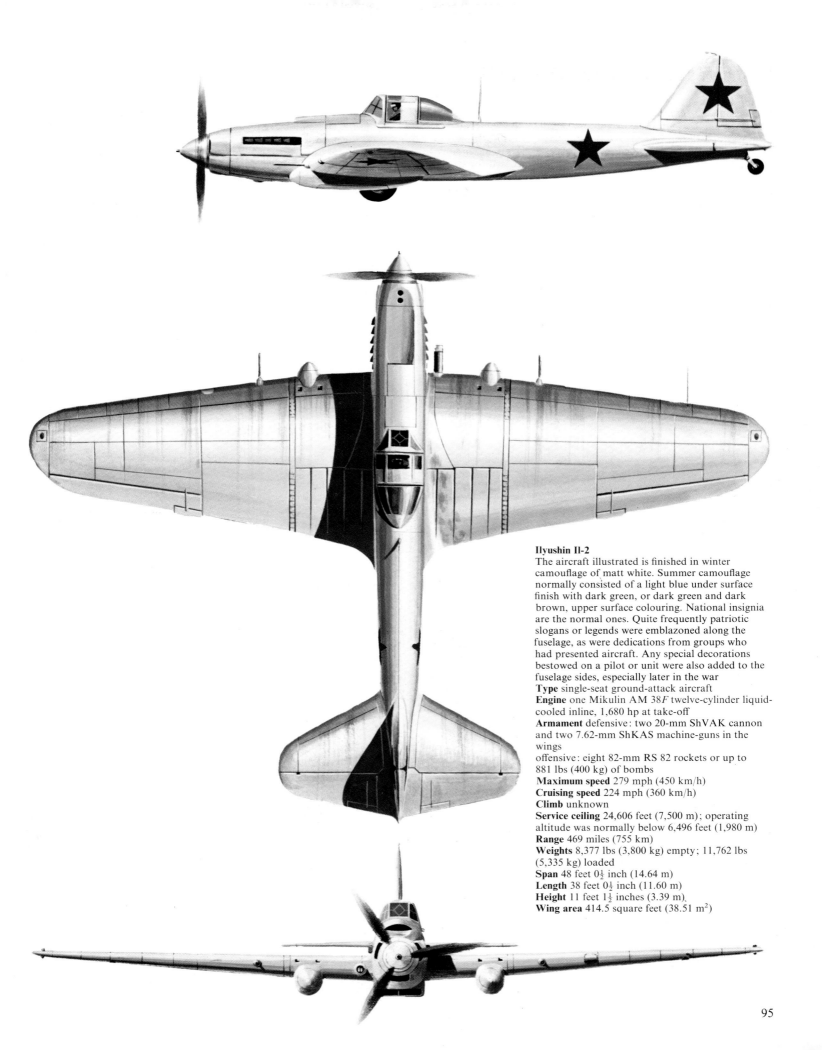

Ilyushin Il-2
The aircraft illustrated is finished in winter
camouflage of matt white. Summer camouflage
normally consisted of a light blue under surface
finish with dark green, or dark green and dark
brown, upper surface colouring. National insignia
are the normal ones. Quite frequently patriotic
slogans or legends were emblazoned along the
fuselage, as were dedications from groups who
had presented aircraft. Any special decorations
bestowed on a pilot or unit were also added to the
fuselage sides, especially later in the war
Type single-seat ground-attack aircraft
Engine one Mikulin AM 38*F* twelve-cylinder liquid-
cooled inline, 1,680 hp at take-off
Armament defensive: two 20-mm ShVAK cannon
and two 7.62-mm ShKAS machine-guns in the
wings
offensive: eight 82-mm RS 82 rockets or up to
881 lbs (400 kg) of bombs
Maximum speed 279 mph (450 km/h)
Cruising speed 224 mph (360 km/h)
Climb unknown
Service ceiling 24,606 feet (7,500 m); operating
altitude was normally below 6,496 feet (1,980 m)
Range 469 miles (755 km)
Weights 8,377 lbs (3,800 kg) empty; 11,762 lbs
(5,335 kg) loaded
Span 48 feet 0½ inch (14.64 m)
Length 38 feet 0½ inch (11.60 m)
Height 11 feet 1½ inches (3.39 m)
Wing area 414.5 square feet (38.51 m²)

Lavochkin Fighters

The Lavochkin La-7 is a classic example of how the life of a basic design can be extended by the skilful refinement of its aerodynamic qualities and the use of more powerful engines. But whilst this process usually takes place at the expense of the aircraft's first handling characteristics, the La-7 actually profited from it, emerging as one of the Soviet Union's ablest fighters of World War II.

The origins of the Lavochkin series of fighters lay in a 1938 requirement for a high-performance monoplane fighter to replace the biplanes and first-generation monoplanes in service with the Red Air Force. Several state design bureaux produced prototypes, that of the team headed by Lavochkin being designated *I-22* and flying in March 1939. (The *I* designation meant *Istrebitel* or Fighter.) When the *I* designation was replaced by a system indicating the designer, the *I-22* became the LaGG-1, the type having been produced by Lavochkin, Gorbunov and Gudkov.

The LaGG-1 was a clean low-wing monoplane powered by an M-105P inline, and was built in small quantities in 1940, before being replaced by the improved LaGG-3. This entered service late in 1940, but was relegated to second-line duties early in 1942. Most Russian fighters of the period featured a higher percentage of wood in their structures than contemporary Western designs. In the case of the Lavochkin fighters, indeed, most of the aircraft's structure was of wood, covered with a specially strengthened plywood skinning. The advantages of this type of construction were that it produced a light, but extremely sturdy, airframe that made little use of expensive strategic materials and, also, the work could be done by less skilled workers.

In October 1941 Semyon Lavochkin began to design a radically improved variant of the LaGG-3, centred around the 1,600-hp Shvetsov M-82 radial engine. The extra 500 hp offered by this engine promised a spectacular performance if it could be built into the basic inline-engined LaGG airframe. To balance the extra drag of the radial there would be the elimination of the inline engine's cooling system, and lighter engine mountings, cowlings and oil system. Flight tests with a converted LaGG-3 powered by an M-82A were very successful, and the type was put into limited production as the LaG-5 (sometimes referred to as the La-3), an interim version pending the arrival of the definitive La-5. (The apparent confusion in nomenclature during this period at the end of 1941 and beginning of 1942 was caused by the departure of Gorbunov and Gudkov within a short time of each other.)

The La-5, which differed from the LaG-5 in having an M-82F (*Forsirovannyi* meaning boosted) engine and a cut-down rear fuselage with an all-round vision canopy, passed its tests with flying colours, and was put into large-scale production in July 1942. Well over 1,000 La-5 fighters had been built by the end of the year. In keeping with the Red Air Force's tactical doctrines, the La-5's maximum speed was obtained at very low level, and the rate of climb was also spectacular at low to medium altitudes (388 mph at 9,842 feet, or 625 km/h at 3,000 m, and 4 minutes 30 seconds to 9,842 feet). Russian pilots normally operated at altitudes lower than 16,404 feet (5,000 m).

The next model to appear, in March 1943, was the La-5FN, which had the 1,650-hp M-82FN (*Forsirovannyi Nyeposredstvenno*—directly boosted) engine, structural refinements, a wing of slightly increased span and reduced chord, and an armament of two 20-mm cannon and four 82-mm rockets. The La-5FN could be distinguished by the large air intake mounted on top of the engine cowling. Maximum speed at 16,404 feet (5,000 m) was 404 mph (650 km/h), and climb to 3,281 feet (1,000 m) a quite remarkable 18½ seconds – nearly twice as fast as most Western types. At the same time the La-5UTI trainer was produced; this had less fuel, only one cannon, and a second cockpit for the instructor.

Lavochkin, meanwhile, was modifying the design to produce an even better type. This emerged late in 1943 as the La-7, reaching front-line units early in 1944. The La-7 was powered by an uprated M-82FNU or M-82FNV engine, and was armed with three 20- or 23-mm cannon and six 82-mm rockets. The La-7 differed from the La-5FN externally in having a cockpit canopy of revised shape, and the oil cooler relocated under the fuselage behind the wing trailing edge. An La-7UTI trainer and liaison aircraft series was also built, as were two La-7R fighters with liquid-fuelled rocket motors in the tail. This last variant had a top speed of over 500 mph at 16,404 feet (805 km/h at 5,000 m). No more were built as the fumes from the rocket's fuel had a very adverse effect on the wooden parts of the La-7's structure.

The final wartime development of the Lavochkin fighter was the La-9, which was similar in basic outline to the La-7, but was in fact a completely new aircraft with a metal structure. It was powered by an M-82FNV engine of 1,870 hp, had a speed of 429 mph (690 km/h) at low altitudes, and possessed the heavy armament of four 20-mm cannon. The definitive Lavochkin fighters, however, were the La-5FN and the La-7, both of which remained in production up to the end of the war. These were excellent low- and medium-altitude fighters, with good speed and armament, rugged, and well able to take on even the latest German fighters with every chance of success at their best altitudes. The two top Russian aces of World War II, Ivan Kojedub (62 victories) and Alexander Pokryshin (59 victories) both flew Lavochkin fighters for most of their careers.

Left: A Lavochkin La-5 of the Czech Mixed Air Division comes in to land during the closing stages of the war in 1945. To improve control at low speeds and whilst manoeuvring, automatic leading-edge slats (seen open in the photograph) were fitted. These were operated by the breaking away of the boundary layer of air flowing over the wings, and proved very successful.

The basic soundness of Lavochkin's design is attested to by the fact that although the type started life as an inline-engined aircraft, later requirements necessitated the substitution of a radial engine. Surprisingly, the alteration required relatively few structural changes, and enhanced the type's performance very considerably. With the Yakovlev fighters the Lavochkin series of fighter aircraft proved one of the most important types in the Red Air Force's front-line inventory during World War II

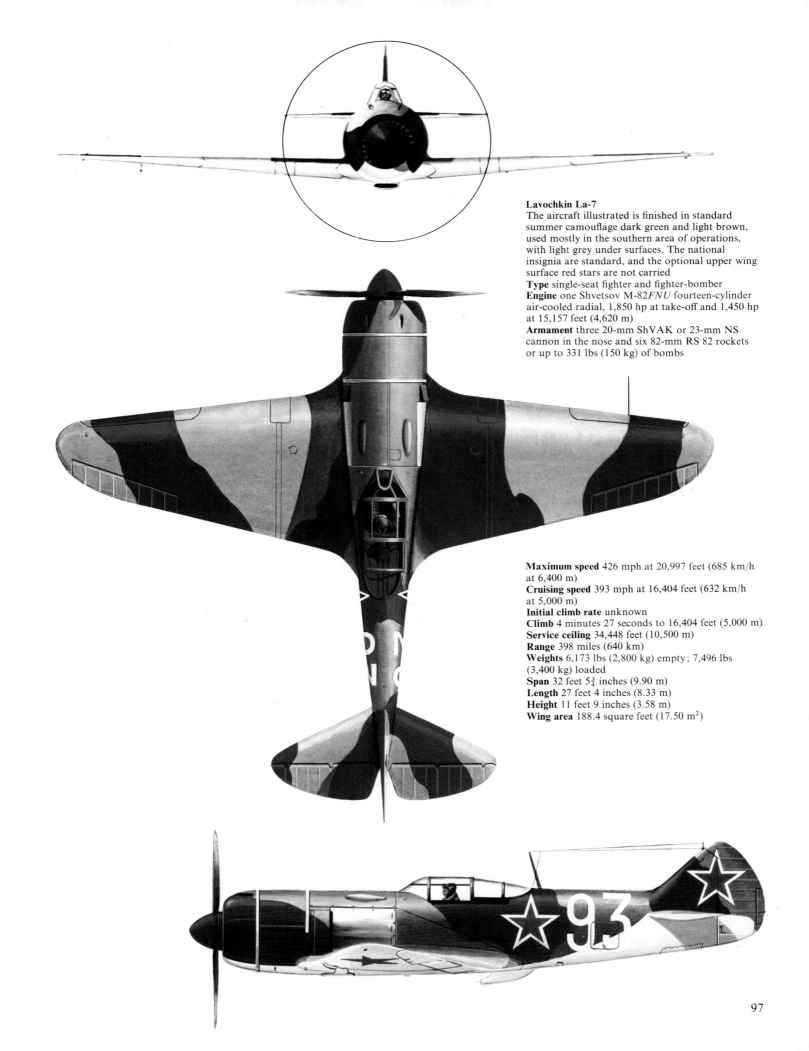

Lavochkin La-7
The aircraft illustrated is finished in standard summer camouflage dark green and light brown, used mostly in the southern area of operations, with light grey under surfaces. The national insignia are standard, and the optional upper wing surface red stars are not carried

Type single-seat fighter and fighter-bomber
Engine one Shvetsov M-82*FNU* fourteen-cylinder air-cooled radial, 1,850 hp at take-off and 1,450 hp at 15,157 feet (4,620 m)
Armament three 20-mm ShVAK or 23-mm NS cannon in the nose and six 82-mm RS 82 rockets or up to 331 lbs (150 kg) of bombs

Maximum speed 426 mph at 20,997 feet (685 km/h at 6,400 m)
Cruising speed 393 mph at 16,404 feet (632 km/h at 5,000 m)
Initial climb rate unknown
Climb 4 minutes 27 seconds to 16,404 feet (5,000 m)
Service ceiling 34,448 feet (10,500 m)
Range 398 miles (640 km)
Weights 6,173 lbs (2,800 kg) empty; 7,496 lbs (3,400 kg) loaded
Span 32 feet 5¾ inches (9.90 m)
Length 27 feet 4 inches (8.33 m)
Height 11 feet 9 inches (3.58 m)
Wing area 188.4 square feet (17.50 m²)

Mikoyan-Gurevich Fighters

The Russian design bureaux led by Semyon Lavochkin and Artem Mikoyan designed aircraft for the Red Air Force both during World War II and during the postwar era. But whilst the war years proved remarkably successful for Lavochkin, Mikoyan had to wait for the years after 1945 for his designs to flourish in the service of his country. This notwithstanding, a series of MiG fighters was built during the war, achieving limited production and combat success, and paving the way for the great line of postwar MiG jet fighters.

The first fighter designed by the MiG team, of Mikoyan and Gurevich, to achieve production status was the MiG-1. Although the Soviet Union had been in the forefront of aviation in the early and middle 1930s, the outbreak of war in September 1939 revealed that the equipment of the Red Air Force was beginning to be outdated compared with the latest aircraft flown by Germany, Great Britain and France. A crash programme of development was therefore instituted, one of the main features of which was a requirement for a high-performance monoplane fighter, issued in December 1939. The MiG team designed its *I-200* to meet this requirement, and by quite extraordinary efforts in design and prototype construction, the first machine flew in April 1940, a mere four months after the issue of the requirement.

Although the handling characteristics of the new fighter left much to be desired, performance (a top speed in the order of 401 mph or 645 km/h) was excellent, and the type was immediately ordered into quantity production as the *I-61*. With the replacement of the *I* designation by an abbreviated form of the designer's or designers' names, the *I-61* became the MiG-1. Deliveries of production aircraft to the Red Air Force began early in 1941, but the performance of these aircraft was sadly reduced from that of the prototype, a maximum speed of 367 mph (590 km/h) being recorded. The reasons for this were the addition of armament and ammunition, armoured protection for the pilot, and the lack of skill on the part of production workers, compared with the skilled craftsmen who had built the prototype. Because of the relative shortness of the fuselage, the MiG-1 was very tricky at take-off and landing, but despite this some 2,100 examples were built. Later production MiG-1 fighters had a better performance than earlier machines as the skill of the production workers increased.

Progressive development of the aircraft led to the introduction of the MiG-3, also originally called the *I-200*, in the autumn of 1941. This model had a 1,350-hp AM-35A engine, a sliding cockpit canopy, and increased fuel tankage. Several thousand MiG-3 fighters were built, but although speed (407 mph at 22,966 feet or 655 km/h at 7,000 m) was excellent, manoeuvrability

was poor, and the type was used mostly for tactical reconnaissance. The MiG-3 was phased out of service in 1943. The MiG-5, which appeared in small numbers during 1943, was based on the MiG-3 airframe, but powered by a 1,600-hp Shvetsov M-82A radial engine. The final wartime variant based on the MiG-1 was the MiG-7, which was built in prototype form only. This was intended as a high-altitude fighter, and featured a pressurized cockpit. Power was provided by a 1,700-hp Klimov M-107A inline engine, but the decline of German air power in late 1944 led to the abandonment of the MiG-7.

The wartime MiG series was characterized by good performance, adequate firepower, and indifferent manoeuvrability. As a result, the brunt of the actual fighting done by the Red Air Force was borne by Lavochkin and Yakovlev aircraft.

Below: Mikoyan-Gurevich MiG-3 fighters on a Russian airfield. A progressive development of the MiG-1 powered by the improved AM-35A engine, the MiG-3 entered service towards the end of 1941, when Russia's fortune was at its lowest ebb, and at first proved a useful type. When the need for fighters was less pressing, however, the MiG-3's lack of manoeuvrability led to its removal from front-line fighter units to other duties, principally high-speed reconnaissance. The type was phased out of service in 1943

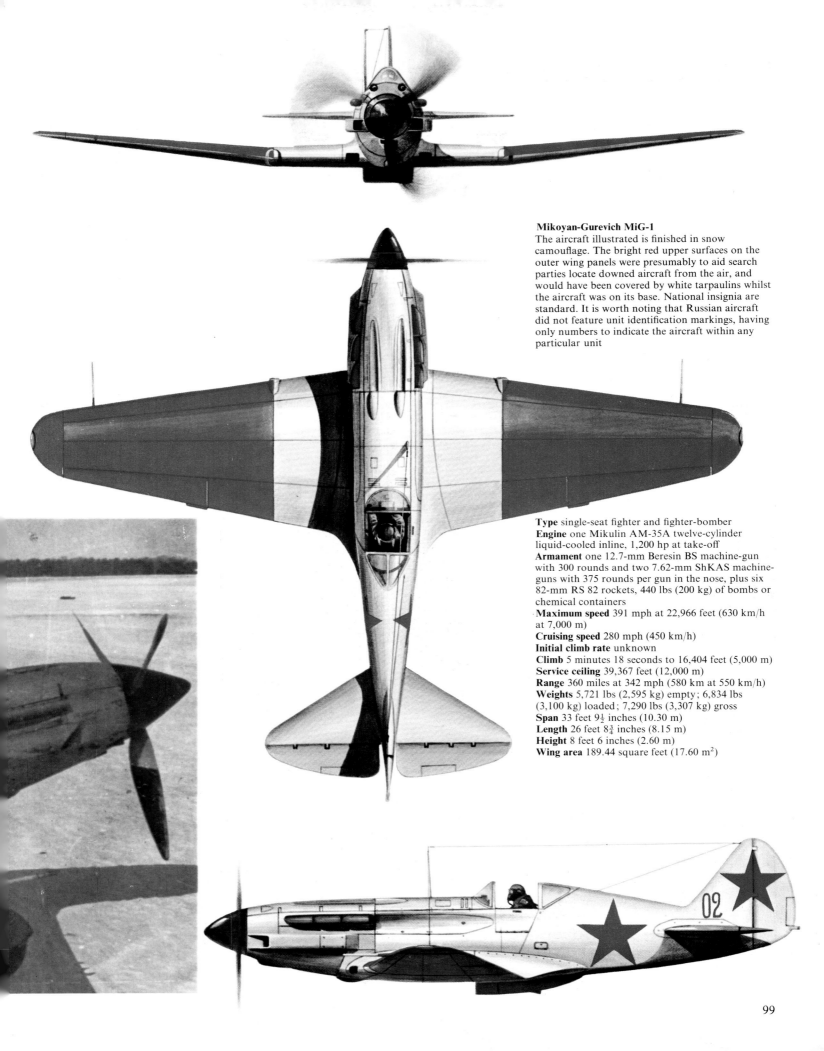

Mikoyan-Gurevich MiG-1
The aircraft illustrated is finished in snow camouflage. The bright red upper surfaces on the outer wing panels were presumably to aid search parties locate downed aircraft from the air, and would have been covered by white tarpaulins whilst the aircraft was on its base. National insignia are standard. It is worth noting that Russian aircraft did not feature unit identification markings, having only numbers to indicate the aircraft within any particular unit

Type single-seat fighter and fighter-bomber
Engine one Mikulin AM-35A twelve-cylinder liquid-cooled inline, 1,200 hp at take-off
Armament one 12.7-mm Beresin BS machine-gun with 300 rounds and two 7.62-mm ShKAS machine-guns with 375 rounds per gun in the nose, plus six 82-mm RS 82 rockets, 440 lbs (200 kg) of bombs or chemical containers
Maximum speed 391 mph at 22,966 feet (630 km/h at 7,000 m)
Cruising speed 280 mph (450 km/h)
Initial climb rate unknown
Climb 5 minutes 18 seconds to 16,404 feet (5,000 m)
Service ceiling 39,367 feet (12,000 m)
Range 360 miles at 342 mph (580 km at 550 km/h)
Weights 5,721 lbs (2,595 kg) empty; 6,834 lbs (3,100 kg) loaded; 7,290 lbs (3,307 kg) gross
Span 33 feet 9½ inches (10.30 m)
Length 26 feet 8¾ inches (8.15 m)
Height 8 feet 6 inches (2.60 m)
Wing area 189.44 square feet (17.60 m²)

Petlyakov Pe-2

Vladimir Petlyakov's Pe-2 was without doubt the best light bomber of World War II. Moreover, so sound was the basic structure and so good the performance that the Pe-2 also bid fair to equal Germany's Junkers Ju 88 and Great Britain's de Havilland Mosquito in the multitude of roles it fulfilled: light bomber, dive-bomber, day fighter, night fighter, reconnaissance aircraft, and advanced trainer. That the type did not undertake further roles was the result of the simplicity of Red Air Force operations rather than any limitations on the part of the aircraft.

The origins of the Pe-2 lay in a Red Air Force requirement of the late 1930s for a high-altitude bomber interceptor. To meet this Petlyakov produced his *VI*-100. (*VI* stands for *Vysotnyi Istrebitel* or High-Altitude Fighter.) The prototype *VI*-100 was ready in the spring of 1939, but was never flown, the Red Air Force cancelling its requirement for such an aircraft, issuing in its place a requirement for a high-altitude bomber. Petlyakov decided to respond to this with a design based on the *VI*-100, using the same turbo-supercharged engines, the same type of pressurized cockpit, and a modified airframe to allow the carriage of bombs in an internal bomb-bay, and remote-control dorsal and ventral defensive machine-guns.

Before a prototype could be built, however, the Red Air Force once again altered its requirement, the accuracy of high-altitude bombing being in doubt. Thus Petlyakov was now instructed to modify his high-altitude bomber into a dive-bomber, the efficiency of which had been proved in the Spanish Civil War. The change in altitude performance required meant that the turbo-supercharged engines could be abandoned, and with them the cabin pressurization equipment. This allowed more room in the aircraft, and meant that the defensive armament could be operated directly by the crew. The new aircraft emerged in December 1939 as the *PB*-100. (*PB* stands for *Pikiruyushchii Bombardirovshchik* or Dive-Bomber.) After service trials, during which the area of the vertical tail surfaces was increased by one-third, the *PB*-100 was pronounced an excellent aircraft, with good diving characteristics when the slatted dive-brakes were extended and a fair turn of speed with them retracted.

The Pe-2, as the *PB*-100 was now designated, was put into large-scale production early in 1940, the tempo of deliveries gaining pace rapidly in 1941. Although only two machines were delivered during 1940, the grand total built finally reached 11,426. The original machine-gun armament consisted of four 7.62-mm weapons, but this was later standardized as three 12.7-mm and two 7.62-mm weapons. The bomb-load was also increased from 1,323 lbs to 2,205 lbs (600 kg to 1,000 kg). The Pe-2's performance was also improved during 1943, when aircraft powered by Klimov VK-105*RF* engines supplanted Klimov M-105*R*-powered machines on the production lines in February. At the same time the airframe was considerably 'cleaned up' aerodynamically by giving the undercarriage doors a better fit, improving the lines of the engine nacelles, and reducing the gap between fixed and movable surfaces. These modifications raised the maximum speed by 25 mph (40 km/h).

As noted above, the Pe-2 was an extremely versatile aircraft, and was modified to perform several roles other than bombing. The first of these, which appeared in the first half of 1941, was the Pe-3. This was structurally akin to the *VI*-100, and was intended as a multi-role fighter. Only limited production of this variant was undertaken as a result of the high priority given to the basic Pe-2. The Pe-3 was powered by the M-105*R* inlines of the early production Pe-2, but was armed with two fixed 20-mm ShVAK cannon and two fixed 12.7-mm UBK machine-guns, and two flexible 12.7-mm machine-guns.

The next Pe-2 variant was the Pe-2*R*. (*R* stands for *Razvedchik* or Reconnaissance.) This reconnaissance aircraft had three cameras in the bomb-bay and a directional autopilot to hold the machine steady during the photography run. Fuel tankage was increased to give a range of 1,056 miles (1,700 km), and the Pe-2*R* was intended for employment by day or night. The Pe-2*UT* was an advanced trainer variant. (*UT* stands for *Uchebno Trenirovochnyi* or Advanced Trainer.) This was intended for operational conversion flying, and had a second cockpit for the instructor, complete with full controls, behind the original cockpit.

For its size the Pe-2 was quite agile, and proved a devastating weapon as a dive-bomber or level bomber. The type's three vices, if they may be called that, were a high landing speed, a tendency to spin after stalling, and extreme sensitivity during landing. In the last, a heavy landing was likely to cause the Pe-2 to bounce high in the air, with disastrous consequences for all but very experienced pilots.

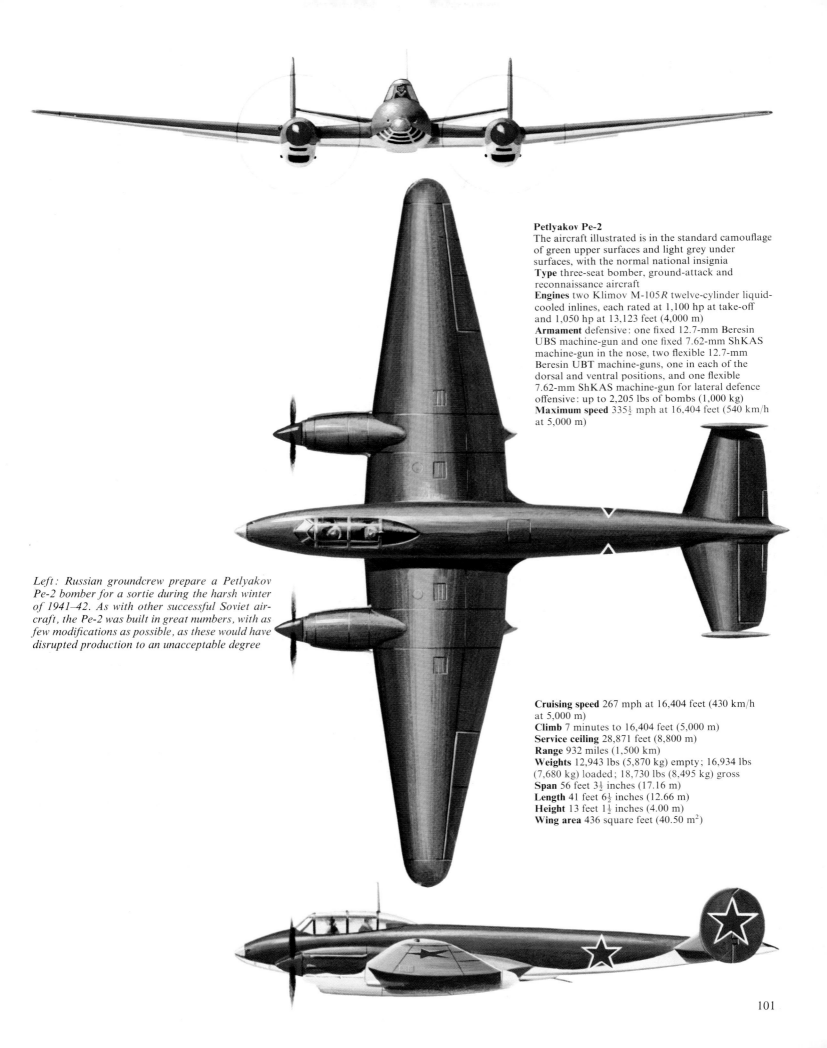

Petlyakov Pe-2
The aircraft illustrated is in the standard camouflage of green upper surfaces and light grey under surfaces, with the normal national insignia
Type three-seat bomber, ground-attack and reconnaissance aircraft
Engines two Klimov M-105*R* twelve-cylinder liquid-cooled inlines, each rated at 1,100 hp at take-off and 1,050 hp at 13,123 feet (4,000 m)
Armament defensive: one fixed 12.7-mm Beresin UBS machine-gun and one fixed 7.62-mm ShKAS machine-gun in the nose, two flexible 12.7-mm Beresin UBT machine-guns, one in each of the dorsal and ventral positions, and one flexible 7.62-mm ShKAS machine-gun for lateral defence offensive: up to 2,205 lbs of bombs (1,000 kg)
Maximum speed 335½ mph at 16,404 feet (540 km/h at 5,000 m)

Left: Russian groundcrew prepare a Petlyakov Pe-2 bomber for a sortie during the harsh winter of 1941–42. As with other successful Soviet aircraft, the Pe-2 was built in great numbers, with as few modifications as possible, as these would have disrupted production to an unacceptable degree

Cruising speed 267 mph at 16,404 feet (430 km/h at 5,000 m)
Climb 7 minutes to 16,404 feet (5,000 m)
Service ceiling 28,871 feet (8,800 m)
Range 932 miles (1,500 km)
Weights 12,943 lbs (5,870 kg) empty; 16,934 lbs (7,680 kg) loaded; 18,730 lbs (8,495 kg) gross
Span 56 feet 3½ inches (17.16 m)
Length 41 feet 6½ inches (12.66 m)
Height 13 feet 1½ inches (4.00 m)
Wing area 436 square feet (40.50 m²)

Polikarpov I-153

The *I-153*, designed by A J Scherbakov, had the dictinction of being, with the Fiat CR 42 *Falco* (Falcon), the fastest biplane fighter to enter service with any of the world's air forces. It was also unique amongst production fighter-biplanes in having a retractable undercarriage.

The *I-153* stemmed from the *I-15* designed by Nikolai Polikarpov in the summer of 1932. This latter had the unusual gull-wing arrangement of the upper flying surfaces, with the centre section divided into two and angled down on each side to meet the fuselage, thus giving the pilot an excellent field of vision forwards and upwards. Considerable numbers of the *I-15* were built before it was succeeded on the production lines by the *I-15bis*. This appeared in 1934, and featured a revised upper wing of greater span with an orthodox centre section raised above the fuselage by conventional cabane struts. A later mark of the M-25 radial engine was installed in a new long-chord cowling. Both the *I-15* and *I-15bis* served with some success in the Spanish Civil War. Production of the *I-15bis*, also known as the *I-152*, did not start until 1936 as a result of delays in the production of the engine.

The *I-153* was developed in 1935 by Scherbakov, one of Polikarpov's subordinates, to capitalize on all the best features of the *I-15* and *I-15bis*, with performance boosted by the use of a more powerful engine and the reduced airframe drag bestowed by a retractable undercarriage. The basic airframe was that of the *I-15bis*, but the wings were those of the earlier *I-15*. The prototype used the M-25B engine of the *I-15bis*, but production aircraft, which were delivered from 1936 onwards, had M-62R radials of 1,000 hp. With 250 hp more available than in the *I-15bis*, the *I-153* attained the respectable speed of 250 mph (400 km/h). With the advent of the latest monoplanes in Western and Japanese service, however, the Russians felt that the performance of the *I-153* must be improved further. The result was the definitive *I-153*, powered by a 1,100-hp M-63R radial. This model had a top speed of 267 mph (430 km/h), and proved a considerable surprise to the Japanese during the border clashes in Mongolia in the summer of 1939.

Experimental developments of the *I-153* were quite numerous, and included: the *I-153BS* of 1939, with a pair of 12.7-mm Beresin machine-guns; the *I-153GK* of 1939, with a turbo-supercharged M-63TK radial and an enclosed pressurized cockpit for high-altitude operations; one prototype with a Merkulov DM-4 ramjet under each lower wing, boosting maximum speed by 16 mph (25 km/h); the *I-190* powered by a 1,000-hp M-88 radial; and the *I-190GK* high-altitude fighter, the M-88 engine version of the *I-153GK*.

The last variant of the *I-153* was the *I-153P*, armed with a pair of 20-mm ShVAK cannon. (*P* stands for *Pushka* or Cannon.) A total of 6,578 fighters of this family was built, the numbers breaking down as 733 *I-15s*, 2,408 *I-15bis*, and 3,437 *I-153s*. This last variant proved more than a match for anything possessed by the Japanese in 1939 and by the Finns in 1940,

providing the little biplane was flown by an experienced pilot to take full advantage of its phenomenal agility. The *I-153* was still in widespread service at the time of the German invasion of June 1940, and performed creditably in the hands of the best pilots. By 1944, however, the type was completely obsolete, and had been relegated to training duties. The *I-153* was also used by the Finns against its former owners, the Germans having sold a number of captured fighters to the Finns.

Below: A Polikarpov I-16 of the Red Air Force in flight. To the Fascists who flew against it in the Spanish Civil War, the I-16 was the 'Rata' or rat; to the Russians it was 'Ishak' or little donkey; to the Germans during World War II it was 'Dienstjäger' or duty fighter. Very apparent in the photograph are the large flat frontal area of the nose and the very short length of the fuselage between the wing and the tailplane, giving great agility in the longitudinal plane; however the compactness of design also made it very tricky to fly

Polikarpov I-153
The aircraft illustrated is finished in standard camouflage of green upper surfaces and blue-grey under surfaces, with the normal national insignia
Type single-seat fighter and fighter-bomber
Engine one Shvetsov M-63R nine-cylinder air-cooled radial, 1,100 hp at take-off
Armament four 7.62-mm ShKAS machine-guns with 650 rounds per gun, plus six 82-mm RS 82 rockets or 331 lbs (150 kg) of bombs
Maximum speed 267 mph at 16,404 feet (430 km/h at 5,000 m)
Cruising speed 186 mph (300 km/h)
Initial climb rate unknown
Climb unknown
Service ceiling 35,137 feet (10,710 m)
Range 298 miles at 186 mph (480 km at 300 km/h) on internal fuel; 560 miles at 174 mph (900 km at 280 km/h) with drop-tanks
Weights 3,168 lbs (1,437 kg) empty; 4,100 lbs (1,860 kg) loaded; 4,431 lbs (2,010 kg) gross
Span 32 feet 9¾ inches (10.00 m)
Length 20 feet 3¼ inches (6.18 m)
Height 9 feet 3 inches (2.82 m)
Wing area 238 square feet (22.11 m²)

Polikarpov I-16

The Polikarpov *I*-16 is another example of how wrong in its assessments of Japanese and Russian aircraft the Western world was in the middle 1930s. When the *I*-16 was first met in combat over Spain in the early months of winter 1936–1937, the type was naively assumed to be a Soviet copy of the American Boeing P-26 fighter. Yet the Polikarpov design was being tested before the first P-26 was delivered to the US Army Air Corps, and, with its enclosed cockpit and wings of cantilever construction, was a far more advanced design than the American fighter. The *I*-16 was the first low-wing monoplane fighter with a retractable undercarriage to enter service anywhere in the world, and thus set the scene for the type of fighter that was to dominate World War II.

The *I*-16, designed by Nikolai Polikarpov and originally known as the *TsKB*-12, was designed in the summer of 1932. The requirement which the new fighter was intended to meet had been issued early in 1932, and called for a fighter that could be produced in quantity by existing methods and factories, and had a performance superior to that of any other fighter in the world. Polikarpov, which had just designed the conventional *I*-15 biplane fighter, therefore had to opt for a simple structure, using inexpensive materials, in an entirely novel design. The first prototype, powered by a 450-hp M-22 radial, flew in December 1933. This had an armament of two 7.62-mm machine-guns, and an undercarriage that had to be retracted manually. Maximum speed was 224 mph (360 km/h). Although the *TsKB*-12's handling characteristics were very

tricky, it was immediately placed in production as the *I*-16 Type 1, with an uprated M-22 of 480 hp and an armament of two 7.62-mm ShKAS machine-guns, which had a higher rate of fire than the previous PV-1 weapons. Service deliveries began in the autumn of 1934.

Meanwhile a newer model had made its first flight in February 1934. This was the *TsKB*-12*bis*, which attained 280 mph (450 km/h) on the 700 hp of its M-25 radial engine. This model was placed in small-scale production as the *I*-16*bis*, being supplanted in June 1934 by the *I*-16 Type 4, which had the M-25 engine and two 7.62-mm ShKAS guns. The *I*-16 Type 5 had minor structural modifications and 9-mm armour protection for the pilot.

The next model, the *I*-16 Type 6, was the first major production variant. This had a 730-hp M-25A radial, and as its weight was greater than that of its predecessors, the rate of climb was affected adversely. The Type 6 was the last *I*-16 model to feature an enclosed cockpit, and was replaced on the production lines in 1937 by the *I*-16 Type 10. Apart from having an open cockpit, the Type 10 differed from the earlier marks in having a 750-hp M-25B radial and four 7.62-mm machine-guns. Also built at the same time was the *I*-16*UTI* trainer, with a second open cockpit in front of the ordinary one. The Type 10 was the first *I*-16 variant to see action, and it proved very successful in the early part of its career in the Spanish Civil War and against the Japanese in Mongolia.

By 1937 the armament of the *I*-16 was beginning to lose ground to that of the latest Western designs, and a programme of improvement was put in hand. The first result of this programme was the *I*-16*P*. (P stands for *Pushka* or Cannon.) This was armed with two 20-mm ShVAK cannon. Next appeared the *I*-16 Type 17, armed with two 20-mm cannon and two 7.62-mm machine-guns. This was the immediate successor of the Type 10 in quantity production. The *TsKB*-18 was an experimental ground-attack fighter with two 7.62-mm machine-guns in the wings and four 7.62-mm PV-1 machine-guns firing obliquely forwards and downwards in the fuselage. Two 110-lb (50-kg) bombs could be carried under the wings, and considerable armour-plate protection for the engine and lower fuselage was provided. The *TsKB*-18 did not enter service, as the Type 18 did. This model introduced the 1,000-hp Shvetsov M-62 radial, but had an armament of four machine-guns. This lack of firepower was rectified in the Type 24, which had two fuselage-mounted 7.62-mm machine-guns and two wing-mounted 20-mm ShVAK

Polikarpov I-16 Type 10
The aircraft illustrated is finished in the standard camouflage of green on the upper surfaces and pale blue on the under surfaces. Note that the national insignia are used on the upper surfaces of the wings
Type single-seat fighter and fighter-bomber
Engine one M-25B nine-cylinder air-cooled radial, 750 hp at 9,842 feet (3,000 m)
Armament two 7.62-mm ShKAS machine-guns with 450 rounds per gun in the nose and two 7.62-mm ShKAS machine-guns with 750 rounds per gun in the wings, plus six 82-mm RS 82 rockets
Maximum speed 282 mph at 9,842 feet (455 km/h at 3,000 m)
Cruising speed 224 mph (360 km/h)
Initial climb rate unknown
Climb 6 minutes 30 seconds to 16,404 feet (5,000 m)
Service ceiling 29,494 feet (8,990 m)
Range 400 miles (645 km)
Weights 2,789 lbs (1,265 kg) empty; 3,704 lbs (1,680 kg) loaded
Span 29 feet 6¾ inches (9.01 m)
Length 20 feet 0¾ inch (6.12 m)
Height 8 feet 5 inches (2.57 m)
Wing area 161.45 square feet (15.00 m²)

cannon. The Type 24 was built in two series, the first being powered by the M-62 engine. The definitive second series, the *I*-16 Type 24B, was powered by a 1,100-hp Shvetsov M-63 radial, giving the aircraft a maximum speed of 323 mph (516 km/h) at sea level. A variant of the Type 24 was the *I*-16*SPB*. (*SPB* stands for *Skorostnyi Pikiruyuschii Bombardirovshchik* or Fast Dive-Bomber.) This had a defensive armament of only two 7.62-mm machine-guns, but could carry two 551-lb (250-kg) bombs on underwing racks.

The Type 24B was the last true *I*-16 production variant, but the basic airframe was used in two other models. The first of these was the *I*-180 which was produced in experimental form in 1938. Power was provided by a 1,100-hp Shvetsov M-88 radial, and maximum speed was 342 mph (550 km/h). The final *I*-16 derivative was the *TsKB*-15. This had an 850-hp M-100 inline engine, and was capable of 311 mph (500 km/h). Armament comprised one 20-mm ShVAK cannon and four 7.62-mm ShKAS machine-guns. A limited number saw service as the *I*-17. The type first flew in September 1934.

The *I*-16 was a great milestone in aviation history, and the *Ishak* or Little Donkey, as the Russians dubbed the type, performed fairly well against the Germans in the first few months of the war. But although the type was very manoeuvrable, the compactness of the basic design made the *I*-16 very tricky to fly and the hand-cranked undercarriage was always a problem to inexperienced pilots.

Tupolev SB-2

The Tupolev *SB*-2, like so many other Russian aircraft of the period immediately before World War II, was a significant landmark in the history of aviation: it marked the emergence of the fast twin-engined medium bomber, a type that was to reach its peak during the war with the Junkers Ju 88, the de Havilland Mosquito, and the Martin B-26 Marauder. As with several other major Russian types, the *SB*-2 owed its origins to another aircraft.

In the early 1930s, under the general supervision of Andrei Tupolev, a team led by Archangelski produced the ANT-29, a twin-engined heavy fighter armed with a pair of 102-mm recoilless cannon. Although the project was abandoned in 1936 as being impractical, the airframe had proved itself adequate during flight trials. Thus when the *VVS-RKKA* (*Voyenno-Vozdushnye Sily Rabocho-Krestyanskoy Krasnoy Armii* or Air Forces of the Workers' and Peasants' Red Army) issued a requirement for a new medium bomber, Archangelski was able to base his design for the *SB*-1 or ANT-39 on the ANT-29. (*SB* stands for *Skorostnyi Bombardirovshchik* or Fast Bomber.) This was a clean mid-wing monoplane, with wings of considerable span and area, powered by a pair of 750-hp M-25 radial engines. The wheels were deliberately designed to retract only half way into the nacelles, to help avoid damage during a crash landing. Defensive armament of the *SB*-1 consisted of three 7.62-mm machine-guns, and the offensive load of 1,102 lbs (500 kg) of bombs.

Progressive development of the ANT-39 led to the ANT-40, named *SB*-2 in service. The prototype, built to an extremely exacting requirement, first flew in 1935, and entered production early in 1936. The airframe was basically the same as that of the *SB*-1, but had completely enclosed crew positions. An undercarriage design that left half of each wheel extending below the engine nacelle, as in the *SB*-1, was employed. Power was provided by a pair of M-100 inline engines. Surprisingly, however, Archangelski chose to place the radiators at the front of the engines, which obviated the advantages that might have been derived from the low frontal area of the inline engines. Performance was considerably enhanced when the M-100*AAU* engine was introduced, and with these engines the *SB*-2 proved a formidable opponent for the Nationalist Fiat CR 32 biplane fighters when it arrived in Spain in October 1936. The Russian bomber had superior level speed, and could outclimb the Italian fighter once it had dropped its bombs. Even the Messerschmitt Bf 109B series had considerable difficulty in catching the *SB*-2.

Late in 1936 the first *SB*-2*bis* flew. This was a considerably improved model, with 960-hp M-103 engines in more orthodox cowlings, the radiators now being placed in ventral positions below each nacelle. The *SB*-2*bis* had the very respectable maximum speed of 282 mph (453 km/h), and with increased fuel tankage over the *SB*-2, a range of 1,430 miles (2,300 km). The type entered production in 1937, and several variants were built. These included the *PS*-40 commercial transport of 1938, a trainer version with an open cockpit for the pupil in front of the ordinary cockpit, and the *SB-RK* dive-bomber. This had two 1,100-hp AM-105*R* engines and a strengthened airframe to allow higher take-off weights. The span was also increased slightly. Maximum speed of the *SB-RK*, which was put into limited production as the Ar-2, was just over 300 mph (485 km/h). This Ar-2 was the last variant of the basic *SB*-2, of which some 6,600 were built.

In the Spanish Civil War and the 'Winter War' with Finland in 1940, the *SB*-2 had proved a very useful aircraft. But with the German invasion of Russia in June 1940 the days of the *SB*-2 were numbered. Protection was inadequate to allow the *SB*-2 to operate at medium altitudes against German fighter opposition, so the type had to operate low down, where German anti-aircraft fire took a heavy toll. The *SB*-2 continued in widespread first-line service up to 1943, but was then gradually phased out, only a few remaining in such service by the end of the war. The type was exported to China, and captured examples were used by the Finns.

Below: An example of the definitive SB-2bis, with inline engines in orthodox cowlings
Bottom: An Avia S-79, the Czech licence-built version of the SB-2. Note the original type of engine cowling, with the radiators in front of the engine in an arrangement visually similar to the appearance of radial engines

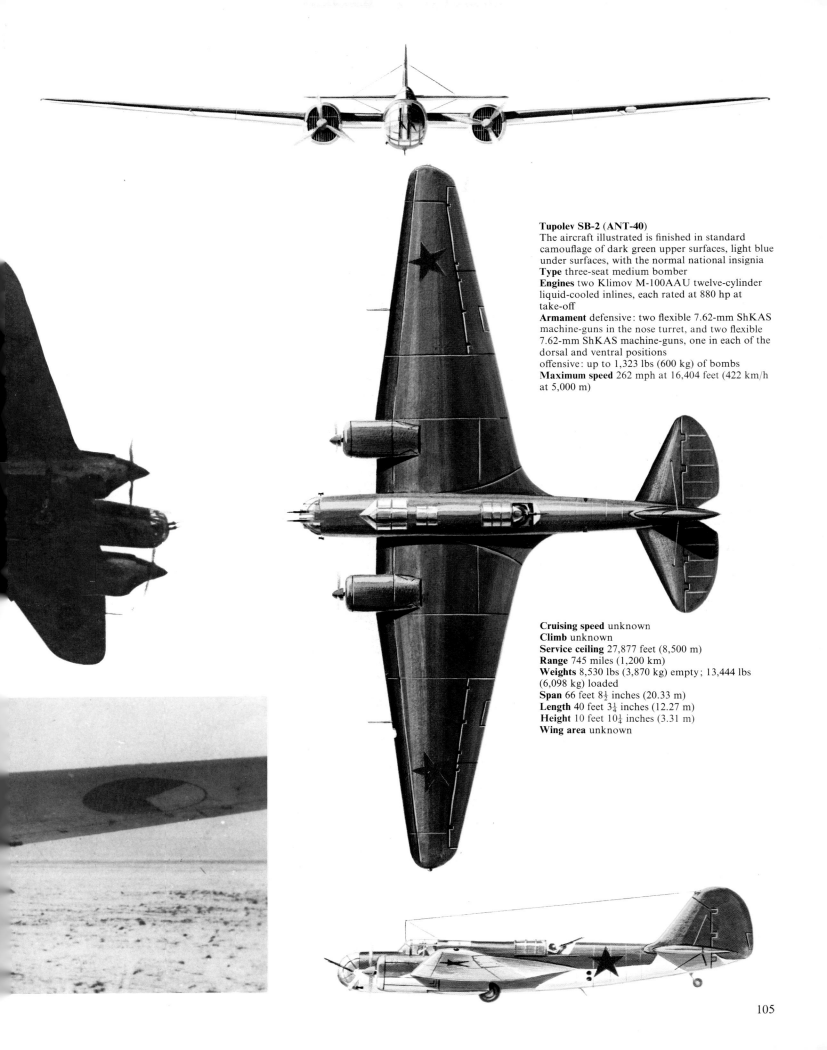

Tupolev SB-2 (ANT-40)
The aircraft illustrated is finished in standard
camouflage of dark green upper surfaces, light blue
under surfaces, with the normal national insignia
Type three-seat medium bomber
Engines two Klimov M-100AAU twelve-cylinder
liquid-cooled inlines, each rated at 880 hp at
take-off
Armament defensive: two flexible 7.62-mm ShKAS
machine-guns in the nose turret, and two flexible
7.62-mm ShKAS machine-guns, one in each of the
dorsal and ventral positions
offensive: up to 1,323 lbs (600 kg) of bombs
Maximum speed 262 mph at 16,404 feet (422 km/h
at 5,000 m)

Cruising speed unknown
Climb unknown
Service ceiling 27,877 feet (8,500 m)
Range 745 miles (1,200 km)
Weights 8,530 lbs (3,870 kg) empty; 13,444 lbs
(6,098 kg) loaded
Span 66 feet 8½ inches (20.33 m)
Length 40 feet 3¼ inches (12.27 m)
Height 10 feet 10¼ inches (3.31 m)
Wing area unknown

Yakovlev Fighters

The Yakovlev series of aircraft was the most widely used of Russian fighters in World War II, and continued in service with the Red Air Force and the services of the Russian satellites long after the end of hostilities. Although its performance seems low, and its structure crude, compared with Western types, the Yak-9 series reigned supreme in the role for which it was designed: low- and medium-altitude tactical fighter. Below 16,404 feet (5,000 m) the Yak-9 had a combination of performance and manoeuvrability that could not be matched by any German fighter.

Design work on the basic aircraft that was developed through the Yakovlev series of fighters began in 1938, in response to a Red Air Force requirement for a replacement for the Polikarpov I-16. Three design teams produced prototypes to meet this need, and all three entered production, the I-26 as the Yak-1, the I-22 as the LaGG-3, and the I-200 or I-61 as the MiG-1. The Yak-1 first flew in March 1939, and quickly attracted the interest of the Russian authorities, including Stalin himself. The type was ordered into production as quickly as possible, and the first unit to re-equip with the new fighter took part in the May Day parade of 1940.

Production Yak-1 fighters were also known as Yak-1IPs. (IP stands for Istrebitel Pushka or Cannon Fighter.) Once its initial teething problems had been corrected in the summer and autumn of 1941, the Yak-1 proved to be one of the few Soviet types able to take on Germany's Messerschmitt Bf 109F and Focke-Wulf Fw 190A on anything approaching equal terms, and quickly became one of the most valued fighters in the Red Air Force's inventory. Meanwhile, the need for an operational trainer for the new generation of fighters had led to the introduction of the Yak-7V, later redesignated Yak-7U. This trainer variant was also known as the UTI-26, and was powered by the Klimov M-105PF of 1,260 hp, the powerplant that was adopted in

late series Yak-1s. With the M-105PF engine, the Yak-1 became the Yak-1M. (M stands for Modificatsion or Modification.) The Yak-1M could be distinguished from its predecessor by its cut down rear fuselage, new all-round vision cockpit canopy and lack of an engine-mounted cannon; production ceased in 1942. The type was later developed into the Yak-3, a parallel version of the Yak-9.

In the autumn of 1941 the Red Air Force formulated a requirement for a single-seat night fighter. Alexander Yakovlev responded to the requirement by producing his Yak-7A, basically a Yak-7U with the second cockpit removed and the armament improved. With the standardization of the M-105PF engine and the cut-down rear fuselage, production examples of the Yak-1M were from this time onwards redesignated Yak-7B. Two variants of the Yak-7 were the experimental Yak-7VRD, with a Merkulov ramjet under each wing, and the Yak-7DI. (DI stands for Distantsyonnyi Istrebitel or Long-Range Fighter.) Only a few examples of the Yak-7DI were built before the type was replaced by a newer variant.

This was designated Yak-9, and was based on the Yak-7DI. Production aircraft started to come off the production lines in December 1942. The powerplant was the standard M-105PF, and the armament one 20-mm cannon and one 12.7-mm machine-gun. In May 1943 the basic Yak-9 was joined by the Yak-9M, which had a second 12.7-mm machine-gun in the nose. At the same time another variant, the Yak-9B, was introduced. (B stands for Bombovoy or Bomber.) This bomber model had the same gun armament as the basic Yak-9, but featured an internal bomb-bay for a load of up to 992 lbs (450 kg) of bombs. Both the Yak-9M and Yak-9B were built in very substantial numbers. By the middle of 1943, Yakovlev fighters in service exceeded both Lavochkin and Mikoyan-Gurevich types by a very handsome margin.

The majority of Russian fighters had been designed to operate over short ranges but as the Red Army began to push forward in 1943, the need for models with increased ranges was strongly felt. Light alloys were now available in fair quantities, and Yakolev again redesigned the wing of his fighter to produce the Yak-9D, which had bigger fuel tanks in the wings, and a range increased by 317 miles (510 km) over that of the basic Yak-9. (D stands for Distantsyonnyi or Long-Range.) Armament was similar to that of the Yak-9, but the ShVAK cannon was replaced by a MPSh cannon of the same calibre. The Yak-9D was further modified with additional internal fuel tankage and provision for a drop-tank under the fuselage, raising the range of the Yak-9DD, as the new type was designated, to 1,367 miles (2,200 km). (DD stands for Dalnodistantsyonnyi or Very Long-Range.)

Late in 1943 the Red Air Force called for a fighter able to deal with the latest generation of German tanks. Yakovlev responded with the Yak-9T. (T stands for Tankovoy or Tank.) The Yak-9T was a derivative of the Yak-9M with a 37-mm NS-37 cannon mounted in place of the 20-mm ShVAK cannon. The final Yakovlev fighter variant to use the well-tried M-105 engine was the Yak-9L, which had the supercharged M-105PD of 1,050 hp at 20,997 feet (6,400 m). (L stands for Lyogkii or Light.)

The next model, the Yak-9U, was powered by the 1,600-hp Klimov VK-107A engine. (U stands for Ulutshennyi or Improved.) The Yak-9U was basically the same aircraft as its predecessors, but was a stronger machine, being of all-metal stressed-skin construction; it began to enter service in the autumn of 1944, and was the last major variant of the Yakovlev piston-engined fighter line. The last Yak-9 variant was the Yak-9P. (P stands for Perekhvatchik or Interceptor.) This differed from the Yak-9U only in having a transparent cover for the direction-finding loop behind the cockpit.

Yakovlev Yak-1

The aircraft illustrated right is finished in the alternative summer camouflage of dark green and dark brown upper surfaces, with light grey under surfaces. National insignia are the usual ones
Type single-seat fighter and fighter-bomber
Engine one Klimov VK-105*PA* twelve-cylinder liquid-cooled inline, 1,100 hp at take-off
Armament one 20-mm ShVAK cannon with 120 rounds firing through the propeller shaft and two 7.62-mm ShKAS machine-guns with 375 rounds per gun in the nose, plus six 82-mm RS 82 rockets
Maximum speeds 364 mph at 16,404 feet (586 km/h at 5,000 m); 310 mph (500 km/h) at sea level
Cruising speed 149 mph at 9,842 feet (240 km/h at 3,000 m)
Initial climb rate unknown
Climb 4 minutes 30 seconds to 16,404 feet (5,000 m)
Service ceiling 32,808 feet (10,000 m)
Range 435 miles at 323 mph (700 km at 520 km/h)
Weights 5,137 lbs (2,330 kg) empty; 6,217 lbs (2,820 kg) loaded
Span 32 feet 9¾ inches (10.00 m)
Length 27 feet 9¾ inches (8.48 m)
Height 8 feet 8 inches (2.64 m)
Wing area 184.5 square feet (17.14 m²)

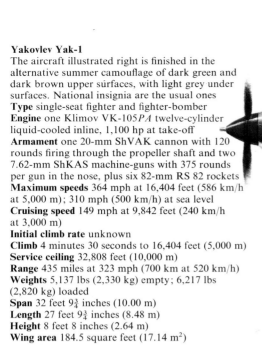

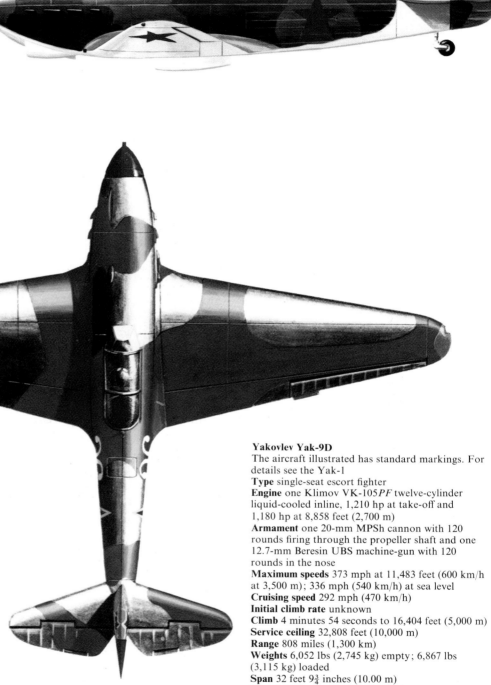

Left: Yakolev Yak-9DD long-range fighters on an airfield in Yugoslavia. Early in the war, emphasis on high performance at short ranges was all important for the Russians, but as the war turned against Germany and the Red Army advanced rapidly, the Red Air Force found itself increasingly in need of longer-ranged tactical aircraft

Yakovlev Yak-9D

The aircraft illustrated has standard markings. For details see the Yak-1
Type single-seat escort fighter
Engine one Klimov VK-105*PF* twelve-cylinder liquid-cooled inline, 1,210 hp at take-off and 1,180 hp at 8,858 feet (2,700 m)
Armament one 20-mm MPSh cannon with 120 rounds firing through the propeller shaft and one 12.7-mm Beresin UBS machine-gun with 120 rounds in the nose
Maximum speeds 373 mph at 11,483 feet (600 km/h at 3,500 m); 336 mph (540 km/h) at sea level
Cruising speed 292 mph (470 km/h)
Initial climb rate unknown
Climb 4 minutes 54 seconds to 16,404 feet (5,000 m)
Service ceiling 32,808 feet (10,000 m)
Range 808 miles (1,300 km)
Weights 6,052 lbs (2,745 kg) empty; 6,867 lbs (3,115 kg) loaded
Span 32 feet 9¾ inches (10.00 m)
Length 27 feet 11½ inches (8.52 m)
Height 9 feet 10 inches (3.00 m)
Wing area 186.75 square feet (17.35 m²)

THE UNITED STATES

Above: A Boeing B-17F, built by Douglas at its Long Beach factory, machine M of an unidentified squadron of the 305th Bombardment Group, 40th Combat Wing, 1st Air Division, US 8th Army Air Force, on a mission over Europe from its base in southern Great Britain. B-17s formed the backbone of the US strategic air forces in the European Theater of Operations

Although some may have doubted the supremacy of the USA before World War II, she was unquestionably the world's most powerful nation in 1945. This was to a large extent attributable to the efforts of the United States Army Air Forces and of the air force of the United States Navy, which also had operational control of the air arm of the formidable United States Marine Corps. (The US Army Air Forces were formed in 1941 from the previous US Army Air Corps, and in turn became the US Air Force only in September 1947.)

The US had entered World War I in April 1917, and most of the squadrons of their air service were equipped with French and British types. Great plans were laid to use American industrial potential to keep the Allied forces supplied with the latest weapons in 1918 and 1919 but it took longer than anticipated to get American production under way, and the war ended in 1918 before much American *matériel* had reached Europe. However, the industrial potential for armaments manufacture remained, and helped to make the United States an overt world power in the 1920s and 1930s.

The postwar history of the US Army and Navy air services was similar to that of the European nations, with financial troubles and public apathy leading to small, but relatively well equipped air forces. Considerable efforts were made to keep up with developments, particularly by the Navy which, because of the geographical situation of the United States, would play an all-important part in any future war. The US Navy was, moreover, one of the few navies in the world to realize that the combination of the aircraft-carrier and high-performance aircraft was to play more than a minor role in future wars. Thus the US Navy was amongst the first of all air forces to introduce aircraft with retractable undercarriages, and to experiment with dive-bombers as a standard weapon.

The USAAC also kept up with developments with record-breaking and racing aircraft, and limited production of a variety of interesting and advanced designs, especially of bomber and attack aircraft. It is worth noting that most American combat aircraft, even late in World War II, were powered by radial engines, which the US forces preferred for their high power-to-

weight ratio and simplicity – the result of having no liquid coolant and its attendant 'plumbing'. The disadvantage of the preference was that radials had a large frontal area, which presented a bigger target in combat, and produced more drag than inlines; this in turn meant that more powerful engines, with increased fuel consumption, had to be used. It is noteworthy that the best US fighter of the war, the North American P-51 Mustang, used an inline engine, but only because this was specified by the British requirement that led to the design of the aircraft.

The US Army Air Forces had long been interested in strategic bombing, and had led the world in the development of fast monoplane bombers capable of carrying large loads over long ranges. The Boeing B-17 Flying Fortress was already in fairly widespread service by the time World War II began in Europe, and the type was to serve in various marks throughout the conflict. The ultimate expression of the heavy bomber concept during World War II was the Boeing B-29 Superfortress, which ushered in the era of true strategic bombing with the dropping of atomic bombs on the Japanese

cities of Hiroshima and Nagasaki in August 1945, at the end of World War II.

The United States also excelled in the field of medium bombers, producing such excellent designs as the Martin B-26 Marauder and the North American B-25 Mitchell. During the war these were fitted with ever heavier gun armaments, and were used almost as attack aircraft and as anti-shipping strike aircraft. In the same class was the Douglas A-20 Havoc, which had started life as a medium bomber and ended as a straight attack aircraft with a useful combination of bombs and gun armament. The Havoc also served extensively with the French and British air forces as the DB-7 and Boston respectively. The Americans had little use for light bombers, but the Martin Maryland and Baltimore aircraft filled the gap between light and medium bomber in relatively small numbers with the US forces and in greater numbers with the Royal Air Force.

The standard US fighter at the beginning of the war was the Curtiss P-40, which also served with the French and British air forces in the guise of the H-75 and Tomahawk/Kittyhawk series respectively. But the standard fighters during the war were the massive Republic P-47 Thunderbolt, the long-range Lockheed P-38 Lightning and the all-round paragon of fighters, the North American P-51 Mustang. As was the case with the British and the Russians, the American need for a pure fighter declined as the war progressed, and American fighters began to appear more and more frequently with bombs and rockets as fighters-bombers. It is worth noting here that the Americans relied on machine-guns rather than cannon as the basic fighter armament, using the excellent Browning 0.50-inch (12.7 mm) weapon. Drop-tanks to increase range also became a common feature of US aircraft later in the war.

The US Navy's standard fighter at the beginning of the war was the Grumman F4F Wildcat, a useful design which was, however, not in the same class as the superlative Mitsubishi A6M series. This position was changed by the advent of the Grumman F6F Hellcat and the Vought F4U Corsair. The latter was perhaps the only rival to the Mustang for the title of the war's best fighter. The standard torpedo-bomber at the beginning of the war was the Douglas TBD Devastator, but this was quickly supplanted by the Grumman TBF Avenger, and the standard dive-bomber throughout the war was the Douglas SBD Dauntless, joined from 1943 onwards by the Curtiss SB2C Helldiver.

The United States also had two superb maritime aircraft: the Consolidated PBY Catalina patrol flying-boat, and the Consolidated B-24 Liberator bomber, which was also used to good effect as a strategic bomber by the USAAF. Many other types were used by the US, and more advanced types were about to enter widespread service as the war ended. These would further have enhanced the US air forces' position as the world's largest and most powerful air power, capable of launching massive raids at every level from short-range tactical attack to long-range strategic bombing.

(It should be noted that in the sections dealing with Great Britain and the United States, the metric measurement of 7.7 mm has been used as the equivalent of both 0.303 and 0.30 inches to avoid confusion. However, the exact metric conversion of 0.303 inch is 7.7 mm, and that of 0.30 inch 7.62 mm.)

Boeing B-17 Flying Fortress

The Boeing B-17 Flying Fortress, which served with the US air forces throughout the World War II period, is perhaps the most celebrated aircraft operated by the United States during the war. Its development during the early 1930s marked the American enthusiasm for pinpoint heavy bombing at a time when most European bomber designs were in the medium bomber category.

The B-17 was designed in 1934 in response to a requirement issued in May by the US Army Air Corps for a multi-engined bomber capable of delivering at least 2,000 lbs (907 kg) of bombs over a minimum range of 1,020 miles at a speed of 200 mph (1,642 km at 322 km/h) or above. As the company was also working on another, larger bomber, the Model 294 or XB-15, the decision to compete for the new aircraft was a risky one. Design and construction work proceeded rapidly, and the prototype Model 299, as the new aircraft was designated by Boeing, first flew in July 1935. This prototype is sometimes erroneously referred to as the XB-17. Power was provided by four 750-hp Pratt & Whitney R-1690 Hornet radials, the defensive armament consisted of five single 0.30-inch (7.7-mm) machine-guns, and a bomb-load of 4,800 lbs (2,177 kg) could be carried. Although the prototype was destroyed in an accident, its performance had been so encouraging that the USAAC ordered a pre-production batch of 14 YB-17s, later redesignated Y1B-17s. The first of these was delivered in December 1936, with 930-hp Wright GR-1820 radials. The first 13 Y1B-17s were finished to this standard, whilst the 14th was completed as the sole Y1B-17A, with turbo-superchargers for its engines. These boosted maximum speed to 311 mph (501 km/h) and service ceiling to over 30,000 feet (9,144 m), and were incorporated on all subsequent B-17 models.

At the end of their trials the Y1B-17s were redesignated B-17s and the Y1B-17A the B-17A. As the US Navy objected to an aircraft that would pre-empt its right to defend America's shores, plans for large-scale procurement of the B-17 by the USAAC had to be cut back. In 1938 the first true production model, the B-17B with a larger rudder, larger flaps and a modified nose, was ordered. Some 39 B-17Bs were built. Production of the B-17C, 38 of which were ordered, began in 1939. This model had a greater take-off weight, improved engines and better armament. The B-17C was followed by 42 B-17Ds in 1941. The B-17D differed only slightly from its predecessor and was the first Flying Fortress variant to enter combat with the USAAF, suffering heavy losses on the ground in the Japanese strikes on Hawaii and the Philippine islands in December 1941.

The next model to enter service was the B-17E, a much modified type incorporating lessons learned in combat by Royal Air Force crews. In 1941 the RAF had received ten B-17Cs, which it renamed Fortress I, and combat experience had shown that the defensive armament of one 0.30-inch (7.7-mm) and six 0.50-inch (12.7-mm) machine-guns was totally inadequate. The first of the 512 B-17Es built was delivered to the USAAF in October 1941, and featured a completely revised defensive armament and a new set of vertical tail surfaces, with much greater area to help control at high altitudes. The armament of this new model now included twin 0.50-inch (12.7-mm) turrets in the tail, dorsal and ventral positions, together with two 0.50-inch waist guns and two 0.30-inch (7.7-mm) nose guns. The bomb-load, which had been 10,496 lbs (4,761 kg) in the B-17C, was increased to 17,600 lbs (7,983 kg) for short ranges. Surprisingly, although the loaded weight had risen 6,350 lbs to 53,000 lbs (2,880 kg to 24,041 kg) and the powerplants were still the 1,200-hp Wright R-1820-65 radials of the B-17C, the B-17E attained a maximum speed of 317 mph at 25,000 feet (510 km/h at 7,620 m), compared with the earlier model's 291 mph (468 km/h) at the same altitude. The B-17E became operational in the Pacific theatre in December 1941, and in the European theatre in July 1941. It was used in the US Eighth Air Force's first raid in Europe on 17 August 1942.

In May 1942, meanwhile, there had appeared the B-17F, based on the combat lessons of the B-17Ds operating in the Pacific in the months immediately after Japan's strike on Pearl Harbor. A new one-piece perspex nose was introduced, and improved R-1820-97 engines, together with a strengthened undercarriage, allowed take-off weight to increase from 54,000 lbs to 65,000 lbs (24,494 kg to 29,484 kg) and finally to 72,000 lbs (32,659 kg). Further additions were made later during production and by front-line units, usually to the amount of armour carried, the defensive armament, and to the fuel tankage in the wings. Finally, the reintroduction of underwing racks allowed a maximum of 20,800 lbs (9,435 kg) of bombs to be carried over very short ranges. Production of the B-17F totalled 3,405 aircraft. Despite these modifications, however, the B-17F still suffered very heavy losses in combat over Europe, especially to German fighters which had discovered that the Flying Fortress's weak spot was the nose.

In an effort to produce a counter to the German head-on attacks prompted by the B-17's poor nose armament, Boeing developed the B-17G, which first flew in July 1943. This model featured a twin 0.50-inch (12.7-mm) machine-gun chin turret, also used on the last B-17Fs, and later production models had improved turbosuperchargers which raised the service ceiling 5,000 feet to 35,000 feet (1,524 m to 10,668 m). Many other modifications were also carried out by front-line units. Production of the B-17G, the last variant of the basic B-17, totalled 8,680 aircraft.

Total production of the B-17 reached 12,731 aircraft, and the Flying Fortress served with distinction as the USAAF's standard daylight heavy bomber over Europe and in South-East Asia and the South-West Pacific. By 1946, however, only a few hundred were left in service. The main failing of the B-17 was that it was designed as a medium bomber, and although later in the war it could carry very heavy bomb-loads, it was only at the expense of range. Another fault was that the type tended to ignite all too easily when hit by enemy gunfire.

Below: B-17G bombers of the 533rd Bombardment Squadron, 381st Bombardment Group, 1st Combat Wing, 1st Air Division, US 8th Army Air Force, set off on a mission over occupied Europe from their base in Great Britain

Boeing B-17G Flying Fortress
The aircraft illustrated is machine D of the 401st Bombardment Squadron (code-letters LL), of the 91st Bombardment Group (marking a black A in a white triangle on the fin), of the 1st Combat Wing of the 8th Air Force's 1st Air Division. The spacing of the individual letter and the squadron letters on each side of the fuselage national insignia show that the period should be before late July 1943, and the group marking that it is after June 1943. This particular aircraft was built by Douglas at Long Beach in California, and was written off after a crash landing at Cambridge on 21 December 1943. Camouflage is the standard olive drab upper surfaces and light grey under surfaces. National insignia, on top of the port wing, under the starboard wing, and on each side of the fuselage, are normal for the period after 17 September 1943, when the blue outline, in place of the earlier red one, was adopted for the white bar
Type ten-seat heavy bomber
Engines four Wright R-1820-97 Cyclone 9 nine-cylinder air-cooled radials, each rated at 1,200 hp at take-off and 1,000 hp at 25,000 feet (7,620 m)
Armament defensive: two flexible 0.50-inch (12.7-mm) Browning M2 machine-guns in the chin turret, two flexible 0.50-inch Browning M2 machine-guns in the ventral turret, two flexible 0.50-inch Browning M2 machine-guns in the dorsal turret, two flexible 0.50-inch Browning M2 machine-guns in the tail turret, and four 0.50-inch Browning M2 machine-guns, one in each of the two nose cheek positions and two waist positions offensive: up to 17,600 lbs of bombs (7,983 kg)
Maximum speed 287 mph (462 km/h) at 25,000 feet (7,620 m) with normal bomb-load

Cruising speed 160 mph (258 km/h) at 25,000 feet (7,620 m) with 4,000-lb (1,814-kg) bomb load
Climb 37 minutes to 20,000 feet (6.096 m)
Service ceiling 35,600 feet (10,851 m)
Range 1,800 miles (2,897 km) at 160 mph (258 km/h) with 4,000-lb (1,814-kg) bomb-load; 3,400 miles (5,472 km) without war load
Weights 36,135 lbs (16,391 kg) empty; 55,000 lbs (24,948 kg) loaded; 65,500 lbs (28,421 kg) gross
Span 103 feet 9½ inches (31.64 m)
Length 74 feet 9 inches (22.78 m)
Height 19 feet 1 inch (5.82 m)
Wing area 1,420 square feet (131.92 m²)

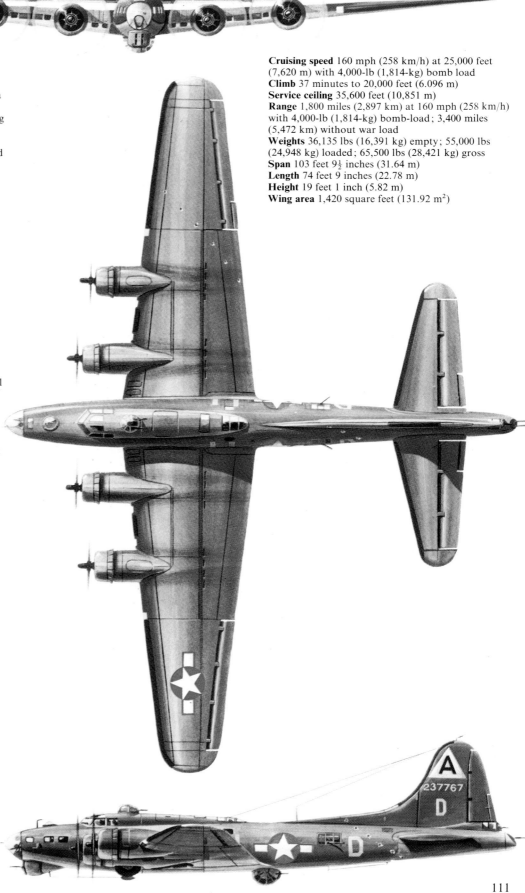

Boeing B-29 Superfortress

If for no other reason, the Boeing B-29 Superfortress will always be remembered as the only aircraft to have used atomic weapons in combat, when Hiroshima and Nagasaki were bombed in August 1945 in the final stages of the war with Japan. The B-29 was also an excellent aircraft, with many advanced features, including remote-control gun turrets and large-scale pressurization of the crew compartments.

US interest in a bomber able to carry a worthwhile load over considerable ranges at high speeds reached back to such designs as the Boeing XB-15 of 1933. Although official interest in such a weapon flagged during the second half of the decade, Boeing continued basic design work on a number of similar projects, culminating in the Model 341, which was estimated to be able to deliver 2,240 lbs (1,016 kg) of bombs over a range of 7,000 miles (11,266 km) at a speed in excess of 400 mph (644 km/h). With the outbreak of World War II in Europe, however, and the possibility of US involvement, the US Army Air Corps once again developed an interest in any weapon that could enable the United States to bomb its enemies over very long ranges. Thus in February 1940 a requirement for a 'Hemisphere Defense Weapon' was issued. This called for a bomber able to deliver 2,000 lbs (907 kg) of bombs over 5,333 miles (8,583 km) at a speed of 400 mph (644 km/h). The bomber also had to have self-sealing fuel tanks, considerable armour protection, a heavy defensive armament, and the ability to carry 16,000 lbs (7,257 kg) of bombs.

Boeing developed its Model 341 design into the Model 345, which met all the requirements but that for speed. Two prototypes, to be called XB-29, were ordered in August 1940. The mock-up was approved in April 1941, and prototype construction began. With the constant deterioration of the world situation in late 1941 and early 1942, the B-29 programme was given top priority in the spring of 1942.

The first XB-29 made its maiden flight in September 1942, preceded by orders for a batch of 14 pre-production YB-29s and more than 1,500 production aircraft. The design was extremely clean, with no steps in the nose outline, and the engine nacelles received special attention. Each of the Wright R-3350 radials used had two turbo-superchargers. The first prototype had no defensive armament, but the second XB-29 was fitted with the system that was intended for production models. This consisted of remote-control Sperry turrets sighted with periscopes. The turrets on production models were also intended to be retractable. The third XB-29 prototype had a system of General Electric turrets controlled from small astrodome bubbles near each turret. This latter system was adopted for production aircraft.

Delivery of the 14 pre-production YB-29s began in June 1943, and units began to work up with the new bomber. Production deliveries began in the autumn of 1943. At the end of the year it was decided not to use B-29s against targets in Europe, but concentrate instead on Japanese targets, in the bombing of which the B-29's great range would be most useful. Pre-production YB-29 aircraft had R-3350-21 radials, but production B-29s had R-3350-23, 23A, or 41 radials, and were allowed to operate at a gross weight of 138,000 lbs (62,595 kg), compared with the 120,000 lbs (54,432 kg) of the XB-29. Production of the B-29 reached 2,527 before the next model, the B-29A, was introduced. This had a wing of 12 inches (30.5 cm) greater span, R-3350-57 or 59 radials, reduced fuel tankage, and a four-gun, instead of a two-gun, front dorsal turret. This turret had also been introduced on the last B-29s, which had dispensed with the 20-mm cannon in the tail turret. In all, 1,119 B-29A bombers were built before production ceased in May 1946.

The first B-29 operation took place in June 1944, and thereafter the tempo of B-29 operations increased rapidly from bases in India and China, and then from the Marianas after their capture. After a relative lack of success with high-explosive bombs, operations with incendiary bombs proved far more successful, devastating vast areas of Japanese cities. With the decline in Japanese airpower, it proved possible to strip all defensive armament and its ancillary equipment, except the tail turret, from the B-29s. This enabled a greater offensive load to be carried. So successful did this field modification prove that a production equivalent, the B-29B, was developed; 311 such aircraft were built.

The last wartime variant of the B-29 was the F-13A, a photographic-reconnaissance aircraft needed to assess the results of B-29 raids on Japan. Additional fuel was carried in the bomb-bay. Variants that achieved only prototype form or project status were the XB-39, with four Allison V-3420 inline engines; the XB-44, with four Pratt & Whitney R-4360 radials, which became the prototype of the B-50 series; and the B-29C, which was to have had improved engines. Development also continued after the war, with cargo, inflight refuelling, air-sea rescue, drone, and reconnaissance variants. By the end of hostilities some 2,000 B-29 models had been delivered to the USAAF. A further 5,000 were cancelled, but production reached a total of 3,960 before ceasing in May 1946.

The B-29 was one of the outstanding aircraft of the war, and played an all-important part in hastening the defeat of Japan. It was an extremely sound, clean design, with good performance and load-carrying capabilities, and excellent defensive armament so long as it was needed.

Below: B-29 Superfortress heavy bombers unload their bombs over a Japanese target. The Superfortress bore the brunt of the long-range US air offensive against Japan, and proved most devastating when using incendiary bombs dropped in clusters at low altitude. Japanese cities, built largely of wood, had little or no defence against such attacks

Boeing B-29 Superfortress

The aircraft illustrated is a machine of the 499th Bombardment Group of the US 20th Air Force. The group markings were a black V above an outlined black square, later changed to a black V alone. The finish of the aircraft is natural metal, camouflage being deemed unnecessary after the virtual elimination of the main strength of the Japanese fighter arm. The natural metal finish also improved the maximum speed. National insignia are the normal ones

Type ten-seat heavy bomber

Engines four Wright R-3350-57 Cyclone eighteen-cylinder air-cooled radials, each rated at 2,200 hp at take-off

Armament defensive: four 0.50-inch (12.7-mm) Browning machine-guns in the front upper turret, two 0.50-inch Browning machine-guns in the rear upper turret, two 0.50-inch Browning machine-guns in the front lower turret, two 0.50-inch Browning machine-guns in the rear lower turret, and two 0.50-inch Browning machine-guns and a 20-mm M2 Type B cannon in the tail turret offensive: up to 20,000 lbs (9,072 kg) of bombs

Maximum speed 358 mph at 25,000 feet (576 km/h at 7,620 m)

Cruising speed 230 mph (370 km/h)

Climb 38 minutes to 20,000 feet (6,096 m)

Service ceiling 31,850 feet (9,708 m)

Range 3,250 miles (5,231 km)

Weights 70,140 lbs (31,815 kg) empty; 133,500 lbs (60,555 kg) loaded; 138,000 lbs (62,596 kg) gross

Span 142 feet 3 inches (43.36 m)

Length 99 feet (30.18 m)

Height 29 feet 7 inches (9.02 m)

Wing area 1,736 square feet (161.28 m²)

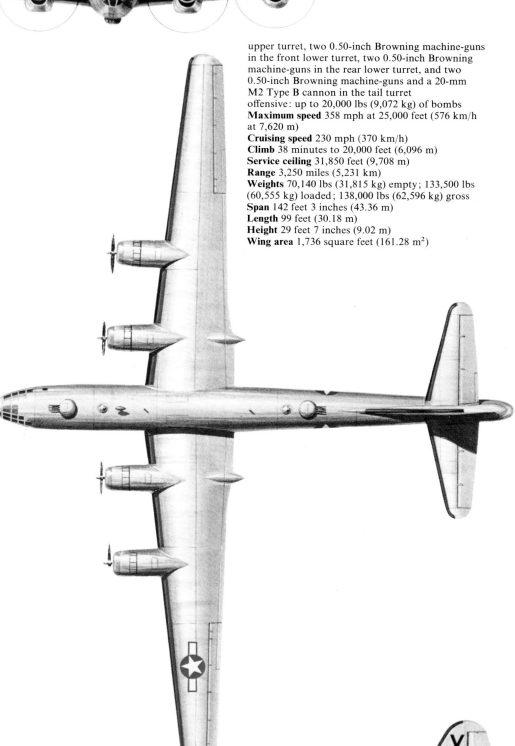

Consolidated B-24 Liberator

Although not as famous as its companion heavy bomber, the Boeing B-17 Flying Fortress, the Consolidated B-24 Liberator was in many respects a superior aircraft. It could not carry the bomb-load of the Flying Fortress, but it did have distinct aerodynamic advantages: a tricycle undercarriage and wings of very high aspect ratio. The first made take-off and landings considerably easier, and the second produced high lift for the minimum drag, resulting in good overall performance. The Liberator also possessed an auto-pilot, and although this proved temperamental at times, it allowed the Liberator to be used to the full advantage of its long range as a maritime-reconnaissance bomber.

The flying surfaces that were the basis of the Liberator's design had first appeared on the Consolidated P4Y flying-boat, and with the US Army Air Corps' interest in long-range heavy bombers with excellent performance at altitude, Consolidated engineers were able to produce a mock-up and plans for a high-performance bomber by combining the wings and tail surfaces of the P4Y with a new fuselage by January 1939. The USAAC insisted on several alterations during February, but in March the first prototype of what was to become the B-24 was ordered.

Prototype construction advanced quickly and smoothly, and the XB-24 first flew in December 1939. This could carry up to 8,000 lbs (3,629 kg) bombs in its capacious fuselage, and had an armament of six hand-held 0.30-inch (7.7-mm) Browning machine-guns. As prototype construction was getting under way, the USAAC had ordered seven YB-24 pre-production aircraft for service evaluation, and these aircraft were delivered during 1941. The only major differences between the two models was the higher take-off weight and the provision of de-icing equipment on the wings and tail for the YB-24s.

During 1940 the USAAC also ordered its first production Liberators under the designation B-24A. Only nine of this model were delivered, as an improved model was being developed. This featured heavier armament and superior engines. The latter had been tested on the XB-24, which had been redesignated XB-24B when the original Pratt & Whitney R-1830-33 Twin Wasps, with mechanically-driven super-

chargers, had been replaced by R-1830-41 units, with exhaust-driven turbo-superchargers. At the same time the engine oil-coolers had been relocated on each side of the engine from positions under each power unit, giving the Liberators' engine nacelles their distinctive elliptical shape when viewed from the front. With these modifications a total of nine production aircraft appeared in 1941 as B-24C Liberators.

Next into service was the first large-scale production version, the B-24D. This had take-off weight increased to 56,000 lbs (25,401 kg), and was powered by R-1830-43 engines, giving the model a top speed of 303 mph at 25,000 feet (487 km/h at 7,620 m) compared with the B-24A's 292 mph at 15,000 feet (469 km/h at 4,572 m). Armament was by now 10 0.50-inch (12.7-mm) machine-guns, and the bomb-load 8,800 lbs (3,991 kg) compared with the B-24A's 4,000 lbs (1,814 kg). Range was also increased by 650 miles (1,046 km) to 2,850 miles (4,586 km). Production of the B-25D began late in 1940, and eventually 2,738 were produced.

The Liberator was about to be declared operational when Japan attacked Pearl Harbor in December 1941. The United States immediately held back delivery of some Liberators ordered by Great Britain, and the type was pressed into service as quickly as possible. The first operational sortie by a B-24 was flown in January 1942 from Java – British Liberators, however, had already flown operationally during 1941. By the middle of 1942 the B-24 was in operation with USAAF units in the Pacific, Alaska, India and the Middle East. During this year the decision was made to concentrate Liberator activities on the Pacific, where their long range, autopilot capability and reliability was to prove invaluable. The type did continue in service elsewhere, however, notably in Europe.

The B-24E was basically the same as the B-24D, but had improved propellers. It was built by Consolidated, Douglas and Ford. The next model, the B-24G, was at first built by North American. The initial 25 were to all intents and purposes identical with the B-24D, but subsequent examples of the 430 built had a nose turret with two 0.50-inch (12.7-mm) machine-guns in a redesigned fuselage. This modification had

been proved essential by combat over Europe, where German fighters had found that the most vulnerable point on both the Liberator and the Flying Fortress was the nose, attacked head-on.

The B-24H was similar to the B-24G, but was built by Douglas, Ford and Consolidated; deliveries totalled 3,100 aircraft. The B-24J was again almost identical with the B-24G and B-24H, and was the most numerous B-24 type – production reached 6,678 aircraft. In place of the Consolidated or Emerson nose-turret used on the two earlier marks, the B-24J introduced a Motor Products turret, and an improved auto-pilot and bombsight were fitted. In fact many B-24G and B-24H aircraft retrofitted with these items were redesignated B-24J. The B-24L featured a Consolidated tail position with two manually-operated 0.50-inch (12.7-mm) machine-guns, and the B-24M had a Motor Products tail turret with two 0.50-inch (12.7-mm) guns. Production of these two models totalled 1,667 and 2,593 respectively. These were the last production Liberator bomber variants, although several other experimental models had been produced.

The Liberator was also used by the US Navy in two patrol-bomber models and three transport models. The bomber variants were the PB4Y-1, basically similar to the B-24D, with an armament of eight 0.50-inch machine guns and a bomb-load of 8,000 lbs (3,628 kg); and the PB4Y-2 Privateer, with a single tail fin and rudder assembly, and an increased armament.

Thus although the Liberator's offensive load was inferior to Allied heavy bombers, this medium bomber served the US Army Air Forces and the US Navy well in a variety of guises, its principal advantages being its excellent range, high speed, and admirable performance at altitude. Production of the Liberator, which also served extensively with the Royal Air Force, exceeded 18,000 making it the most numerous US aircraft of World War II.

Below: A Consolidated B-24J Liberator of the 565th Bombardment Squadron, 389th Bombardment Group, 2nd Combat Wing, 2nd Air Division, US 8th Army Air Force. The high-set wings and elliptical nacelles are shown to advantage

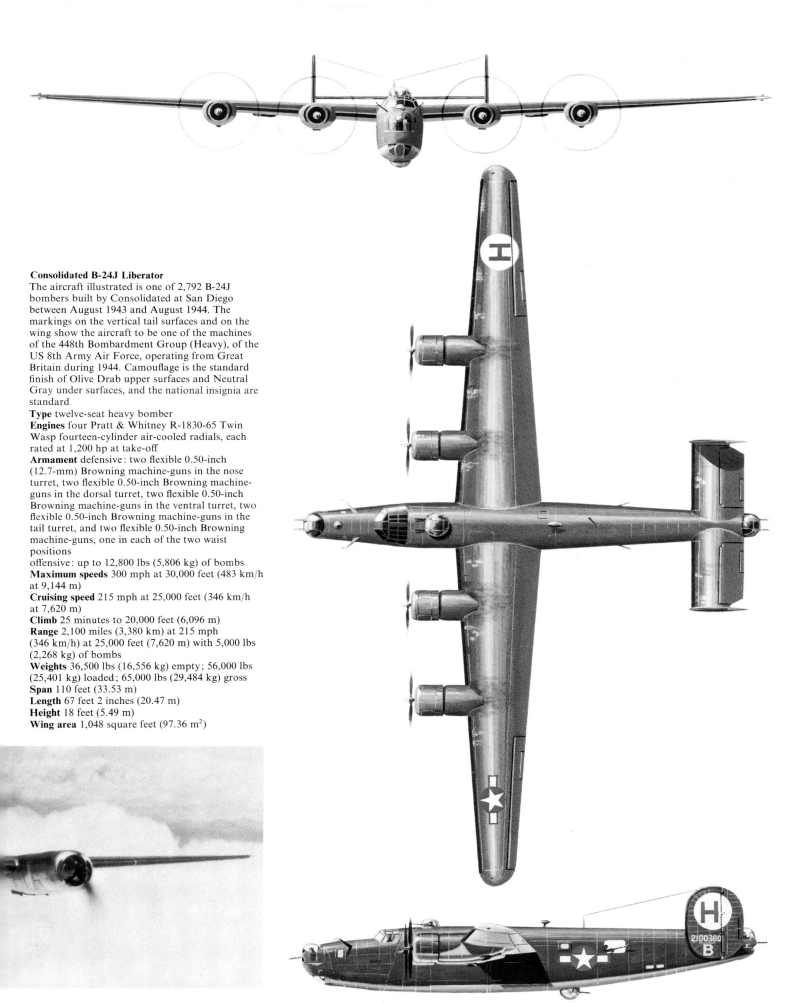

Consolidated B-24J Liberator
The aircraft illustrated is one of 2,792 B-24J
bombers built by Consolidated at San Diego
between August 1943 and August 1944. The
markings on the vertical tail surfaces and on the
wing show the aircraft to be one of the machines
of the 448th Bombardment Group (Heavy), of the
US 8th Army Air Force, operating from Great
Britain during 1944. Camouflage is the standard
finish of Olive Drab upper surfaces and Neutral
Gray under surfaces, and the national insignia are
standard
Type twelve-seat heavy bomber
Engines four Pratt & Whitney R-1830-65 Twin
Wasp fourteen-cylinder air-cooled radials, each
rated at 1,200 hp at take-off
Armament defensive: two flexible 0.50-inch
(12.7-mm) Browning machine-guns in the nose
turret, two flexible 0.50-inch Browning machine-
guns in the dorsal turret, two flexible 0.50-inch
Browning machine-guns in the ventral turret, two
flexible 0.50-inch Browning machine-guns in the
tail turret, and two flexible 0.50-inch Browning
machine-guns, one in each of the two waist
positions
offensive: up to 12,800 lbs (5,806 kg) of bombs
Maximum speeds 300 mph at 30,000 feet (483 km/h
at 9,144 m)
Cruising speed 215 mph at 25,000 feet (346 km/h
at 7,620 m)
Climb 25 minutes to 20,000 feet (6,096 m)
Range 2,100 miles (3,380 km) at 215 mph
(346 km/h) at 25,000 feet (7,620 m) with 5,000 lbs
(2,268 kg) of bombs
Weights 36,500 lbs (16,556 kg) empty; 56,000 lbs
(25,401 kg) loaded; 65,000 lbs (29,484 kg) gross
Span 110 feet (33.53 m)
Length 67 feet 2 inches (20.47 m)
Height 18 feet (5.49 m)
Wing area 1,048 square feet (97.36 m^2)

Consolidated PBY Catalina

The Consolidated PBY flying-boat, named Catalina by the Royal Air Force, was one of the best aircraft of its type during World War II together with the British Short Sunderland and the Japanese Kawanishi H8K 'Emily'. But being smaller and therefore lighter than the other two types, the PBY was also capable of adaptation into an amphibian, and as such is still in service today with several operators, and is bidding fair to rival the ubiquitous Douglas DC-3 Dakota for longevity.

The origins of the Catalina lay in a requirement issued by the US Navy during 1933 for a replacement for its first generation of monoplane and sesquiplane flying-boats. The new boats were to make the fullest use of the latest technological advances, and to be possessed of a high performance. Both Consolidated and Douglas built prototypes, but only the Consolidated type entered widespread service.

Originally designated XP3Y-1, and designed by Isaac M Laddon (later the chief designer of the B-24 Liberator bomber), the new flying boat was ordered in October 1933 and first flew in March 1935. It was a handsome aircraft, with a parasol wing mounted on a pylon above the fuselage, braced by four struts, and the unusual feature of retractable floats at the wingtips. This saved a considerable amount of drag, with benefits to the overall performance. Power was provided by a pair of Pratt & Whitney R-1830-58 Twin Wasp radials of 825 hp each, and armament consisted of four flexible 0.30-inch (7.7-mm) Browning machine-guns and up to 2,000 lbs (907 kg) of bombs.

Prototype flight trials were so encouraging that the type was ordered into production in June 1935 as the PBY-1. As the new production line was being readied, the XP3Y-1 was modified to an improved standard as the XPBY-1, with a less angular fin and rudder and the more powerful R-1830-64 engines of 900 hp each. The revised prototype flew in May 1936, and was handed over to the navy in October, at about the same time as production PBY-1s began to enter service. PBY-1 production totalled 60 aircraft; it was replaced by the PBY-2 (50 built), PBY-3 (66 built), and PBY-4 (33 built) which were constructed during 1937 and 1938. The later models were similar to the PBY-1 in all respects except the powerplant – 1,000-hp R-1830-66 radials in the PBY-3 and 1,050-hp R-1830-72 radials in the PBY-4.

The PBY-5 was powered by a pair of 1,200-hp R-1830-92 radials and had a revised shape to the vertical tail surfaces. More immediately apparent, however, was the replacement of the sliding hatches for the waist guns by prominent blisters on each side of the hull midway between the wings and the tailplane. These blisters had been pioneered on the PBY-4, all but one of which had had the new positions. Deliveries of the PBY-5 began in September 1940.

Before production of the PBY-5 was complete, Consolidated had unveiled their latest version of the series, which was an amphibious model with a retractable tricycle undercarriage, the main members pulling up to positions on the sides of the hull, and the nose-wheel up into a compartment in the under surface of the bows. The whole arrangement was very neat, and although it reduced performance slightly, this was more than counterbalanced by the versatility it bestowed on the type. The US Navy immediately converted the last of its orders for the PBY-5 to the PBY-5A, as the new type was designated, and placed orders for another 134 PBY-5A boats in November 1940, only three days after the first flight of the prototype.

Further orders for the type, now named Catalina in agreement with the British, were placed in 1941 and 1942: 586 PBY-5s, 627 PBY-5As, and 225 PBY-5Bs, the last for transference to Great Britain under Lend-Lease. By this time the offensive armament of the type had been increased from the 2,000-lb (907-kg) bomb-load of the PBY-1 to 4,000 lb (1,814 kg) of bombs, depth-charges or torpedoes on the PBY-5A, with increases in the defensive armament to two 0.50- (12.7-mm) and three 0.30-inch (7.7-mm) machine-guns.

Production was also undertaken in Canada by Vickers and Boeing. The former built 230 Catalinas as OA-10A amphibians for the USAAF, and 149 as Cansos for the Royal Canadian Air Force. Boeing built 362 as Catalinas and Cansos, the latter being the RCAF designation for the aircraft. In the United States, meanwhile, the Naval Aircraft Factory had undertaken an improvement programme for the type, and this in 1941 led to the introduction of the PBN-1 Nomad. This had an improved hull and float design, and a taller fin and rudder assembly. A 0.50-inch (12.7-mm) machine-gun replaced the 0.30-inch (7.7-mm) weapon in the bows, and deliveries, including 138 for Russia, began in February 1943. This model was also built by Consolidated as the PBY-6A with two 0.50-inch (12.7-mm) guns in the bows and search radar mounted in a radome over the cockpit.

Contracts for Catalina production were cancelled at the end of the war in Europe, after 3,290 examples had been built in Canada and the United States. This production alone made the Catalina the most numerous flying-boat type of all time, and many more were built under licence in Russia. The Catalina proved an admirable type, with excellent range characteristics, good cruise, and a powerful offensive armament.

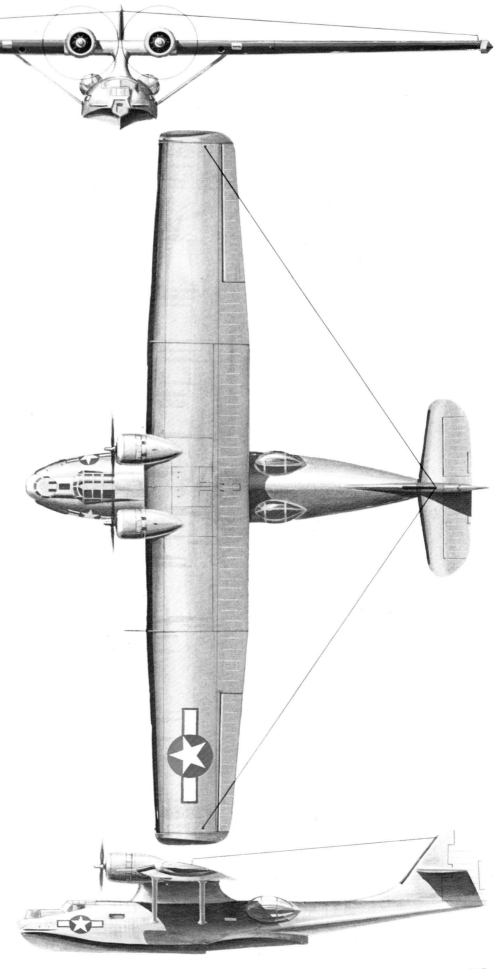

Consolidated PBY-5 Catalina
The aircraft illustrated is finished in an overall light grey colour scheme. Note the positioning of the national insignia on the bows rather than behind the wings – a feature common to all US Navy patrol flying-boats
Type seven- to nine-seat patrol-bomber flying boat
Engines two Pratt & Whitney R-1830-92 Twin Wasp fourteen-cylinder air-cooled radials, 1,200 hp each at take-off
Armament defensive: two flexible 0.50-inch (12.7-mm) Browning machine-guns, one in each of the two waist positions, one flexible 0.30-inch (7.7-mm) Browning machine-gun in the bow turret, and one flexible 0.30-inch Browning machine-gun in the ventral tunnel
offensive: up to 4,000 lbs (1,814 kg) of bombs, two torpedoes or four 325-lb (147-kg) depth charges
Maximum speed 189 mph at 7,000 feet (304 km/h at 2,134 m)
Cruising speed 115 mph (185 km/h)
Initial climb rate 690 fpm (210 m/minute)
Climb unknown
Service ceiling 18,100 feet (5,517 m)
Range 2,990 miles (4,812 km)
Weights 17,526 lbs (7,950 kg) empty; 26,200 lbs (11,884 kg) loaded; 34,000 lbs (15,422 kg) gross
Span 104 feet (31.70 m)
Length 63 feet 10 inches (19.46 m)
Height 20 feet 2 inches (6.15 m)

Below: A Naval Air Factory PBN-1 Nomad patrol flying-boat. This revised version of the Catalina featured improved armament and heightened vertical tail surfaces. An equivalent version, designated PBY-6A, was built by Consolidated. This was an amphibious model, and also had sea search radar mounted in a small radome above the cockpit

Curtiss P-40 Kittyhawk

The Curtiss P-40 series of fighters formed the basis of the US Army Air Corps' fighter (or pursuit according to the contemporary American terminology) squadrons at the beginning of World War II, and served in greater numbers than any other US fighter of the period except the North American P-51 Mustang and Republic P-47 Thunderbolt. Although it was a robust, sound design, the P-40 Warhawk was outclassed by the fighters of both Germany and Japan, and only found its true *métier* as a fighter-bomber in the South Pacific, North Africa and Italy.

The P-40 was essentially a conversion of the earlier P-36, an Allison V-1710 inline replacing the Pratt & Whitney R-1830 radial of the tenth production P-36 to produce the XP-40. This prototype, which first flew in October 1938, had its radiator located under the rear fuselage initially, but this was soon moved to the more familiar position under the nose. Official trials in May 1939 found the XP-40 to be the best of the competitors, and an immediate order for 524 P-40 production models was placed. The order for this first major type, distinguished by its 1,040-hp V-1710-33 engine, lack of wheel fairings, and carburettor intakes above the nose, was later cut back to 200 aircraft with the development of improved models. The French air force ordered the P-40, but these were delivered to the RAF as Tomahawk Is after the fall of France.

In March 1941 the next model, the P-40B (named Tomahawk II by the British), made its first flight. This had armour protection for the

pilot, and two 0.30-inch (7.7-mm) machine-guns in the wings supplemented the two 0.50-inch (12.7-mm) guns mounted in the upper nose of the P-40. Production of the P-40B reached 131 before the P-40C was introduced. This latter type had made its first flight in April 1941, and differed from its predecessors in having self-sealing fuel tanks and an additional pair of 0.30-inch (7.7-mm) guns in the wings. Some 193 P-40C fighters were built. Aircraft of the B and C series were the first of the type to be flown in combat by the USAAF, over Pearl Harbor and the defeats in South-East Asia. The P-40 suffered heavily at the hands of the more experienced Japanese pilots, flying the supremely agile Mitsubishi A6M. But the type enjoyed greater success in operations with the American Volunteer Group in China.

Later in 1941 the P-40D emerged with a slightly altered appearance. This was the result of the fitting of the V-1710-39 engine, which allowed the fuselage to be shortened by six inches and reduced in cross area. At the same time the machine-guns in the nose were deleted, and those in the wings were increased in calibre to 0.50-inch (12.7-mm). The most profound visual difference concerned the radiator, which was enlarged and moved right up under the nose.

The next model, the P-40E, was the second most numerous model after the P-4N, a total of 2,320 being built. This model, which had six 0.50-inch (12.7-mm) guns in the wings, was slightly heavier than its predecessor, and was 6 mph (10 km/h) slower at 354 mph (570 km/h).

The P-40E kept the racks for bombs and drop-tanks introduced on the P-40D, and was the first of the P-40 series to be used by the USAAF in action against the Germans. As with many other aircraft, it was suggested that the installation of a Rolls-Royce Merlin in the P-40 would improve performance considerably. The result was the P-40F, introduced late in 1941, and powered by a Rolls-Royce Merlin 28 of 1,300 hp. In this model, of which 1,311 were built, the carburettor air intake on top of the nose was deleted, and after the first 260, the rear fuselage was lengthened by 20 inches (50.8 cm) to improve control at low speeds.

The P-40K was produced at the same time as the P-40E, and was powered by an Allison V-1710-73 inline of 1,325 hp. Top speed of the type was 360 mph (579 km/h), compared with the 373 mph (600 km/h) of the Merlin-powered P-40E, but the model was the heaviest of the series at 10,000 lbs (4,536 kg). The first examples had the original short fuselage, with a dorsal extension to the fin, but later models incorporated the P-40E's lengthened fuselage. Production of the P-40K reached 1,300, with an additional 600 P-40Ms, basically the P-40K with a V-1710-81 powerplant.

The P-40G, of which 59 were produced in mid-1940, was a conversion of the original

Below: A 'kill' symbol is added to the fuselage of a Curtiss P-40 of the 26th Fighter Squadron, 51st Fighter Group, in China, where the type was flown with considerable success

P-40 to take the six-gun wing of the P-40E. The P-40H was never built, and the P-40J abandoned. The next model was therefore the P-40L, an improved version of the P-40F, which was lightened by the removal of two guns, and a reduction in fuel capacity and armour protection. Although the weight saved amounted to only 250 lbs (113 kg), giving little improvement in performance, 700 were built.

Introduced in 1943, the P-40N was the most numerous of the P-40 series built, 5,220 being built before production stopped in 1944. The P-40N was a lightweight model, powered by the V-1710-81 inline of 1,200 hp. Weight was reduced to 8,850 lbs (4,014 kg) by the removal of two wing guns, the front fuel tank, and several structural alterations, raising top speed to 378 mph (608 km/h). Later models had the two guns restored, as well as racks for a bomb-load of up to 1,500 lbs (680 kg). After the 1,977th machine, the powerplant was altered to the V-1710-99 engine, and after 3,023 of these had been delivered, the V-1710-115 engine was introduced. The last models of the series were three XP-40Qs, which had four-bladed propellers and wing-mounted radiators for their 1,425-hp Allison V-1710-121 engines.

Curtiss P-40D Kittyhawk I
The aircraft illustrated is machine B of No. 250 'Sudan' Squadron (code-letters LD), flown in the Western Desert by Squadron-Leader M T Judd in 1942. Camouflage is the standard Ministry of Aircraft Production Pattern No. 1 for single-engined monoplanes, in the Middle East colour scheme of Dark Earth and Middle Stone upper surfaces, and Azure Blue under surfaces. National insignia are ordinary, but the arrow motif is an individual one.
Type single-seat fighter and fighter-bomber
Engine one Allison V-1710-39 twelve-cylinder liquid-cooled inline, 1,150 hp at take-off and 11,700 feet (3,566 m)
Armament six 0.50-inch (12.7-mm) Browning machine-guns with 281 rounds per gun in the wings, plus up to 700 lbs (318 kg) of bombs
Maximum speeds 350 mph at 15,000 feet (563 km/h at 4,572 m)
Cruising speed 258 mph (415 km/h)
Initial climb rate 2,580 fpm (786 m/minute)
Climb 11 minutes to 20,000 feet (6,096 m)
Service ceiling 30,600 feet (9,327 m)
Range 1,150 miles (1,851 km)
Weights 6,208 lbs (2,816 kg) empty; 7,740 lbs (3,511 kg) loaded; 8,809 lbs (3,996 kg) gross
Span 37 feet 4 inches (11.38 m)
Length 31 feet 2 inches (9.50 m)
Height 10 feet 7 inches (3.23 m)
Wing area 236 square feet (21.93 m²)

Curtiss SB2C Helldiver

The Curtis SB2C Helldiver was one of the US Navy's most potent weapons at the end of World War II. Yet the SB2C had an eventful and not very successful early career that at one time made it look doubtful if the type would ever enter quantity production.

It was developed in 1939 to replace the Curtiss SBC Helldiver biplane dive-bomber then in quantity production for the navy, who realizing that the day of biplanes for carrier use were numbered, ordered prototypes of two new monoplane dive-bombers: the Brewster SB2A Buccaneer and the Curtiss SB2C Helldiver. The design of both aircraft was similar, with large, straight-tapered wings set on a massive fuselage, and possessed considerable strength – a quality much needed in dive-bombers. The Buccaneer was not a particularly successful aircraft, and the 771 built were used mostly for training.

The main burden of replacing the Douglas Dauntless as the US Navy's major dive-bomber therefore devolved upon the Helldiver, the prototype of which, the XSB2C-1, first flew in December 1940. Quantity production had been ordered the previous month, and the crash of the prototype just a few days after its maiden flight did not deter the navy. The programme to get the Helldiver into service, however, was seriously hampered by the 881 modifications that the design team had to incorporate. Chief amongst these were the revision of the vertical tail surfaces, which had to be enlarged considerably, the fuel tankage, which had to be greatly improved and increased, and the armament, which was altered from the prototype's two 0.30-inch (7.7-mm) machine-guns in the upper nose to four 0.50-inch (12.7-mm) guns in the wings. As these and other alterations were being carried out, a new factory to produce the Helldiver was set up, and the first production SB2C-1 flew in June 1942.

As navy squadrons were working up with the new aircraft, the armament was again changed, the four 0.50-inch (12.7-mm) guns in the wings being replaced by a pair of 20-mm cannon. The rear gunner's defensive armament, of two 0.30-inch (7.7-mm) machine-guns, and the offensive load, 1,000 lbs (453 kg) of bombs carried in the internal bomb-bay, remained unchanged. Production of the SB2C-1, with the four guns in the wings, totalled 200, and that of the SB2C-1C, with two cannon, 778. Despite the fact that production was at last beginning to gather momentum, the first service unit did not receive its aircraft until December 1942, and it was not until November 1943, 11 months later, that the Helldiver first went into action, in the Pacific.

Only one XSB2C-2, a floatplane conversion of the SB2C-1, was produced, and the next model to enter production, early in 1944, was the SB2C-3. This had the improved R-2600-20 radial of 1,900 hp, driving a four-bladed propeller. The SB2C-4 was powered by the same engine, but differed from its predecessor in having provision for eight 5-inch (12.7-cm) rocket projectiles or a further 1,000 lbs of bombs to be carried under the wings. A derivative of the SB2C-4, the SB2C-4E, also carried a search radar set. Production of the SB2C-3 and the

SB2C-4 and its -4E variant by the parent company totalled 1,112 and 2,045 respectively.

The last model to be built in quantity was the SB2C-5, which had increased fuel tankage. SB2C-5 production reached 970 examples, the first being delivered in February 1945. Only two examples of the XSB2C-6 were built. This model was to have been delivered in large numbers, and had the more powerful R-2600-28 engine and a longer fuselage. Production of the Helldiver was also undertaken by two Canadian manufacturers: Fairchild delivered 300 XSBF-1, SBF-1, SBF-3 and SBF-4E aircraft, and Canadian Car and Foundry produced 894 SBW-1, SBW-3, SBW-4, SBW-4E and SBW-5 machines, the portions of the designations after the hyphen denoting what model of the basic type each aircraft was. Some 26 Helldivers built by the Canadian Car and Foundry factory were handed over to the Fleet Air Arm, which did not use the Helldiver operationally, however. Curtiss had also built some 900 Helldivers under the designation A-25A for the US Army Air Forces, but most of these went to the US Marine Corps.

The Helldivers took over an ever-increasing portion of the dive-bombing role from the aging Douglas SBD Dauntless during 1944, but never entirely replaced the older type as production could not keep pace with demand. Nevertheless, the Helldiver played the dominant role in the Pacific campaign, and proved itself a formidable weapon against the remnants of the Japanese surface fleet and the various Japanese garrisons on the Pacific islands. After delivering its bombs with great accuracy, the Helldiver was still able to cause considerable damage with its rockets and its two cannon. So successful was the type that it was kept in service for several years after the war.

Curtiss SB2C-1 Helldiver

The aircraft illustrated is finished in the standard camouflage for the late war years: deep blue upper surfaces and light grey under surfaces. The outer panels of the wings are also painted in deep blue on the under surfaces so that when the wings are folded, the upturned under surfaces will present the same colour as the upper surfaces to anyone looking down. National insignia are standard, in the slightly larger size used by the US Navy in comparison with the US Army Air Forces. The white star in the centre of the roundel is not in fact pure white, but has a small amount of blue mixed in, this being a normal practice on blue-camouflaged aircraft

Type two-seat naval dive-bomber and reconnaissance aircraft

Engine one Wright R-2600-8 Double Cyclone fourteen-cylinder air-cooled radial, 1,700 hp at take-off and 1,450 hp at 7,800 feet (2,377 m)

Armament defensive: four fixed 0.50-inch (12.7-mm) Browning machine-guns in the wings and two flexible 0.30-inch (7.7-mm) Browning machine-guns in the rear cockpit
offensive: up to 1,000 lbs (454 kg) of bombs

Maximum speeds 281 mph at 12,400 feet (452 km/h at 3,780 m)

Cruising speed unknown

Climb unknown

Service ceiling 24,700 feet (7,529 m)

Range 1,110 miles (1,786 km)

Weights 10,363 lbs (4,701 kg) empty; unknown loaded; 15,076 lbs (6,838 kg) gross

Span 49 feet 8¾ inches (15.16 m)

Length 36 feet 8 inches (11.18 m)

Height 13 feet 2 inches (4.01 m)

Wing area 422 square feet (39.21 m²)

Below: A fine air-to-air study of the US Navy's best dive-bomber, the Curtiss Helldiver. The model illustrated is an SB2C-4E, which had provision for a small radar set. The antenna can be seen under the port wing

Douglas A-20 Havoc

The Douglas A-20 series of attack aircraft has never acquired the same fame as the legendary de Havilland Mosquito of Great Britain or the Junkers 88 of Germany, but it was nevertheless a remarkable aeroplane which deserves greater attention than it has received, for it was a potent and versatile fighting machine.

Design of the Douglas Model 7A, which was finally to be developed into the A-20 series, began in 1936 as a private venture by a team under Ed Heinemann. Although no official requirement had been issued, Douglas felt confident that the army would need a high-performance attack bomber, and decided to start work on such an aircraft. The prototype of this aircraft, designated Model 7B, first flew in October 1938, and immediately attracted interest – from France. Douglas redesigned the basic aircraft in view of the French requirements, and thus developed the DB-7, whose prototype flew in August 1939. France ordered large quantities of the DB-7, but only a few were flown operationally during the defeat of France in May and June 1940. Some aircraft were flown to safety in Great Britain by their crews, and the rest of the French order was delivered to the RAF. In British service the DB-7 was named Boston I and II, the former being used as a trainer and the latter as an operational bomber.

The French order had been for 105 aircraft, and at the same time the USAAC ordered substantial quantities of two types derived from the DB-7: 63 A-20 attack bombers and 143 A-20A modified attack bombers. The A-20 was powered by a pair of turbosupercharged Wright R-2600-7 radials, and was capable of 390 mph (628 km/h), the highest speed recorded by any A-20 variant. The A-20s were never used in their intended role, however, 60 being converted to P-70 night fighters with British radar in a 'solid' nose and four cannon in a pack under the fuselage; and three to F-3 photographic-reconnaissance aircraft. The A-20As were used as attack bombers however. They were powered by a pair of unsupercharged R-2600-3 radials, and despite being lighter than the A-20 were capable of only 349 mph (562 km/h). The machine-gun armament was increased by adding a 0.30-inch (7.7-mm) gun to the rear of each nacelle, in addition to the standard four forward-firing, two dorsal and one ventral guns. A bomb-load of 2,600 lbs (1,179 kg) could also be carried.

The A-20A was similar in all important respects to the British Boston III, and many of the latter were ordered by the RAF. The US Navy also received one A-20A as the BD-1, and eight A-20Bs under the designation BD-2, without armament. Only the prototype XA-20B was built for the army, this having twin 0.50-inch (12.7-mm) gun turrets in the nose, dorsal and ventral positions. The production A-20B aircraft, of which 999 were built, were in fact earlier in design than either the A-20 or the A-20A, being the American version of the French DB-7A. The navy's BD-2 was derived from this. Power was provided by two R-2600-11s, and the fuselage was 5 inches (12.7 cm) longer than normal as a result of a different pattern of nose glazing. The A-20B was not ordered until late in 1940.

It is worth noting that at this time the British had produced five variants of the Boston under the designation Havoc for nocturnal operations: the Havoc I intruder, the Havoc II with a 'solid' nose mounting 12 0.303-inch machine-guns, the Havoc III night fighter, the Havoc IV intruder, and the Turbinlite Havoc with an airborne searchlight to illuminate German bombers.

The next model, the A-20C, was the first American model to see combat. This was basically the same as the British Boston III, and entered production during 1941, a total of 948 being built. Power was provided by 1,600-hp R-2600-23 radials, and as weight had risen to 25,600 lbs (11,339 kg), speed dropped to 342 mph (550 km/h). The two guns in the engine nacelles were deleted, however, and provision was made to carry one 2,000-lb (907-kg) torpedo under the fuselage. Only 17 A-20Es were produced, all conversions of A-20As to the standard of the A-20B, powered by R-2600-11 radials. Production of the next model, the XA-20F, an A-20A converted to mount a 37-mm cannon in the nose and two 0.50-inch (12.7-mm) machine-guns in each of the dorsal and ventral turrets, only amounted to the prototype. The A-20D had been cancelled.

The A-20G was the most numerous mark of the A-20 series, 2,850 being built, in several versions. The first featured a 'solid' nose with four M2 cannon and two 0.50-inch (12.7-mm) machine-guns in the nose, and single guns in the ventral and dorsal positions; next came a model with six 0.50-inch (12.7-mm) guns in the nose; and finally a variant with a wider fuselage to mount a Martin dorsal turret with a pair of 0.50-inch machine-guns, underwing racks to enable a further 2,000 lbs (907 kg) of bombs to be carried, and a drop-tank under the fuselage, the last extending endurance to over 10 hours. The increase in weight to 30,000 lbs (13,607 kg) reduced speed to 317 mph (510 km/h). The A-20H was basically the same, and 412 were built. The A-20H had 1,700-hp R-2600-29 radials, which

boosted speed to 322 mph (518 km/h). The final two variants, the A-20J and A-20K, were produced (450 of the former and 413 of the latter) in response to need for better bombing and navigation facilities. The two models were based on the A-20G and A-20H respectively, and were known as the Boston IV and V in RAF service. Both had a one piece perspex nose which increased length by 7 inches (17.8 cm). In all, 7,385 aircraft had been built before production ceased in September 1944.

The A-20 series played an important part in the war, serving not only with the US forces, but also with those of France, Holland, Great Britain and Russia. The last, in particular, made great use of the nearly 3,000 aircraft she received in the attack role. The Havoc, as the type was called in American service, was a sturdy and manoeuvrable aircraft, with excellent offensive capabilities with gun, bomb and torpedo, and good performance even in the later heavily loaded variants. Although the Havoc was phased out of production late in 1944, it had given birth to another type, the A-26 Invader, which would have been built in great quantities had the war continued longer. As it was, the Invader proved a formidable and worthy successor to the Havoc.

Below: A partially camouflaged Douglas A-20G attack aircraft. Earlier models had had a transparent nose for the bomb-aimer, but this feature was dispensed with in favour of a solid nose fitted with armament to enhance the type's ground-attack capabilities. At first the guns fixed in the new nose were four 20-mm cannon and two 0.50-inch (12.7-mm) machine-guns; this was later altered to six 0.50-inch guns. Field modifications also led to several other armament dispositions. The A-20G's predecessor, the A-20C, was often retrofitted with a solid nose for four 0.50-inch (12.7-mm) and four 0.30-inch (7.7-mm) machine-guns. By the end of the war the DB-7/A-20 family had been developed into a fine attack weapon with excellent offensive capabilities

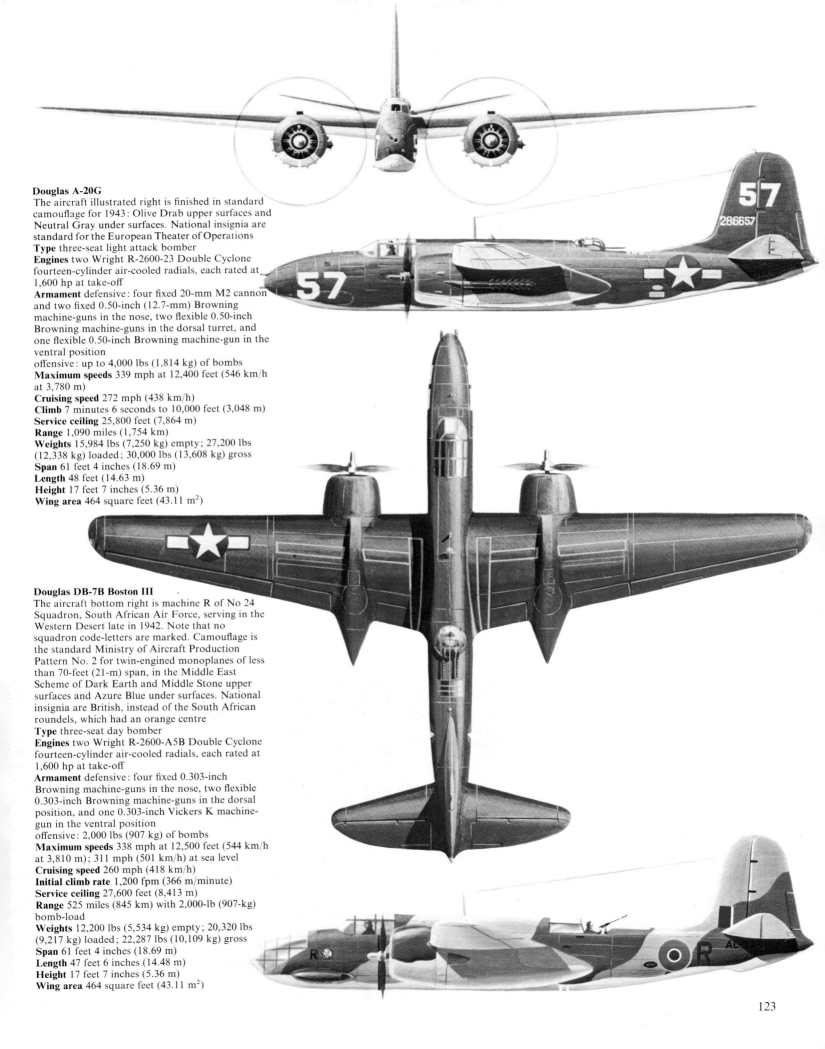

Douglas A-20G
The aircraft illustrated right is finished in standard camouflage for 1943: Olive Drab upper surfaces and Neutral Gray under surfaces. National insignia are standard for the European Theater of Operations
Type three-seat light attack bomber
Engines two Wright R-2600-23 Double Cyclone fourteen-cylinder air-cooled radials, each rated at 1,600 hp at take-off
Armament defensive: four fixed 20-mm M2 cannon and two fixed 0.50-inch (12.7-mm) Browning machine-guns in the nose, two flexible 0.50-inch Browning machine-guns in the dorsal turret, and one flexible 0.50-inch Browning machine-gun in the ventral position
offensive: up to 4,000 lbs (1,814 kg) of bombs
Maximum speeds 339 mph at 12,400 feet (546 km/h at 3,780 m)
Cruising speed 272 mph (438 km/h)
Climb 7 minutes 6 seconds to 10,000 feet (3,048 m)
Service ceiling 25,800 feet (7,864 m)
Range 1,090 miles (1,754 km)
Weights 15,984 lbs (7,250 kg) empty; 27,200 lbs (12,338 kg) loaded; 30,000 lbs (13,608 kg) gross
Span 61 feet 4 inches (18.69 m)
Length 48 feet (14.63 m)
Height 17 feet 7 inches (5.36 m)
Wing area 464 square feet (43.11 m²)

Douglas DB-7B Boston III
The aircraft bottom right is machine R of No 24 Squadron, South African Air Force, serving in the Western Desert late in 1942. Note that no squadron code-letters are marked. Camouflage is the standard Ministry of Aircraft Production Pattern No. 2 for twin-engined monoplanes of less than 70-feet (21-m) span, in the Middle East Scheme of Dark Earth and Middle Stone upper surfaces and Azure Blue under surfaces. National insignia are British, instead of the South African roundels, which had an orange centre
Type three-seat day bomber
Engines two Wright R-2600-A5B Double Cyclone fourteen-cylinder air-cooled radials, each rated at 1,600 hp at take-off
Armament defensive: four fixed 0.303-inch Browning machine-guns in the nose, two flexible 0.303-inch Browning machine-guns in the dorsal position, and one 0.303-inch Vickers K machine-gun in the ventral position
offensive: 2,000 lbs (907 kg) of bombs
Maximum speeds 338 mph at 12,500 feet (544 km/h at 3,810 m); 311 mph (501 km/h) at sea level
Cruising speed 260 mph (418 km/h)
Initial climb rate 1,200 fpm (366 m/minute)
Service ceiling 27,600 feet (8,413 m)
Range 525 miles (845 km) with 2,000-lb (907-kg) bomb-load
Weights 12,200 lbs (5,534 kg) empty; 20,320 lbs (9,217 kg) loaded; 22,287 lbs (10,109 kg) gross
Span 61 feet 4 inches (18.69 m)
Length 47 feet 6 inches (14.48 m)
Height 17 feet 7 inches (5.36 m)
Wing area 464 square feet (43.11 m²)

Douglas C-47 Skytrain

At the end of World War II General of the Army, Dwight D Eisenhower – commander of the Western Allies in the final reduction of Germany – included the C-47 with the jeep, bazooka and atom bomb as the four weapons that had most helped win the war. And although no finer testimonial could be needed, it is worth noting that the type had entered service, in civilian form, three years before World War II and is

service in January 1942. (It is worth noting that although the name Dakota is often used for all DC-3 derivatives, both civil and military, the name is strictly relevant only to C-47s supplied to the RAF, which applied this name to its new transport.)

All military DC-3s were powered by Pratt & Whitney Twin Wasp radials, the initial C-47 model, of which 953 were built, having the 1,200-hp R-1830-92 version. Next came 4,931 C-47A models, which differed from their predecessors only in having 24-volt instead of 12-volt electrical systems. By this time the Burma Road had been cut, and as *matériel* and fuel had to be

flown into China over the 'Hump', need was felt for a C-47 derivative with improved altitude performance. The C-47B was intended to fill this gap, power being provided by a pair of R-1830-90 or -90B radials with high-altitude blowers for their superchargers. Some 3,108 C-47Bs were produced, as well as 133 TC-47Bs, a special modification with R-1830-90C engines intended as flying classrooms for navigational training. The US Navy also received 458 C-47 types under the designation R4D.

The C-47 was further developed after the war. Production finally reached 10,123 examples of the military versions.

still in service, in both military and civilian garb, 30 years after the end of the war. There was nothing glamorous about the C-47's service in World War II, just a multitude of necessary tasks (transport, casualty evacuation, liaison, paratroop transport and glider towing) carried out often and well.

The Douglas Commercial (DC) family, from which the C-47 was derived, began with the DC-1 of 1933, which was never put into production, being followed almost immediately by the improved DC-2. This latter was ordered in considerable numbers by civilian users, and also by the USAAC. But in December 1935 the prototype DC-3 airliner was flown, and the army immediately evinced an interest in a military version of the type, which was slightly larger than its predecessor and capable of carrying 3,000 lbs (1,361 kg) more payload. Pending production of a suitable military model, the USAAC accepted a variety of hybrid DC-2/DC-3 conversions to add to its fleet of DC-2 models, designated C-32 and C-34. The hybrids all had DC-3 outer wing panels married to DC-2 fuselages and centre sections. These were designated C-38 (trooper with Wright Cyclone radials), C-39 (cargo transport with Wright Cyclones) and C-41 (trooper with Pratt & Whitney Twin Wasp radials). The US Navy had also acquired DC-2s under the designation R2D-1.

The first military DC-3 version was the C-53 Skytrooper, of which 405 production examples were eventually built. This differed little from the civilian airliner, being intended for personnel transport and having an unreinforced floor and a single entry door in the port side of the fuselage, and entered service in October 1941. The definitive version of the DC-3 for military use, however, was to be the C-47 Skytrain, which entered

Above right: The single experimental XC-47C, fitted with Edo-designed floats. Note the wheels retracted into the underside of the twin floats which also contained additional fuel
Right: C-47s in the classic role of paratroop dropping, in this case over Arnhem

Douglas C-47B Skytrain
The aircraft illustrated is finished in standard camouflage of Olive Drab and Neutral Gray, with the normal national insignia. Note the large double loading doors in the fuselage side, peculiar to military versions of the DC-3
Type four-seat troop and cargo transport, paratroop dropper and glider tug
Engines two Pratt & Whitney R-1830-90 Twin Wasp fourteen-cylinder air-cooled radials, each rated at 1,200 hp at take-off
Armament none
Payload 27 armed troops or 10,000 lbs (4,536 kg) of freight
Maximum speeds 230 mph at 8,800 feet (370 km/h at 2,682 m)
Cruising speed 207 mph (333 km/h)
Initial climb rate 1,130 fpm (344 m/minute)
Climb 9 minutes 36 seconds to 10,000 feet (3,048 m)
Service ceiling 24,100 feet (7,346 m)
Range 1,600 miles (2,575 km)
Weights 18,200 lbs (8,255 kg) empty; 26,000 lbs (11,794 kg) loaded; 30,000 lbs (13,608 kg) gross
Span 95 feet 6 inches (29.11 m)
Length 63 feet 9 inches (19.43 m)
Height 17 feet (5.18 m)
Wing area 987 square feet (91.70 m²)

Grumman F4F Wildcat

The Grumman F4F Wildcat was the US Navy's standard carrier-borne fighter in the first two years of the war, and was as such called upon to to bear the brunt of the Japanese air offensive, spearheaded by the redoubtable Mitsubishi A6M. It is greatly to the credit of the F4F that although it was aerodynamically inferior to the Japanese fighter, it put up a sturdy resistance, capitalizing on its firepower, strength and high diving speed to counter the Zero's agility.

The F4F was the first monoplane designed by Grumman, and its descent from the long line of Grumman biplane fighters was easily seen in its tubby fuselage and the type of undercarriage used, with the wheels retracting up into the fuselage. The origins of the F4F lay in a 1935 navy requirement for a high-performance fighter. Brewster tendered its F2A monoplane, which was eventually to enter service as the Buffalo, and to safeguard itself against any possible failure of the as yet untried monoplane concept for carrier use, the navy also ordered a prototype of the Grumman F4F biplane.

In 1936, however, experimental work on the F2A and the increasingly evident obsolescence of the biplane concept led Grumman to redesign their fighter as a mid-wing monoplane, designated XF4F-2 to distinguish it from the XF4F-1. The navy ordered the monoplane prototype in July 1936, and this aircraft made its first flight in September 1937, immediately proving itself superior to the Brewster F2A in terms of speed. In other respects, however, the Brewster fighter was superior, and on the conclusion of the trials in June 1938 the Brewster F2A was selected for quantity production.

Despite this, the performance of the XF4F-2 was felt to be good enough to warrant further development, and an XF4F-3 was ordered. This had a 1,200-hp Pratt & Whitney XR-1830-76 radial engine with a two-stage supercharger in place of the first model's 1,050-hp R-1830-66, blunt-tipped wings and more angular vertical tail surfaces. The XF4F-3 first flew in February 1939, and immediately proved to have very good

performance, a speed of 334 mph (537 km/h) being recorded. Flight trials revealed problems with engine cooling, but nevertheless the navy in August 1939 ordered the type into production, in a form derived from the second XF4F-3. This latter was further improved, with a more vertical fin and rudder assembly and the tailplane raised above the line of the wings. An armament of four 0.50-inch (12.7-mm) machine-guns in the wings was standardized after several experimental installations of guns of 0.30-(7.7-mm) and 0.50-inch (12.7-mm) calibres in the fuselage and wings.

The first production F4F-3 flew in February 1940, and soon impressed navy pilots with its speed, which was slightly superior to contemporary US land-based fighters, and its rate of climb, which was definitely superior to that of USAAC fighters. The new Grumman fighter was also released for export, and orders were soon received from France, Greece and Great Britain. In the last the F4F was known initially as the Martlet.

Deliveries of the F4F-3 to the navy began in December 1940, and by the end of 1941 many US Navy and US Marine Corps fighter squadrons were equipped with the new aircraft. During 1940 a small number of F4F-3As were also ordered. These had R-1830-90 engines with single-stage superchargers, as trouble was still being experienced with the two-stage superchargers of the R-1830-76. F4F-3 production totalled 285, and that of the F4F-3A 95.

Next to appear was the F4F-4, which first flew in April 1941. This had manually-folding wings to facilitate carrier use of the type. The F4F-4 entered service in time to play a major part in the Battles of the Coral Sea and Midway, which helped turn the tide of Japanese conquest in the South-West Pacific. Production of the F4F-4 reached 1,169 with Grumman, and the Eastern Aircraft Division of the General Motors corporation built another 1,140 under the designation FM-1. The latter model differed from the Grumman F4F-4 principally in having

four 0.50-inch machine-guns in the wings instead of the six guns introduced on the Grumman F4F-4.

Only two XF4F-5 models were built, these being powered by the 1,200-hp Wright R-1820-40 radial, the first being flown in December 1940. A single XF4F-6 was built in the autumn of 1940 to test the installation of the R-1830-90 radial with a single-stage supercharger for the F4F-3A. The F4F-7 was similar to the F4F-4, but was intended for the long-range reconnaissance role. With no armament and extra fuel, raising the gross weight to 10,328 lbs (4,685 kg), the first of the 100 ordered flew in December 1941, all but 79 being cancelled early in 1942. The F4F-7 had the extraordinary range, for a single-seater, of 3,500 miles (5,633 km). The final Grumman derivative of the F4F was the XF4F-8, of which two were built late in 1942 as prototypes of the Eastern FM-2. This last Wildcat model was developed to meet the need for a lightened fighter that could operate from the smaller flight decks of the escort-carriers then coming into widespread service. In conjunction with a lightening of the airframe, a 1,350-hp Wright R-1820-56 radial was used, the armament of four wing-mounted 0.50-inch machine-guns being retained, as on the FM-1. In all, Eastern built 4,127 FM-2s and 340 Wildcat VIs, the latter being the Fleet Air Arm equivalent of the FM-2.

As has been noted, the F4F family was the US mainstay against Japanese naval aircraft during the first two years of the war against the Nipponian empire. In the right circumstances the Wildcat could hold its own against Japanese fighters, but its real strength lay in attacking Japanese bombers. Aircraft of the latter category featured highly in the 6.9 to 1 ratio of kills to losses enjoyed by the Wildcat throughout the war. And where the Wildcat's career left off, the F6F Hellcat picked up.

Below: A Grumman F4F-4 Wildcat in the markings of late 1942, after the red centre to the white star had been deleted

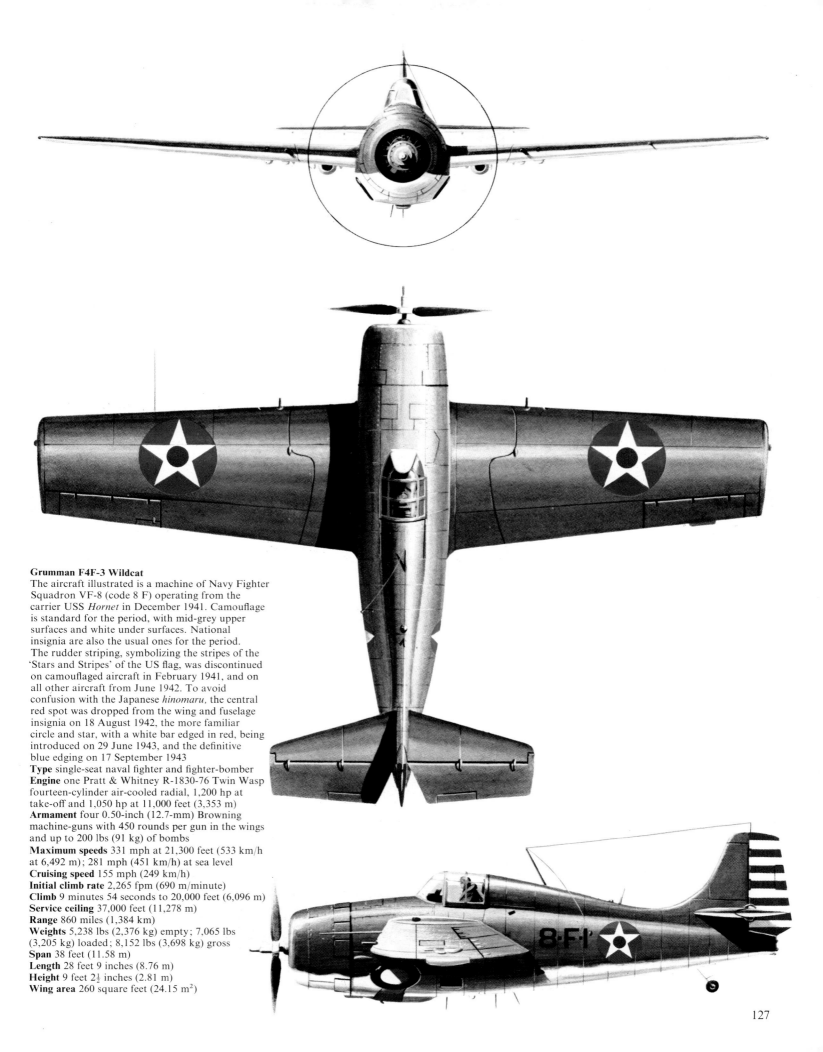

Grumman F4F-3 Wildcat

The aircraft illustrated is a machine of Navy Fighter Squadron VF-8 (code 8 F) operating from the carrier USS *Hornet* in December 1941. Camouflage is standard for the period, with mid-grey upper surfaces and white under surfaces. National insignia are also the usual ones for the period. The rudder striping, symbolizing the stripes of the 'Stars and Stripes' of the US flag, was discontinued on camouflaged aircraft in February 1941, and on all other aircraft from June 1942. To avoid confusion with the Japanese *hinomaru,* the central red spot was dropped from the wing and fuselage insignia on 18 August 1942, the more familiar circle and star, with a white bar edged in red, being introduced on 29 June 1943, and the definitive blue edging on 17 September 1943

Type single-seat naval fighter and fighter-bomber
Engine one Pratt & Whitney R-1830-76 Twin Wasp fourteen-cylinder air-cooled radial, 1,200 hp at take-off and 1,050 hp at 11,000 feet (3,353 m)
Armament four 0.50-inch (12.7-mm) Browning machine-guns with 450 rounds per gun in the wings and up to 200 lbs (91 kg) of bombs
Maximum speeds 331 mph at 21,300 feet (533 km/h at 6,492 m); 281 mph (451 km/h) at sea level
Cruising speed 155 mph (249 km/h)
Initial climb rate 2,265 fpm (690 m/minute)
Climb 9 minutes 54 seconds to 20,000 feet (6,096 m)
Service ceiling 37,000 feet (11,278 m)
Range 860 miles (1,384 km)
Weights 5,238 lbs (2,376 kg) empty; 7,065 lbs (3,205 kg) loaded; 8,152 lbs (3,698 kg) gross
Span 38 feet (11.58 m)
Length 28 feet 9 inches (8.76 m)
Height 9 feet 2½ inches (2.81 m)
Wing area 260 square feet (24.15 m²)

Grumman F6F Hellcat

The F6F Hellcat was the lineal descendant of the F4F Wildcat, and was intended to provide the US Navy with a carrier-borne fighter better able to match Japanese types than its predecessor. The necessary increase in performance was to be attained by refining the aircraft aerodynamically with a larger, more streamlined airframe, and by providing a considerably more powerful engine. Design work began on the new fighter early in 1941, and in June of that year, the navy ordered two prototypes: the XF6F-1, powered by a Pratt & Whitney R-2800-10W, and the XF6F-2, powered by an R-2800-21 radial with a supercharger. Subsequent modifications, many of them the result of combat experience with the Wildcat, led to the redesignation of the two prototype aircraft as the XF6F-3 and XF6F-4 respectively.

Large production orders had been placed before the first flight of the XF6F-3 in June 1942, and the first production F6F-3 flew only five weeks later. Service deliveries began in early 1943, and the type entered combat for the first time in August 1943. Thus a mere two years had elapsed between the ordering of the prototype, and the production aircraft's blooding in combat. By this time production of the Wildcat had been transferred to the Eastern Aircraft Division of the General Motors Corporation, and the Grumman factories were able to concentrate on the Hellcat. Production was switched to the F6F-5 in April 1944, but by this time 4,423 F6F-3s had been built, 18 as F6F-3Es with APS-4 radar in a small streamlined pod under the starboard wing, and 205 as F6F-3N night fighters with APS-6 radar in a similar pod. The Royal Navy also received 252 F6F-3 fighters under the designation Hellcat I.

Only one prototype XF6F-4 fighter was built. This, based on the second original prototype, was powered by a Pratt & Whitney R-2800-27 radial by the time it made its first flight in March 1943. The type did not achieve production status, leaving the F6F-5 to succeed the F6F-3 in this capacity. The first F6F-5 made its maiden flight in April 1944, and the type was immediately placed in large-scale production. It differed from the F6F-3 in having increased armour

protection for the pilot, a redesigned engine cowling, a modified windscreen for the cockpit, improved armament and a more powerful engine. The armament improvement was effected by adding the capability of carrying two 1,000-lb (453-kg) bombs under the centre section and six 5-inch (12.7-cm) rockets under the outer wing panels, and on later aircraft of the mark by enabling the innermost pair of the six 0.50-inch (12.7-mm) machine-guns to be replaced by a pair of 20-mm cannon. The more powerful engine was the Pratt & Whitney R-2800-10W, which had an emergency power rating of 2,220-hp with the use of water injection, signified by the W suffix to the engine designation. As with the F6F-3, a night-fighter version with APS-6 radar was produced under the designation F6F-5N. Of the 6,436 F6F-5s built, 1,189 were F6F-5Ns and 930 were supplied to the Royal Navy as Hellcat IIs.

The final wartime development of the Hellcat was the model with a Pratt & Whitney R-2800-18W radial. Only two prototypes were built as XF6F-6s, the first flying in July 1944. The Hellcat continued to serve with the navy in the immediate postwar years, two other models being developed.

These were the F6F-5P, fitted with cameras as photographic-reconnaissance aircraft, and the F6F-5K, equipped as target drones for missile testing. Some of these were also used as flying bombs during the Korean War in the early 1950s.

The Hellcat was a remarkably successful aircraft, being credited with some 75 per cent of all air-to-air kills recorded by US carrier-based aircraft in World War II. In addition to these 4,947 victories, land-based Hellcats brought down a further 209 enemy aircraft, bringing the type's total to 5,156 enemy aircraft destroyed by US Hellcats. In all, the 12,272 Hellcats built proved very useful, for apart from their capabilities in air-to-air combat they also had a powerful punch in the ground-attack role, as Japanese island garrisons found to their cost in the last two years of the war.

Below: Grumman F6F Hellcat fighter-bombers warm up prior to a sorties from the light aircraft-carrier USS Cowpens
Bottom: An F6F-5 Hellcat in flight. This model differed from the F6F-3 principally in having provision for six 5-inch (12.7-cm) rockets to be carried under the wings

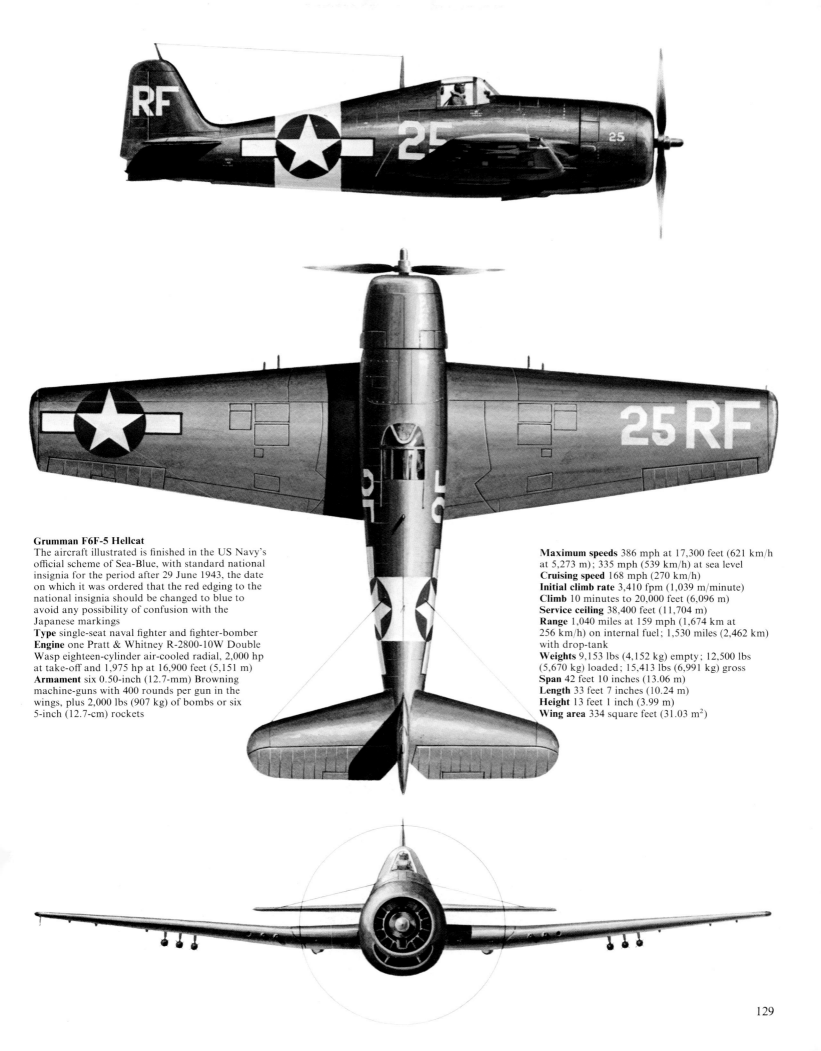

Grumman F6F-5 Hellcat

The aircraft illustrated is finished in the US Navy's official scheme of Sea-Blue, with standard national insignia for the period after 29 June 1943, the date on which it was ordered that the red edging to the national insignia should be changed to blue to avoid any possibility of confusion with the Japanese markings

Type single-seat naval fighter and fighter-bomber
Engine one Pratt & Whitney R-2800-10W Double Wasp eighteen-cylinder air-cooled radial, 2,000 hp at take-off and 1,975 hp at 16,900 feet (5,151 m)
Armament six 0.50-inch (12.7-mm) Browning machine-guns with 400 rounds per gun in the wings, plus 2,000 lbs (907 kg) of bombs or six 5-inch (12.7-cm) rockets

Maximum speeds 386 mph at 17,300 feet (621 km/h at 5,273 m); 335 mph (539 km/h) at sea level
Cruising speed 168 mph (270 km/h)
Initial climb rate 3,410 fpm (1,039 m/minute)
Climb 10 minutes to 20,000 feet (6,096 m)
Service ceiling 38,400 feet (11,704 m)
Range 1,040 miles at 159 mph (1,674 km at 256 km/h) on internal fuel; 1,530 miles (2,462 km) with drop-tank
Weights 9,153 lbs (4,152 kg) empty; 12,500 lbs (5,670 kg) loaded; 15,413 lbs (6,991 kg) gross
Span 42 feet 10 inches (13.06 m)
Length 33 feet 7 inches (10.24 m)
Height 13 feet 1 inch (3.99 m)
Wing area 334 square feet (31.03 m²)

Grumman TBF Avenger

Introduced into combat during the Battle of Midway in June 1942, just as the United States' tide of defeat was beginning to turn, the Grumman TBF Avenger had a disastrous initial career. But once its crews had learned the best way in which to use their aircraft, the Avenger was destined to become, with the Curtiss SB2C Helldiver, one of the major scourges of Japanese ships, both naval and mercantile. The Avenger was also used with great success by several of the United States' allies, and served with the US Navy itself in a variety of roles up to 1954.

The Avenger was designed early in 1941 in answer to a navy requirement for a replacement for its Douglas TBD Devastator torpedo-bomber. Although the company had never built such a type before, the designers set to work with a will, basing their work on the F4F Wildcat fighter: a tubby fuselage, mid-mounted wings and angular flying surfaces. Two prototype XTBF-1s were ordered in April 1940, and construction soon began. The offensive load of one torpedo or 2,000 lbs (907 kg) of bombs could be carried in the capacious internal bomb-bay, and a defensive armament of one fixed forward-firing 0.50-inch (12.7-mm) machine-gun on the engine cowling, one flexible 0.50-inch gun in a powered dorsal turret, and one flexible 0.30-inch (7.7-mm) gun in a ventral position was incorporated.

The navy had already placed orders for 286 production aircraft some eight months before the first prototype flew in August 1941, and the TBF was accepted for service in December 1941. The first production aircraft reached the navy

in January of the following year, and units began to work up on the new torpedo-bomber as quickly as possible. Despite the disaster of its first air combat, in which five of the six TBF-1s despatched were shot down, orders for the type grew, with Grumman unable to match production with demand. The Eastern Aircraft Division of the General Motors Corporation was therefore asked to undertake production of the Avenger, as well as continuing production of the other Grumman type it was building, the Wildcat fighter. Eastern began to deliver Avengers, with the designation TBM-1, in November 1942, eight months after orders had been placed. Grumman also continued production until early in 1944, in that time building 1,525 TBF-1s and 764 TBF-1Cs, the latter having two fixed 0.50-inch guns in the wings in place of the initial single gun in the engine cowling. Eastern built 550 TBM-1s and 2,332 TBM-1Cs to a similar specification. Other versions of the basic TBF-1 mark were the TBF-1D with radar, the TBF-1CP with special cameras as a reconnaissance aircraft, the TBF-1E with radar, and the TBF-1L with a small searchlight in the bomb-bay; Eastern built similar models. The Royal Navy accepted 395 Avengers of the TBF-1B type under the designations first of Tarpon and then of Avenger I, and then 334 TBM-1Cs as Avenger IIs.

The last Avenger models built by Grumman were three prototypes: one XTBF-2, with a Wright XR-2600-10 radial, and two XTBF-3s, with Wright R-2600-20 engines. The former was not persevered with, but the latter went into

production in Eastern factories as the TBM-3. Eastern itself built another four prototypes as TBM-3s. Apart from their more powerful engines, delivering an additional 200 hp, the aircraft of the TBM-3 family were similar to the TBM-1 aircraft, and were built in the same sub-series, with D, P, E and L suffixes to their designations. The TBM-3H incorporated a special search radar set. The final wartime version of the Avenger was to have been the TBM-4, but only three XTBM-4 prototypes were built to test the strengthened airframe.

Total Avenger production reached 9,839, with Grumman contributing 2,293 and Eastern the other 7,546. British orders for the type amounted to 1,058 aircraft, but only 921 were delivered to the Royal Navy, a further 63 going to the Royal New Zealand Air Force. In British service the TBM-3 was designated Avenger III, the TBM-3E Avenger AS Mark 4, and the cancelled TBM-4 Avenger IV.

After the war the type gained great popularity as an anti-submarine aircraft, fitted with radar in a radome under the fuselage and with the dorsal turret deleted. As such it was supplied to several US allies. A transport version, the TBM-3R, with a capacity of seven passengers, was also produced for ferrying out personnel to aircraft-carriers at sea.

Below: An Eastern-built TBM-3, in service with the Fleet Air Arm as an Avenger III. The 0.30-inch (7.7-mm) machine-gun in the ventral 'step' came as a severe shock to many Axis fighter pilots, who took the type for an F4F or F6F

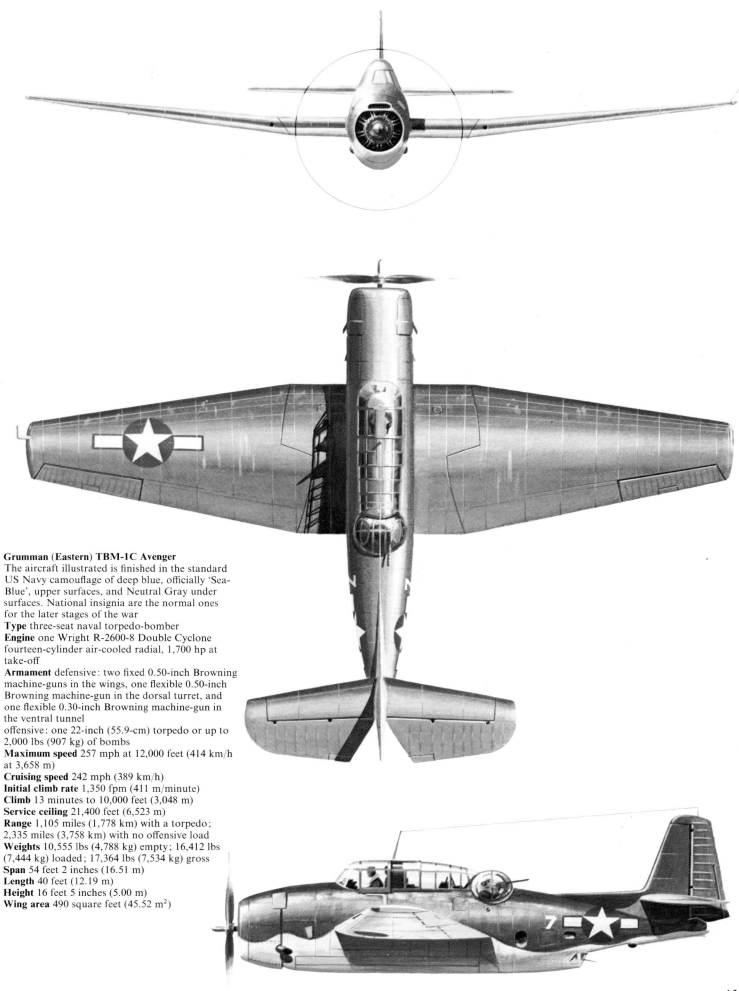

Grumman (Eastern) TBM-1C Avenger
The aircraft illustrated is finished in the standard US Navy camouflage of deep blue, officially 'Sea-Blue', upper surfaces, and Neutral Gray under surfaces. National insignia are the normal ones for the later stages of the war
Type three-seat naval torpedo-bomber
Engine one Wright R-2600-8 Double Cyclone fourteen-cylinder air-cooled radial, 1,700 hp at take-off
Armament defensive: two fixed 0.50-inch Browning machine-guns in the wings, one flexible 0.50-inch Browning machine-gun in the dorsal turret, and one flexible 0.30-inch Browning machine-gun in the ventral tunnel
offensive: one 22-inch (55.9-cm) torpedo or up to 2,000 lbs (907 kg) of bombs
Maximum speed 257 mph at 12,000 feet (414 km/h at 3,658 m)
Cruising speed 242 mph (389 km/h)
Initial climb rate 1,350 fpm (411 m/minute)
Climb 13 minutes to 10,000 feet (3,048 m)
Service ceiling 21,400 feet (6,523 m)
Range 1,105 miles (1,778 km) with a torpedo; 2,335 miles (3,758 km) with no offensive load
Weights 10,555 lbs (4,788 kg) empty; 16,412 lbs (7,444 kg) loaded; 17,364 lbs (7,534 kg) gross
Span 54 feet 2 inches (16.51 m)
Length 40 feet (12.19 m)
Height 16 feet 5 inches (5.00 m)
Wing area 490 square feet (45.52 m²)

Lockheed P-38 Lightning

The Lockheed P-38 fighter was one of the most controversial aircraft of World War II, being for the most part either greatly liked or intensely disliked by its pilots. It was built in lesser numbers than either the Republic P-47 Thunderbolt or the North American P-51 Mustang, yet served in more theatres and proved a more versatile aircraft. It was not as manoeuvrable as other single-seat fighters, nor as fast, yet earned a healthy respect from German pilots, who nicknamed the Lightning the *gabelschwanz Teufel* or 'forked-tail Devil'.

The P-38 was designed in 1937 by a team under H L Hibbard to a USAAC requirement for a high-altitude interceptor. As no single engine with the requisite power was available, the Lockheed team opted for the twin-engined format that was currently in vogue for single-seaters with European designers. (This trend produced several interesting designs, including the British Westland Whirlwind and the German Focke-Wulf 187.) The question of basic layout was neatly solved by twin booms which contained the engines, turbo-superchargers and radiators, and the main members of the tricycle undercarriage, as well as supporting the tail surfaces. An armament of one 23-mm cannon and four 0.50-inch (12.7-mm) machine-guns grouped in the nose of the central nacelle, which also housed the pilot, was intended. This was very heavy for US aircraft of the time, yet despite this, the unorthodox layout and the very high loaded weight, the USAAC ordered a prototype XP-38 in June 1937.

Construction of the XP-38 began a month later, and it first flew in January 1939. The performance of the XP-38, which was powered by a pair of 960-hp Allison V-1710-11/15 inlines, was good and 13 pre-production YP-38s were ordered, despite the total destruction of the XP-38 during flight trials and trouble with tailplane buffeting. The YP-38s were powered by Allison V-1710-27/29 engines of 1,150-hp each, and had a revised armament of one 37-mm Oldsmobile cannon, two 0.50-inch Browning and two 0.30-inch (7.7-mm) Colt machine-guns. Production contracts had been awarded in September 1939, and the first P-38, with armament restored to that of the XP-38, flew in June 1941. Only 30 P-38s were built, the rest of the first batch of 66 being finished as P-38Ds, the initial combat model. The incidence of the tailplane was altered on the latter, it having been discovered that this was principally to blame for the buffeting encountered by earlier aircraft. Production of the P-38E, with a 20-mm Hispano cannon and revised nose, totalled 210; the first was delivered in March 1942, but 99 of these became F-4 models for photographic-reconnaissance, with cameras replacing the armament in the nose. The Lightning, as all models after the D were named, was ordered by Great Britain; the order was cancelled, however, after two examples had been tested as performance without the turbo-superchargers, which were not released for export, was too low for British requirements.

Airframes built to the British order were bought by the USAAF after the cancellation of the British requirement and finished as P-38Fs, with 1,325-hp V-1710-49/53 engines. The P-38F for the USAAF had also replaced the P-38E in production early in 1942, and featured racks under the centre section for two 1,000-lb (454-kg) bombs, two 22-inch (55.9-cm) torpedoes or drop-tanks. A combat setting for the flaps was also introduced on the P-38F to give the type enhanced manoeuvrability, especially in turns. Of the 527 P-38Fs built, 20 were converted to F-4A photographic-reconnaissance aircraft by replacing the armament with cameras. The P-38F was the first model to enter combat, in August 1942, but the type was not used in substantial numbers until the Allied landings in French North Africa during November 1942.

The P-38G, which differed from the P-38F in having V-1710-51/55 engines and some equipment changes, replaced the P-38F in production during June 1942; 1,082 examples were built before production ceased in March 1943. It was G-model Lightnings that were involved in the type's most celebrated single action of the war: in April 1943 fighters of this type, operating from Henderson Field on Guadalcanal, intercepted and shot down a transport carrying the Imperial Japanese Navy's commander-in-chief, Admiral Yamamoto, over 500 miles (805 km) from their base. As with other Lightnings, photographic-reconnaissance models of the P-38G were produced.

In May 1943 the first of 601 P-38Hs entered service. This model was powered by a pair of 1,425-hp V-1710-89/91 engines, and could carry a maximum of 1,600 lbs (726 kg) on each of the two underwing pylons. When very long-range fuel tanks were carried on these pylons, the already excellent operating radius of the Lightning was extended yet further from 850 miles (1,368 km) of the P-38G. The F-5C, of which 128 were built, was the photographic-reconnaissance

model of the P-38H. In August 1943 the P-38J appeared, and in this model the external appearance of the Lightning was substantially altered for the first time. Powered by a pair of the same powerplants as its predecessor, the P-38J introduced 'chin' radiators under each engine. The improved cooling allowed the engines to develop their full power, boosting the P-38J's speed to 420 mph (676 km/h). Of the 2,970 P-38Js built, several hundred were converted to the F-5E and F-5F photographic-reconnaissance model before the P-38L appeared in June 1944. This was the most numerous P-38 model, 3,923 being built. It was powered by a pair of 1,600-hp V-1710-111/113 engines, and was the first Lightning model to carry rocket projectiles, five 5-inch (12.7-cm) weapons on 'Christmas tree' installations under each wing. Again, several hundred were converted to F-5E, F-5F and F-5G photographic-reconnaissance standard. The last P-38 model to see service, in the closing stages of the war against Japan, was the P-38M. This was a conversion of the P-38L to make a two-seat night-fighter.

Captain Richard Bong, the leading US ace with 40 kills, flew only the Lightning, so the type was clearly an excellent machine in the right hands. Yet the strength of feeling both for and against the type raged during the war, and has abated little since amongst ex-pilots and air historians. It would seem fair to assess the type as being less forgiving than most other types to inexperienced pilots, but in the right hands an excellent aircraft for the high-altitude interception role for which it was designed.

Below: A beautiful study of a Lockheed P-38H Lightning. Note the turbo-superchargers on top of each boom and the radiators on each side of the booms. Armament is one 20-mm cannon and four 0.50-inch (12.7-mm) machine-guns

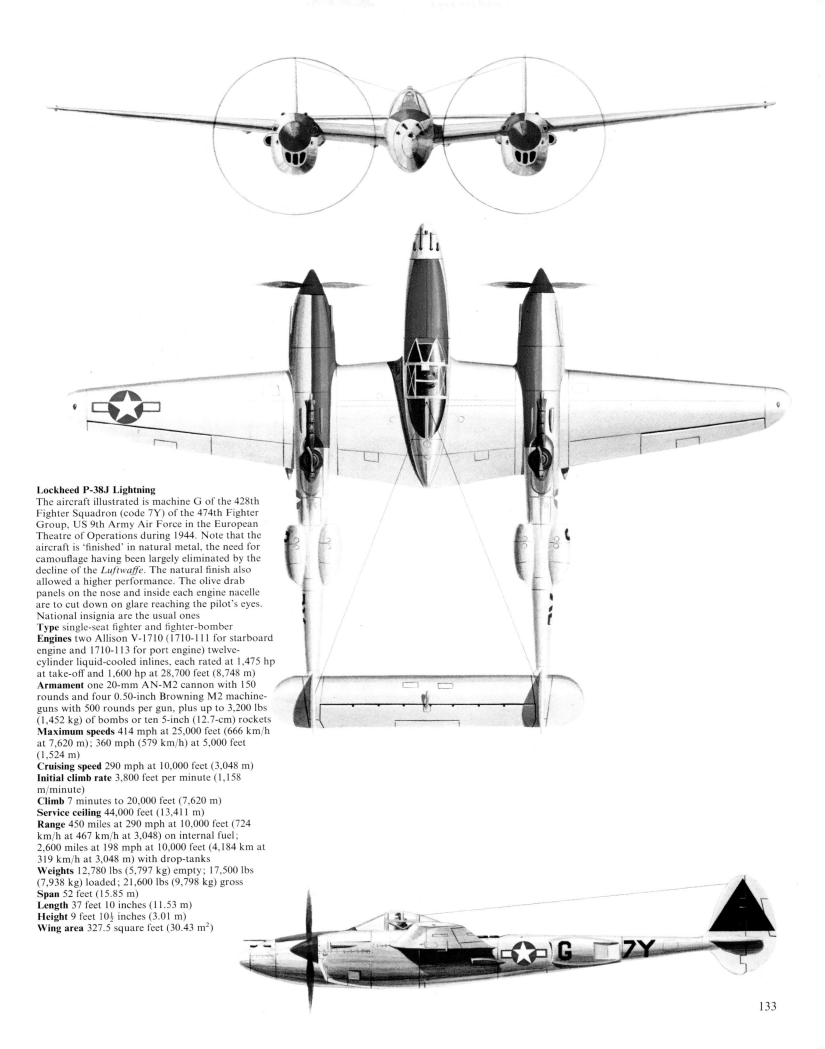

Lockheed P-38J Lightning

The aircraft illustrated is machine G of the 428th
Fighter Squadron (code 7Y) of the 474th Fighter
Group, US 9th Army Air Force in the European
Theatre of Operations during 1944. Note that the
aircraft is 'finished' in natural metal, the need for
camouflage having been largely eliminated by the
decline of the *Luftwaffe*. The natural finish also
allowed a higher performance. The olive drab
panels on the nose and inside each engine nacelle
are to cut down on glare reaching the pilot's eyes.
National insignia are the usual ones

Type single-seat fighter and fighter-bomber
Engines two Allison V-1710 (1710-111 for starboard
engine and 1710-113 for port engine) twelve-
cylinder liquid-cooled inlines, each rated at 1,475 hp
at take-off and 1,600 hp at 28,700 feet (8,748 m)
Armament one 20-mm AN-M2 cannon with 150
rounds and four 0.50-inch Browning M2 machine-
guns with 500 rounds per gun, plus up to 3,200 lbs
(1,452 kg) of bombs or ten 5-inch (12.7-cm) rockets
Maximum speeds 414 mph at 25,000 feet (666 km/h
at 7,620 m); 360 mph (579 km/h) at 5,000 feet
(1,524 m)
Cruising speed 290 mph at 10,000 feet (3,048 m)
Initial climb rate 3,800 feet per minute (1,158
m/minute)
Climb 7 minutes to 20,000 feet (7,620 m)
Service ceiling 44,000 feet (13,411 m)
Range 450 miles at 290 mph at 10,000 feet (724
km/h at 467 km/h at 3,048) on internal fuel;
2,600 miles at 198 mph at 10,000 feet (4,184 km at
319 km/h at 3,048 m) with drop-tanks
Weights 12,780 lbs (5,797 kg) empty; 17,500 lbs
(7,938 kg) loaded; 21,600 lbs (9,798 kg) gross
Span 52 feet (15.85 m)
Length 37 feet 10 inches (11.53 m)
Height 9 feet 10½ inches (3.01 m)
Wing area 327.5 square feet (30.43 m²)

133

Martin B-26 Marauder

Aesthetically a very attractive aircraft, the B-26 Marauder was in fact a tricky aeroplane to fly, and early in its career it earned an unenviable reputation as a death-trap for its crews. The reason for this lay in its high wing-loading, the consequence in turn of the stringent USAAC requirement the design had to meet. In January 1939 the army issued a requirement for a new medium bomber of very high performance. Realizing that the performance needed at the upper end of the operating range could not be met by an aircraft with a low wing-loading, the USAAC deliberately omitted any reference to landing and stalling speeds, thereby tacitly admitting that what had previously been unacceptable speeds for these two factors would now be accepted.

Martin replied to the requirement with a beautifully streamlined aircraft with very small flying surfaces and two large engines. So pressing was the need for the new design that the army ordered over 1,000 examples into immediate production in September 1939, waiving the normal procedure of X and Y prototype and pre-production models for testing. This was perhaps an unwise step, as Peyton M Magruder's design had the highest wing-loading to date of any US aircraft. The first B-26, powered by a pair of 1,850-hp Pratt & Whitney R-2800 Double Wasp radials and armed with one 0.30-inch (7.7-mm) machine-gun each in the nose and tail positions, and two 0.50-inch (12.7-mm) guns in the dorsal turret, made its maiden flight in November 1940. The first few aircraft were reserved for testing and evaluation, and full-scale production got under way in 1941.

The designation B-26 was applied to the first 201 aircraft built. These had R-2800-5 engines, and were capable of carrying a bomb-load of 5,800 lbs (2,631 kg). Top speed, the highest of the whole series at a gross weight of just over 30,000 lbs (13,608 kg), was 315 mph (507 km/h). Conversion to the new aircraft was of necessity a lengthy process, and the first Marauder unit did not become operational until December 1941. Operational conversions were further delayed by the introduction of the heavier (32,200-lb or 14,606 kg)) B-26A in the second half of 1941. The increased weight came from the extra fuel tanks in the bomb-bay, a change from 0.30- to 0.50-inch calibre guns in the nose and tail positions, and the provision of shackles for a 22-inch (55.9 cm) torpedo under the fuselage. Production of the B-26A, which was powered by R-2800-9 or R-2800-39 radials, reached 139; the B-26B entered production in May 1942.

Several sub-marks of the B-26B were built,

corresponding to the various batches of aircraft built. The first batch had R-2800-5 radials of 1,850-hp each, and an increased weight of 36,500 lbs (16,556 kg); this latter was occasioned by an increase in armour protection for the crew, the addition of a ventral gun in a 'tunnel', and the doubling of the armament in the tail position to two 0.50-inch guns. The second batch had 1,920-hp R-2800-41 or -43 radials, two 0.50-inch machine-guns for beam defence in place of the first batch's ventral 0.30-inch gun, and a lengthened leg for the nosewheel, to increase the incidence of the wing and improve take-off performance.

A more radical change was made in another batch. In an effort to reduce the wing-loading, and therefore the problems of handling the aircraft at low speeds, the span of the wing was increased by 6 feet to 71 feet (1.8 m to 21.6 m), thereby adding another 56 square feet (5.2 sq m) to the area of the wing. This should have helped matters considerably, but it was negated by a further increase in weight to 38,200 lbs (17,327 kg) due to the addition of a second gun to the nose armament, and the location of four new guns, all fixed, two on each side of the nose. At the same time a Martin-Bell tail turret replaced the older position, and the size of the vertical tail surfaces was increased. Production of this sub-model amounted to 2,477 aircraft.

The sole XB-26D and XB-26E were experimental aircraft, the first to test thermal de-icing equipment, and the second to assess the effects of moving the dorsal turret forward. Neither was put into production, and the next major model therefore became the B-26F, of which 300 were built in 1943. In a further effort to improve the type's take-off and landing characteristics, the incidence of the wing was increased by 3½ degrees. Other, detailed modifications were also included. The final combat model of the Marauder was the B-26G, which only slightly differed from the B-26F. Before production of the type terminated in March 1945, 893 B-26Gs and 57 TB-26Gs had been built, the latter as trainers and target tugs.

The final Marauder model was the XB-26H, which was used to test a four-wheel bicycle undercarriage under the fuselage, similar to that finally used on the Boeing B-47 jet bomber. Total B-26 production came to 5,157. The Marauder was also used by the Royal Air Force: 52 Marauder I (B-26A), 19 Marauder IA (B-26B), 100 Marauder II (B-26C), and 350 Marauder III (B26F and G). The B-26B and C were also converted into target tugs in the United States as they were withdrawn from front-line service under the designation AT-23, 208 B and 350 C models being converted.

Although the service introduction of the Marauder had been far from smooth, and considerable difficulty had been experienced at first in combat, the Marauder came into its own in the closing stages of the war, when its high speed and heavy armament turned it into a formidable tactical support aircraft. Its high wing-loading was always a problem, but as pilots became more experienced as the war progressed, they learned how to cope with this, and the losses of B-26s became proportionally the lowest of any US combat type.

Left: Martin B-26C Marauder light bombers in action over enemy territory. The aircraft partially hidden by the machine in the foreground has just released its load of six 500-lb (227-kg) bombs

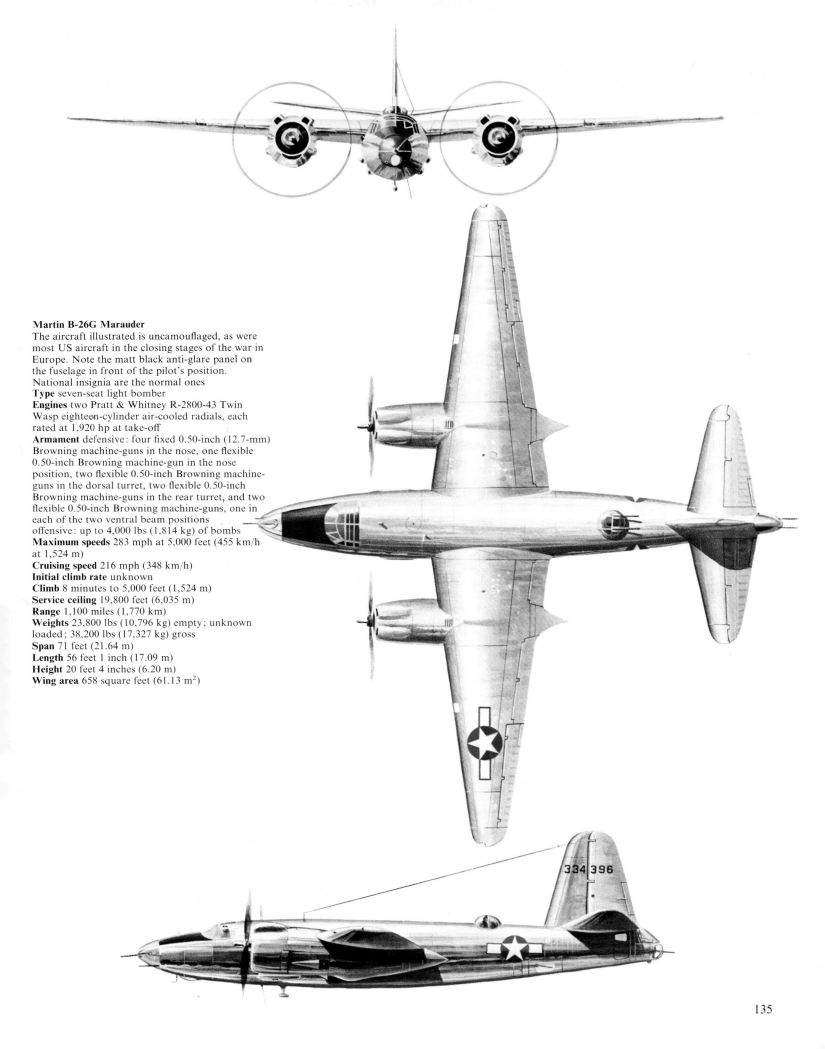

Martin B-26G Marauder
The aircraft illustrated is uncamouflaged, as were
most US aircraft in the closing stages of the war in
Europe. Note the matt black anti-glare panel on
the fuselage in front of the pilot's position.
National insignia are the normal ones
Type seven-seat light bomber
Engines two Pratt & Whitney R-2800-43 Twin
Wasp eighteen-cylinder air-cooled radials, each
rated at 1,920 hp at take-off
Armament defensive: four fixed 0.50-inch (12.7-mm)
Browning machine-guns in the nose, one flexible
0.50-inch Browning machine-gun in the nose
position, two flexible 0.50-inch Browning machine-
guns in the dorsal turret, two flexible 0.50-inch
Browning machine-guns in the rear turret, and two
flexible 0.50-inch Browning machine-guns, one in
each of the two ventral beam positions
offensive: up to 4,000 lbs (1,814 kg) of bombs
Maximum speeds 283 mph at 5,000 feet (455 km/h
at 1,524 m)
Cruising speed 216 mph (348 km/h)
Initial climb rate unknown
Climb 8 minutes to 5,000 feet (1,524 m)
Service ceiling 19,800 feet (6,035 m)
Range 1,100 miles (1,770 km)
Weights 23,800 lbs (10,796 kg) empty; unknown
loaded; 38,200 lbs (17,327 kg) gross
Span 71 feet (21.64 m)
Length 56 feet 1 inch (17.09 m)
Height 20 feet 4 inches (6.20 m)
Wing area 658 square feet (61.13 m²)

North American B-25 Mitchell

The North American B-25 Mitchell formed, with the Douglas A-20 Havoc and the Martin B-26 Marauder, the mainstay of the tactical support units of the USAAF during World War II. The Mitchell, in particular, turned out to be a versatile and popular aircraft. Although its bomb-load was not very high, it was capable of carrying a heavy gun armament for both offensive and defensive purposes, and was much feared by German, Italian and Japanese pilots. It was a Mitchell unit, also, that made the daring raid on Tokyo from the carrier USS *Hornet* in April 1942 – despite the fact that the Mitchell had never been intended for carrier operations, being a large, land-based medium bomber.

The genesis of the B-25 series lay in a 1938 USAAC requirement for a medium bomber, to which North American designed their private-venture NA-40. This was a neat three-seat aircraft, with a shoulder-mounted wing, twin vertical tail surfaces, a heavy defensive armament and two 1,100-hp Pratt & Whitney R-1830-56C3-G radial engines. The NA-40 flew for the first time in January 1939, and after its engines had been replaced by 1,350-hp Wright GR-2600-A71 units in February, the type was handed over to the USAAC for official testing in March. The NA-40 was lost in an accident soon after the trials began, but so impressive had been its performance that the USAAC instructed North American to proceed with a larger version. This emerged as the NA-62, with a wider fuselage, double the bomb-load, the wings dropped slightly, and the crew increased to five.

North American completed the redesign by September 1939, and the USAAC immediately ordered 184 production machines, designated B-25, without the normal lengthy programme of prototypes and pre-production machines. Work began as quickly as possible, and the first B-25 was ready for flight in August 1940. It was powered by two 1,700-hp Wright R-2600-9 radials and a weight of 27,310 lbs (12,388 kg) half as much again as that of the NA-40. Early flight trials were successful apart from a lack of

directional stability, which was cured by reducing the dihedral on the outer wing panels. As there were no prototypes as such, the first production B-25s were retained for testing, the initial nine having full dihedral, and the subsequent 15 having the reduced dihedral outer panels. These 24 aircraft should be considered as prototype, testing and evaluation models, the first combat type being the B-25A, of which 40 were built.

The B-25A was basically similar to the later B-25s, but had armour protection for the flight crew and self-sealing fuel tanks; combat experience in Europe, passed on to the Americans by the British, had shown that these were absolutely essential for fighting aircraft. Deliveries to the USAAF began in 1941, and at the end of the year several units were operational with the Mitchell. The B-25B was also produced in 1941, 120 being built in all. Again this was similar to its predecessor, but had certain armament differences: Bendix turrets with two 0.50-inch (12.7-mm) machine-guns in each for the dorsal and ventral positions, and the deletion of the single hand-held 0.50-inch gun in the tail position. Gross weight had also risen to 28,460 lbs (12,909 kg). It was Mitchells of this model that took part in the Doolittle raid on Tokyo already mentioned. In 1941 production of the next model, the B-25C, began in California while at the same time an almost identical model, the B-25D, was built in Texas.

Three experimental models followed, all based on the B-25C. The XB-25E tested a thermal de-icing device, whilst the XB-25F tested an electrical de-icing device. And the XB-25G had a trial installation of one of the heaviest guns to be used by any aircraft in World War II – an M4 75-mm field gun obtained from the army. The tests with this gun proved so successful that the B-25G, armed with a 75-mm gun, was put into production. Each of the 21 shells carried weighed 15 lbs (6.8 kg), and had to be loaded individually by the navigator. With this gun, which was aimed with the aid of a pair of 0.50-inch (12.7-mm) machine-guns in the nose, the 405 B-25Gs

became devastating anti-shipping weapons, when the target could be hit.

The B-25G was followed into production by the B-25H, which was fitted with the lighter T13E1 75-mm gun and a multitude of other guns to make it the most heavily armed B-25 model of all. Although 1,000 B-25Hs were built, the 75-mm gun did not prove very successful in the Pacific and Far East, where most B-25Hs were deployed.

The model that followed, the B-25J, was the most numerous Mitchell derivative, some 4,318 being built. This had the older type of forward fuselage, with a considerable amount of glazing, and an armament of one flexible and two fixed 0.50-inch machine-guns. The rest of the aircraft was the same as the B-25H. The powerplants which had been R-2600-13 or -29 radials in the B-25H, were replaced by R-2600-92 engines in the B-25J. With the decline in Japanese air power in 1944, B-25s could operate at very low level, where the bombardier or bomb-aimer was not needed, and a new nose with eight 0.50-inch guns was designed. At the same time the Mitchell was given the capability of carrying eight 5-inch (12.7-cm) rocket projectiles under the wings.

The Mitchell was built in considerable numbers, the USAAF receiving 9,816 and others of the Allies some 2,500 more. For its size the Mitchell was relatively agile, and this proved a great asset in the roles in which it excelled: low-level bombing and 'on the deck' attack on strongpoints and shipping. All in all the Mitchell played a part that would be difficult to over-estimate. Moreover, unlike many other medium bombers and attack aircraft, the Mitchell was able to rely on its own defences to protect itself against enemy fighters, and could therefore dispense with fighter escort to a great extent.

Below: A North American B-25J Mitchell in service with the Royal Air Force as a Mitchell III. Note the restoration of the 'bombardier' nose in place of the 75-mm gun of the B-25H which had not proved very successful

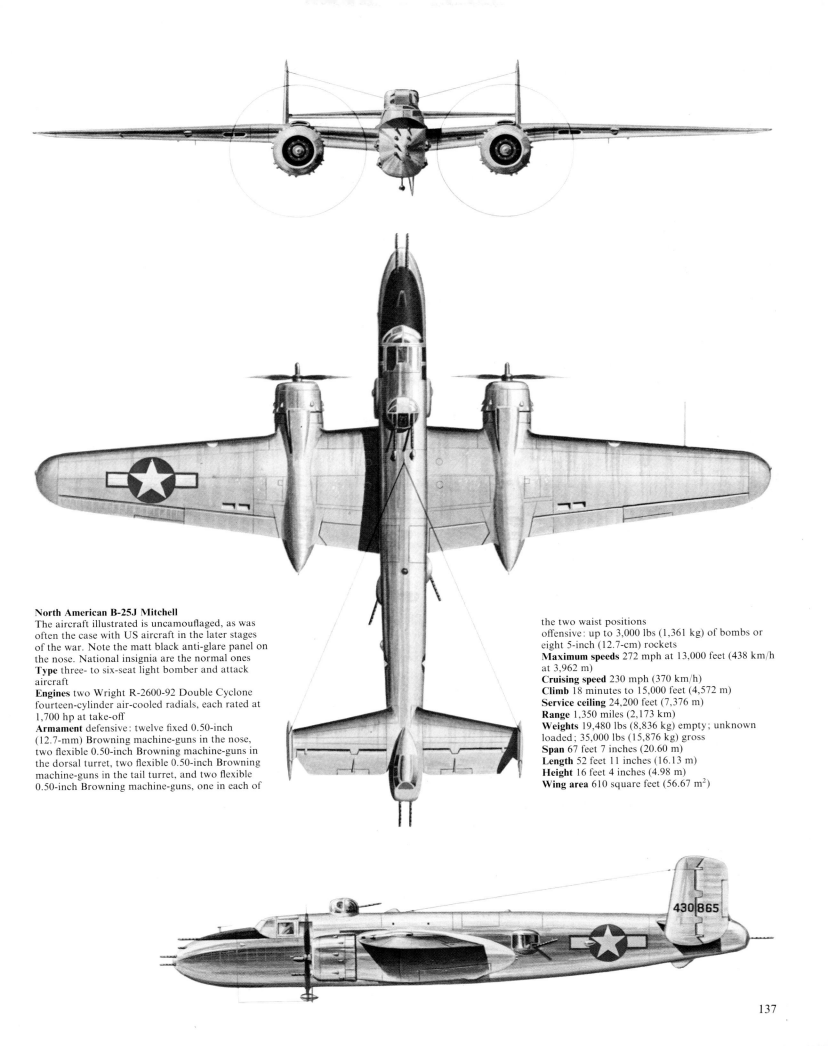

North American B-25J Mitchell
The aircraft illustrated is uncamouflaged, as was often the case with US aircraft in the later stages of the war. Note the matt black anti-glare panel on the nose. National insignia are the normal ones
Type three- to six-seat light bomber and attack aircraft
Engines two Wright R-2600-92 Double Cyclone fourteen-cylinder air-cooled radials, each rated at 1,700 hp at take-off
Armament defensive: twelve fixed 0.50-inch (12.7-mm) Browning machine-guns in the nose, two flexible 0.50-inch Browning machine-guns in the dorsal turret, two flexible 0.50-inch Browning machine-guns in the tail turret, and two flexible 0.50-inch Browning machine-guns, one in each of the two waist positions
offensive: up to 3,000 lbs (1,361 kg) of bombs or eight 5-inch (12.7-cm) rockets
Maximum speeds 272 mph at 13,000 feet (438 km/h at 3,962 m)
Cruising speed 230 mph (370 km/h)
Climb 18 minutes to 15,000 feet (4,572 m)
Service ceiling 24,200 feet (7,376 m)
Range 1,350 miles (2,173 km)
Weights 19,480 lbs (8,836 kg) empty; unknown loaded; 35,000 lbs (15,876 kg) gross
Span 67 feet 7 inches (20.60 m)
Length 52 feet 11 inches (16.13 m)
Height 16 feet 4 inches (4.98 m)
Wing area 610 square feet (56.67 m²)

North American P-51 Mustang

The North American P-51 Mustang is one of the truly great aircraft of all time. Although the early Mustang models, powered by an Allison inline engine, were good low-level aircraft, it was not until the introduction of the Rolls-Royce Merlin engine in later models that the Mustang came into its own. The basic simplicity of the design, coupled with its beautiful lines, had great potential for development, and the Mustang was to excel in two fields: as a hard-hitting low-level fighter-bomber, and a long-range high-altitude escort fighter. In the former capacity the Mustang could deliver a formidable volume of gunfire, rockets and bombs, and in the latter, with the aid of drop-tanks, became the first Allied fighter to penetrate as far as Berlin or Tokyo. The Mustang was a great fighter; what makes this all the more remarkable is the fact that it was designed to a British specification, and that it was one of few aircraft to be designed during the war to enter very widespread service.

At the beginning of 1940 the British were shopping for combat aircraft in the United States. Failing to find a fighter that could meet the requirements that combat had shown to be essential, the British asked North American, who had little experience in the field, if it could produce a fighter to British specifications within the remarkably short time of 120 days. The aircraft had to have good performance, an armament of eight machine-guns, armour protection for the pilot, self-sealing fuel tanks, and an inline engine, the last in keeping with all British single-engined fighters of the period.

The prototype NA-73, as the design was called, was ready three days before the British deadline and could immediately be seen to possess exceptional lines, with laminar-flow wings, low-drag fuselage features, and an overall cleanliness of airframe. After the 1,100-hp Allison V-1710-P3R inline had been fitted, the prototype made its maiden flight in October 1940 and entered immediate production, the first deliveries beginning in December. These Mustang I aircraft had an armament of four 0.30-inch (7.7-mm) and two 0.50-inch (12.7-mm) machine-guns in the wings, and two 0.50-inch guns in the fuselage.

As part of the original export permission, it had been specified that two NA-73s should be supplied to the US army for evaluation and the fourth and tenth aircraft were handed over and tested as XP-51s. The USAAF ordered 150 of this model, armed with four 20-mm cannon, as P-51s so that they could be supplied to Great Britain as Mustang IAs under Lend-Lease. After the Japanese attack on Pearl Harbor, however, the USAAF kept some examples.

The first Mustang model ordered for the USAAF themselves was the A-36A, a ground-attack version which had first flown in September 1942. Armament consisted of six 0.50-inch guns in the wings and two 500-lb (227-kg) bombs under the wings; deliveries of the 500 ordered were completed by March 1943. Because of the type of Allison engine fitted to these early models, the first Mustangs were used by the USAAF and RAF as low-level ground-attack and army co-operation aircraft respectively, but some urgency was now attached to giving the Mustang an engine that would deliver its best power at a higher altitude. A partial solution was found in the Allison V-1710-81 of 1,200 hp, which was used in the P-51A; a total of 310 of this type was ordered in 1942. The uprated Allison engine had only partially solved the problem of the Mustang's lack of adequate performance above medium altitude and a new solution had to be found. The answer in fact lay in a British proposal to abandon the Allison engine in favour of the Rolls-Royce Merlin. Experimental installations were carried out in the United States and Great Britain with engines built in each country; the American version was selected for major production. Conclusive trials, which had shown that the Merlin boosted the Mustang's top speed by some 50 mph (80 km/h) to 441 mph (710 km/h) and generally altered the type's high-altitude performance out of all recognition, were concluded in September 1942, and the type was ordered into large-scale production. Two identical models, the P-51B and the P-51C, were built in California and Texas. At first deliveries were made of aircraft with 1,300-hp V-1650-3 engines, but later the V-1650-7 of 1,695 hp was

fitted. Armament of both the P-51C and D started as four 20-mm cannon, but was later altered to six 0.50-inch (12.7-mm) guns. Drop-tanks could be carried, increasing the maximum range to 2,080 miles (3,348 km). Production of the P-51B reached 1,988, and of the P-51C 1,750.

The next model, the P-51D, was built in greater numbers than all other Mustangs put together. The main distinguishing feature of this model was a complete revision of the cockpit lines to improve the pilot's field of vision. The rear fuselage was cut down, and a smoothly lined one-piece perspex canopy was fitted in place of the earlier framed hood. The six-gun armament was standardized, as was the V-1650-7 engine, and after a few aircraft had been delivered, a dorsal fillet was added to the fin to aid directional stability. This fillet was also added retrospectively to many P-51B and C aircraft. Production of the P-51D amounted to 7,956 aircraft, of which 280 were supplied to the RAF as Mustang IVs.

The final production model was the P-51H with power provided by a 2,218-hp V-1650-9 engine, the cockpit shortened, extra fuel tankage provided, and a taller fin and rudder assembly fitted. The P-51H was 1,100 lbs (499 kg) lighter than the P-51D and was the fastest of all Mustang variants at 487 mph (784 km/h). Only 555 had been built before further orders were cancelled after the surrender of Japan.

The Mustang was in every respect a great aircraft, well loved by its pilots and the crews of bombers it escorted, and greatly feared by German and Japanese pilots. With the Merlin engine the Mustang possessed great speed, rate of climb and acceleration. Combined with a high level of manoeuvrability, this made the type a fighter to be respected – and its lines made it a type to be remembered.

Below: Four US 8th Air Force North American P-51 Mustang fighters. Three distinct types are visible: leading is a D without a dorsal fillet; nearest is a D with such a fillet; and furthest away is a B with the original type of framed cockpit canopy

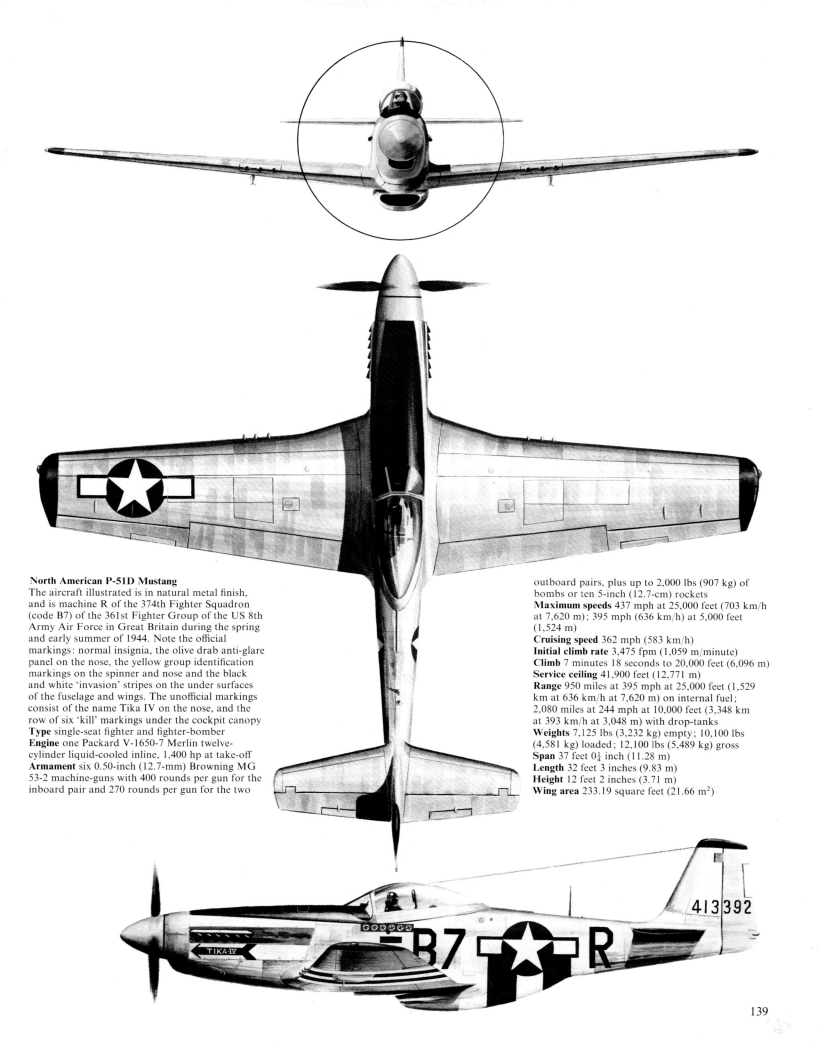

North American P-51D Mustang

The aircraft illustrated is in natural metal finish, and is machine R of the 374th Fighter Squadron (code B7) of the 361st Fighter Group of the US 8th Army Air Force in Great Britain during the spring and early summer of 1944. Note the official markings: normal insignia, the olive drab anti-glare panel on the nose, the yellow group identification markings on the spinner and nose and the black and white 'invasion' stripes on the under surfaces of the fuselage and wings. The unofficial markings consist of the name Tika IV on the nose, and the row of six 'kill' markings under the cockpit canopy
Type single-seat fighter and fighter-bomber
Engine one Packard V-1650-7 Merlin twelve-cylinder liquid-cooled inline, 1,400 hp at take-off
Armament six 0.50-inch (12.7-mm) Browning MG 53-2 machine-guns with 400 rounds per gun for the inboard pair and 270 rounds per gun for the two

outboard pairs, plus up to 2,000 lbs (907 kg) of bombs or ten 5-inch (12.7-cm) rockets
Maximum speeds 437 mph at 25,000 feet (703 km/h at 7,620 m); 395 mph (636 km/h) at 5,000 feet (1,524 m)
Cruising speed 362 mph (583 km/h)
Initial climb rate 3,475 fpm (1,059 m/minute)
Climb 7 minutes 18 seconds to 20,000 feet (6,096 m)
Service ceiling 41,900 feet (12,771 m)
Range 950 miles at 395 mph at 25,000 feet (1,529 km at 636 km/h at 7,620 m) on internal fuel; 2,080 miles at 244 mph at 10,000 feet (3,348 km at 393 km/h at 3,048 m) with drop-tanks
Weights 7,125 lbs (3,232 kg) empty; 10,100 lbs (4,581 kg) loaded; 12,100 lbs (5,489 kg) gross
Span 37 feet 0¼ inch (11.28 m)
Length 32 feet 3 inches (9.83 m)
Height 12 feet 2 inches (3.71 m)
Wing area 233.19 square feet (21.66 m²)

Republic P-47 Thunderbolt

The Republic P-47 Thunderbolt was the largest and heaviest single-seat, single-piston engined fighter ever to enter service, and was excelled in size and weight only by the experimental Boeing XF8B-1 shipboard fighter of 1943. Like North American's P-51 Mustang, the Thunderbolt was conceived and built wholly during the war years, but was also the logical conclusion of the series of barrel-shaped Republic fighters that had started in the 1930s with the P-35 and progressed to the P-43 Lancer of 1940. The P-47 was also the last radial-engined fighter to serve in quantity with the USAAF.

The first two designs to bear the designation P-47, the XP-47 and XP-47A, in fact bore little resemblance to the eventual Thunderbolt, being designed in 1940 to meet USAAC requirements for a light fighter. Although the USAAC evinced interest in both types, reports of air combat over Europe convinced the authorities that they would have to re-equip American fighter units with a machine that would excel the 400-mph (644 km/h) performance of the XP-47 and XP-47B, as well as possess a far heavier armament and be fitted with armour protection and self-sealing fuel tanks.

In view of the new requirements, the Republic team under Alexander Kartveli undertook a complete reworking of the initial designs to produce the XP-47B. This was powered by a 2,000-hp Pratt & Whitney R-2800 Double Wasp radial, and no effort was made to pare down weight at the expense of performance or combat capacity. In fact the armament proposed – eight 0.50-inch machine-guns in the wings – was extremely heavy by the standards of the time. Although the projected gross weight of 12,000 lbs (5,443 kg) would make the type the heaviest fighter to date ordered, the USAAF gave Republic the order to go ahead with a prototype in September 1940.

The mechanical centre of the new fighter was its large radial engine and its associated turbo-supercharger; Kartveli started with the problem of where to place the latter, and then built up the fuselage around the two major components. To help balance the aircraft the supercharger was placed in the rear fuselage. This in turn meant that the air for the supercharger to compress had to be drawn in through the nose, ducted back to the supercharger and then led forward again to the engine; the engine exhaust gases to drive the supercharger were led back from the engine, and after use exhausted under the rear fuselage. To utilize the engine's output efficiently a four-bladed propeller of large dimensions was needed and this entailed provision of a long undercarriage to enable the propeller to clear the ground. A large amount of fuel had to be carried, and the structure necessary to deal with the recoil forces of the eight machine-guns needed to be sturdy, and so the XP-47B, which flew for the first time in May 1941, was of necessity a very bulky, heavy aircraft. Top speed was 412 mph (663 km/h), fully justifying the order for 773 production models placed by the USAAF during the previous September.

Deliveries of the P-47B, which differed from the prototype in having a sliding instead of a hinged cockpit canopy and an R-2800-2 engine, began in 1942, and eventually 171 were built. The P-47B was used in combat for the first time over Europe, and experience against German fighters in April and May 1943 showed that although the new fighter lacked adequate manoeuvrability and rate of climb, its weight bestowed a phenomenal dive, and its structure the ability to absorb battle damage that would destroy any other fighter.

Production of the 602 P-47Cs began in the last quarter of 1942. This model had provision for a drop-tank under the fuselage, and the fuselage itself was lengthened by some 13 inches (33 cm) to increase manoeuvrability. The drop-tank increased range from 550 to 1,250 miles (885 to 2,012 km), and the installation of the R-2800-59 engine of 2,300 hp added to the P-47C's rate of climb considerably, as well as improving other performance figures. This engine, with water injection to boost power to 2,535 hp for emergency combat use, was standardized on later production examples of the next model, the P-47D. This was built in larger numbers (12,608) than any other model, and also had a pylon under each wing for additional drop-tanks. These gave the P-47D a range of 1,800 miles (2,897 km), enabling Thunderbolts to play a useful part in long-range escort duties. Later in the P-47D's career, the drop-tank pylons were converted to enable the type to carry bombs up to a total weight of 2,500 lbs (1,134 kg); with these the P-47 became an effective fighter-bomber from the end of 1943. To improve vision a bubble canopy was introduced on late P-47Ds.

The introduction of the latest German aircraft and the V-1 flying bomb led to the development of the P-47M late in 1944. This model was intended only as a fighter, and all fighter-bomber equipment was removed from the 130 models built. The last Thunderbolt production model – the P-47N – was intended for use in the Pacific theatre, in which very long range was essential. This was similar to the P-47M, but had wings increased in span by 22 inches (55.9 cm) to 42 feet 7 inches (12.98 m). The engine was the 2,800-hp R-2800-77, and increased fuel capacity made the P-47N the longest-ranged Thunderbolt of all at 2,350 miles (3,782 km). Fighter-bomber equipment was restored, and the dorsal fillet was larger than that pioneered on the P-47D. Production of the P-47N amounted to 1,816 before the end of the war against Japan brought cancellation of the remaining 5,934 Thunderbolts on order. In all, production of the Thunderbolt had amounted to 15,683 aircraft.

The type was also used by the Free French, Russian and British air forces. The British designated the 340 early P-47Ds delivered Thunderbolt I, and the 590 late P-47Ds and subsequent models Thunderbolt II.

Below: The largest piston-engined single-seat fighter to serve in World War II: the Republic P-47 Thunderbolt. Shown here is a D model, the first to have a bubble canopy

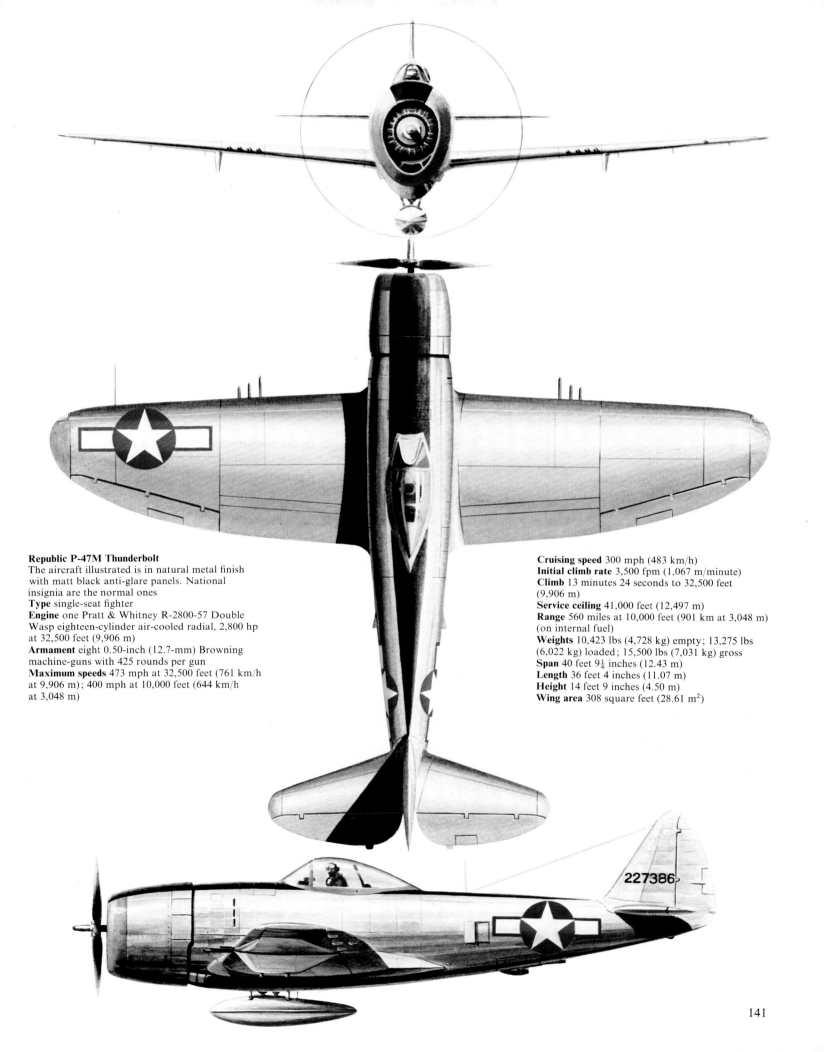

Republic P-47M Thunderbolt
The aircraft illustrated is in natural metal finish
with matt black anti-glare panels. National
insignia are the normal ones
Type single-seat fighter
Engine one Pratt & Whitney R-2800-57 Double
Wasp eighteen-cylinder air-cooled radial, 2,800 hp
at 32,500 feet (9,906 m)
Armament eight 0.50-inch (12.7-mm) Browning
machine-guns with 425 rounds per gun
Maximum speeds 473 mph at 32,500 feet (761 km/h
at 9,906 m); 400 mph at 10,000 feet (644 km/h
at 3,048 m)

Cruising speed 300 mph (483 km/h)
Initial climb rate 3,500 fpm (1,067 m/minute)
Climb 13 minutes 24 seconds to 32,500 feet
(9,906 m)
Service ceiling 41,000 feet (12,497 m)
Range 560 miles at 10,000 feet (901 km at 3,048 m)
(on internal fuel)
Weights 10,423 lbs (4,728 kg) empty; 13,275 lbs
(6,022 kg) loaded; 15,500 lbs (7,031 kg) gross
Span 40 feet 9¼ inches (12.43 m)
Length 36 feet 4 inches (11.07 m)
Height 14 feet 9 inches (4.50 m)
Wing area 308 square feet (28.61 m²)

141

Vought F4U Corsair

The Vought F4U was undoubtedly the best carrier-borne fighter of World War II, and could with some justification make a bid for the title of best fighter of the war. It was an extremely potent fighter, and as a fighter-bomber proved so efficient against the Japanese that they nicknamed it the 'Whistling Death'.

The origins of the Corsair lay in a 1938 US Navy requirement for a fighter that could match the performance of any landplane. Vought produced the V-166B design to meet this requirement, and in June 1938 the company received a contract to build one prototype. The design had been produced by a team under Tex B Beisel, and was very striking in appearance. To obtain the necessary high performance the new fighter was designed around the Pratt & Whitney XR-2800 Double Wasp radial, with the fuselage being kept to the minimum dictated by the engine. The wing arrangement was very ingenious, the inverted gull planform providing the necessary area in a reduced overall span. As the wing also folded at its angle, this helped keep the folded height of the aircraft down. The backward-retracting undercarriage was also located at the angle of the wing, which enabled the length of the legs to be kept short, with resultant saving in weight.

The first Corsair, the XF4U-1 prototype, made its maiden flight in May 1940, and quickly showed its paces, being capable of more than 400 mph (644 km/h). At the time it was the only US fighter that could fly at this speed. Armament consisted of one 0.30- (7.7-mm) and one 0.50-inch (12.7-mm) gun in the fuselage, and one 0.50-inch gun in each wing, as well as 10 small bombs to be dropped on enemy bomber formations. At the end of June 1941 the navy placed orders for 584 production F4U-1 models.

The first of these flew in June 1942, and deliveries began in October. These aircraft were powered by the R-2800-8 engine in place of the prototype's R-2800-4, and had two more guns in the wings. The most noticeable difference was the relocation of the cockpit three feet (91 cm) further back, to allow extra fuel to be carried in the fuselage. This unfortunately reduced the forward view of the pilot when the aircraft was on the ground, and the navy decided that the Corsair could not be operated from aircraft-carriers. The first F4U-1s therefore went to units of the US Marine Corps operating from land bases and entered combat with the marines for the first time in February 1943.

The Vought production facilities could not match demand, and the Corsair was accordingly manufactured by Brewster as the F3A-1 and by Goodyear as the FG-1. Later models built by all three companies had the raised cockpit canopy introduced on Vought's 689th Corsair. Other early models were: the FG-1A with fixed wings; the F4U-1C with four 20-mm cannon in place of earlier production models' six wing-mounted 0.50-inch machine-guns; and the F4U-1D/FG-1D/F3A-1D with water-injected R-2800-8W engines, provision for a drop-tank under the fuselage, and shackles for one 1,000-lb (454-kg) bomb or four 5-inch (12.7-cm) rockets under each wing to turn the Corsair into a fighter-bomber. Production of these first models by the three companies involved totalled 8,663, and of these 370 were delivered to the Royal New Zealand Air Force and 2,012 to the Royal Navy's Fleet Air Arm. The first Corsair operations from carrier decks were by the Fleet Air Arm in April 1944, although successful trials had been carried out some nine months before. It was at this time that the US Navy finally cleared the Corsair for carrier operations.

As the Corsair was beginning to make its mark on operations in the Pacific, work on a night-fighter version, the XF4U-2, was making progress. This prototype was not in fact completed; and although work on three XF4U-3s, using the turbo-supercharged R-2800-16 engine, started in March 1942, the first aircraft did not fly until 1946. Only 13 of the 27 similar Goodyear FG-3s were completed. The next production model was therefore the F4U-4, the first of which flew in April 1944. Power was provided by the 2,100-hp R-2800-18W engine with water injection. The extra 350 hp of this engine, when water injection was used, raised top speed of the Corsair by 21 mph (34 km/h) to 446 mph (718 km/h). Other versions of the F4U-4 were the F4U-4C armed with four 20-mm cannon; the F4U-4N night fighter with four cannon and APS-5 radar in a wing-mounted pod; the F4U-4E with four cannon and APS-4 radar; the Goodyear FG-4 equivalent of the F4U-4; and the F4U-4P photographic-reconnaissance model with cameras. Total production of the F4U-4 series reached 2,556 aircraft including the 200 FG-4s.

These were the last wartime variants of the Corsair, and although many aircraft contracts were cancelled in September 1945, the excellent Vought fighter was kept in production, with development plans slightly curtailed. The last Corsair was delivered in December 1952, after the type had been in production for more than 10 years. In combat the Corsair had served principally with the US Navy and Marine Corps in the Pacific theatre, some 64,051 missions being flown in all. Corsairs achieved the remarkable ratio of 11 kills to one loss in action against Japanese fighters, destroying 2,140 aircraft for the loss of only 189 of their own number. And in the fighter-bomber role the Corsair also achieved remarkable results, being able to deliver its large offensive load with considerable speed and great accuracy.

Below: Vought F4U-4 fighter-bombers, perhaps the US Navy's most versatile aircraft of World War II, and certainly the most successful naval fighter of that war

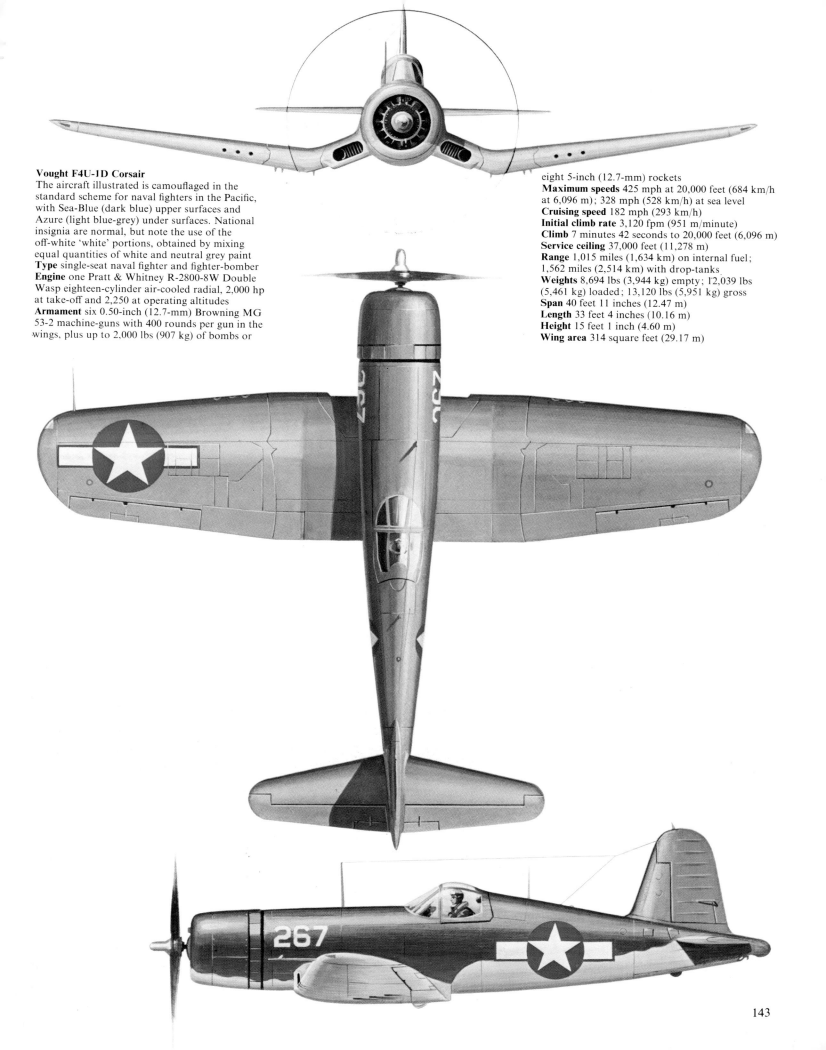

Vought F4U-1D Corsair
The aircraft illustrated is camouflaged in the
standard scheme for naval fighters in the Pacific,
with Sea-Blue (dark blue) upper surfaces and
Azure (light blue-grey) under surfaces. National
insignia are normal, but note the use of the
off-white 'white' portions, obtained by mixing
equal quantities of white and neutral grey paint
Type single-seat naval fighter and fighter-bomber
Engine one Pratt & Whitney R-2800-8W Double
Wasp eighteen-cylinder air-cooled radial, 2,000 hp
at take-off and 2,250 at operating altitudes
Armament six 0.50-inch (12.7-mm) Browning MG
53-2 machine-guns with 400 rounds per gun in the
wings, plus up to 2,000 lbs (907 kg) of bombs or

eight 5-inch (12.7-mm) rockets
Maximum speeds 425 mph at 20,000 feet (684 km/h
at 6,096 m); 328 mph (528 km/h) at sea level
Cruising speed 182 mph (293 km/h)
Initial climb rate 3,120 fpm (951 m/minute)
Climb 7 minutes 42 seconds to 20,000 feet (6,096 m)
Service ceiling 37,000 feet (11,278 m)
Range 1,015 miles (1,634 km) on internal fuel;
1,562 miles (2,514 km) with drop-tanks
Weights 8,694 lbs (3,944 kg) empty; 12,039 lbs
(5,461 kg) loaded; 13,120 lbs (5,951 kg) gross
Span 40 feet 11 inches (12.47 m)
Length 33 feet 4 inches (10.16 m)
Height 15 feet 1 inch (4.60 m)
Wing area 314 square feet (29.17 m)